Rch Wa

Masterworks of the German Cinema

Masterworks of the German Cinema

Introduction by Dr. Roger Manvell

The Golem · Nosferatu
M · The Threepenny Opera

Lorrimer Publishing, London

Published by Lorrimer Publishing Limited
47 Dean Street, London W1
First printing

SBN: 0-85647-021-X

Manufactured in Great Britain by Villiers Publications Ltd,
London NW5

CONTENTS

ACKNOWLEDGEMENTS

The publishers wish to thank the following individuals and organisations for their help in preparing this volume: Dr. Rudolph S. Joseph of the Stadtmuseum of Munich, for providing stills from *The Golem* and *The Threepenny Opera;* to the British Film Institute for the use of stills from *Nosferatu* and *M;* to Nero Films International and *L'Avant-Scene du Cinema* for the use of stills from *M;* to Lotte H. Eisner and Secker & Warburg, Ltd., for permission to reprint extracts from *The Haunted Screen;* to The Tantivy Press for permission to reprint the section on *M* from *The Cinema of Fritz Lang* by Paul M. Jensen; to Longmans, Green & Co., Ltd., for permission to reprint extracts from *Celluloid* by Paul Rotha.

INTRODUCTION

by Dr. Roger Manvell

The post-war period in Germany after the Armistice in 1918 was one of great social, political and economic disruption. With the sudden abdication of the Kaiser in November, Germany had changed abruptly into a republic, the Weimar republic set up following the elections of January, 1919. The new government had a socialist slant, and immediately came under attack from both the extreme Right and extreme Left for signing the Versailles treaty with the Allies — the so-called ' stab in the back ' for an Army which many Germans felt had been deserted rather than defeated. After spectacular successes by the Army in France early in the year, the government had sued for peace in October 1918 following serious reverses of which the public were less aware. Unrest immediately after the war had taken the form of uprisings by the self-styled Soldiers' Councils modelled on the Soviet pattern. The Councils had taken temporary control in some German states, notably Bavaria, to the disgust of such right-wing patriots as Corporal Adolf Hitler, who remained in the Army until 1920. The Nationalists formed armed bands, the Frei Korps, to oppose the Left, and Germany in 1919 faced the serious possibility of civil war.

Europe was the scene of revolutionary activity in many areas, with the collapse of unstable monarchies. The Russian revolution represented either a beacon or a menace according to your political standpoint. Germany, however, remained essentially a bourgeois nation, dominated by the values of the middle class and, over them, the authoritarian outlook of the landowners (Junkers), industrialists, and the Army hierarchy. The Allies, with a wary eye on Soviet Russia and the Left in the German nation itself, permitted a German Army to remain in being with a ceiling of 100,000 men. In the circumstances, the Frei Korps became a natural outlet for ex-officers and ex-soldiers with extreme Right-wing views. Violence was an everyday occurrence in the streets, notably in Munich, centre of the Bavarian revolution which lasted until May 1919. In 1920 the right-wing Kapp putsch failed to overthrow the Reich government in Berlin; the more moderate Right had already taken over in Bavaria, the scene of Hitler's abortive putsch of November, 1923, which he hoped would lead (like Mussolini's action in Italy) to an eventual march on Berlin. Meanwhile, ministers had been murdered — Erzberger, who had signed the peace treaty of 1918, and the Jewish Walther Rathenau, who had supported the terms of the peace treaty. During the period up to 1923, the confidence of the wage earner in the society in which he lived collapsed with the fall of the mark, which was only stabilized in November 1923 after it had fallen from 4 to the dollar to 130,000,000,000. In contrast, from 1924 towards the end of the decade, when another severe recession was to set in following the Wall Street crash, German industry passed into a period of boom.

In spite of these conditions of national instability, 1919-1924 was to be the great period of the German silent cinema, starting with the extraordinary, but perhaps somewhat historically over-rated film, *The Cabinet of Doctor Caligari* (1919). Even during the war years there had been some official recognition of the importance of the cinema in the national culture and tradition (termed, in wartime, national 'morale'), and the important production combine UFA had been formed in 1917 with strong financial backing by the government. UFA was to be the source (or part source) of many outstanding films, such as *Madame Dubarry, Dr Mabuse the Gambler, The Golem, The Chronicle of the Greyhouse, Faust, The Last Laugh, The Love of Jeanne Ney, Metropolis, The Blue Angel, Emil and the Detectives,* and *Congress Dances.*

German cinema in the 1920s was characterized by the extraordinarily high quality of its studio production. This was the period in which the direction of cinematography was in the hands of artists of the calibre of Fritz Arno Wagner, with his magnificent atmospheric, shadowed, claustrophobic lighting (*Destiny, Nosferatu, Warning Shadows, Chronicles of the Greyhouse, The Love of Jeanne Ney,* and later *The Threepenny Opera, Westfront 1918, Kameradschaft,* and *M*), and Karl Freund, with his skill in special effects and luminous, stylized, theatrical pictorialization (*The Golem, The Last Laugh, Faust, Vaudeville, Metropolis*). Other great studio cameramen of the period included Guido Seeber, Eugen Schüfftan, and Gunther Krampf. Theatricality was, in fact, the outstanding characteristic of the German 'art' cinema, largely because so many directors, designers, and performers came from the celebrated theatrical stable of Max Reinhardt's Deutsches Theater, which was paramount both before and after the war. Reinhardt trained or employed, among many others, Ernst Lubitsch (as an actor), Paul Wegener, Emil Jannings, Conrad Veidt, Wilhelm Dieterle, Karl Grune and the Dutch actor-director, Henrik Galeen. F. W. Murnau was also a stage director for Reinhardt. Others who came to the film from the theatre, either as actors or directors, included G. W. Pabst, Werner Krauss, Robert Wiene, Fritz Kortner, and Peter Lorre. They brought a stylized theatricality into their work for the silent screen. Reinhardt, though never identified with expressionism, was celebrated for the use of chiaroscuro effects of light and shadow on the stage, and these effects reappeared in the early German cinema and merged naturally with the more specifically expressionist design the German film was to adopt.

Design, like photography, became an outstanding factor in the German film. The post-war period saw expressionism adopted in the 'art' cinema. It is true that expressionism, already present in art and literature, reached the cinema comparatively late, largely through the influence of such expressionist films as *Caligari* and *From Morn to Midnight* (Karl Heinz Martin, 1919). It became a cult during the period of social malaise in Germany; it was naturally favoured more by artists and intellectuals than by the general public. Indeed, *The Cabinet of Dr Caligari* was very sparsely screened initially. It had been made in a small studio with a budget of only some $18,000. But expressionism was to spread its influence into the design and presentation of many more broadly stylized theatrical films of the time, such as Murnau's *Faust* or Lang's *Metropolis*. Lotte Eisner, in *The Haunted Screen*, has attempted the difficult task of describing this strange urge, so characteristic of German predilection for the darkly mystical and magical, the romantic haunting of forests and isolated dwellings, and the persecution of mankind by evil forces vaguely and symbolically conceived:

> The Expressionist does not see, he has "visions". According to Edschmid [in *Uber den Expressionismus in der Literatur*], "the chain of facts: factories, houses, illness, prostitutes, screams, hunger" does not exist; only the interior vision they provoke exists. Facts and objects are nothing in themselves: we need to study their essence rather than their momentary and accidental forms. It is the

> hand of the artist which " through them grasps what is behind them " and allows us to know their real form, freed from the stifling constraint of a " false reality ". The Expressionist artist, not merely receptive but a true creator, seeks, instead of a momentary, accidental form, the *eternal, permanent meaning* of facts and objects.

In the semi-popular form adopted by the cinema, expressionism merged with the more theatrical concepts of the supernatural and the horrific. Man became the victim of forces originating in his darker imaginings, creatures conjured by " Gothic " fancies — vampires, magicians, hypnotists, demented scientists, archetypal criminals and the like seeking absolute power over their individual victims or over mankind as a whole. To these forces of darkness were opposed the idealism of the soul — loyalty, love, self-sacrifice, usually demonstrated by innocent youth and beauty in the face of evil old age and foul decay. For Siegfried Kracauer in his celebrated book, *From Caligari to Hitler,* these characteristics in German cinematic art were clearly indicative of Germany's capitulation to Hitler at the turn of the 1920s and 1930s, a thesis he develops to the point of exaggeration and over-simplification. Certainly, social and psychological instability in the period up to 1924 may have encouraged the production of these " nightmares " which have ever since been picked on as the outstanding works of the German cinema of the time, though the pressures which finally led the voters of 1930-1933 to put Hitler in power were surely far less " metaphysical ".

The designers initially associated with expressionism were the artists who collaborated on the sets for *Caligari* — Hermann Warm, who later worked with Lang on *Destiny,* with Galeen on *The Student of Prague,* with Pabst on *The Love of Jeanne Ney,* and later with Dreyer on *The Passion of Joan of Arc* and *Vampyr;* and Walther Röhrig, who worked on *Destiny, The Golem, The Chronicle of the Greyhouse, The Last Laugh,* and *Faust.* Designers influenced by the expressionists also included Erno Metzner (*Sumurun, The Loves of Pharoah, Diary of a Lost Girl*), while Lang himself (a designer in his own right) carried aspects of theatrical expressionism into the settings for his later German films, such as *M* and *The Last Will of Dr Mabuse.* Pabst, too, although identified with a growing movement towards realism (scarcely true of his silent period) adopted the same dark, shadowy stylization, with its doom-laden atmosphere, in such films as *Secrets of the Soul, The Love of Jeanne Ney, The Joyless Street, Pandora's Box* and *The Threepenny Opera.*

The Golem (1920, directed and scripted by Paul Wegener, with Henrik Galeen; camera, Karl Freund, Guido Seeber; design, Hans Poelzig) was Wegener's third Golem film (*The Golem,* 1914; *Der Golem und die Tänzerin,* 1917). Born in 1874, he had joined Reinhardt in 1906 after a varied career in the theatre, remaining in association with him until 1920, though also making many films. He had showed in such films as *The Student of Prague* and *Der Rattenfänger von Hameln* a marked interest in period subjects and fantasy. Wegener was also an impressive character actor, and was later to become a recognized artist under the Nazis, though never identified with them. *The Student of Prague* had introduced the concept of the Doppelgänger, the shadow or double of a human being who develops an independent, evil existence and preys on its human counterpart. Wegener had been among the first to recognize the peculiar properties of the film camera, and as early as 1916 had forecast a cinema using " fantastic images which would provoke absolutely novel associations of ideas in the spectator ", including the abstract film of moving shapes as well as films of fantasy. "Light and darkness in the cinema play the same role as rhythm and cadence in music ", he said. The possibilities of magic visual effects latent in the cinema drew Wegener to the Golem theme, a legend of the Prague ghetto associated with the sixteenth-century figure of the Rabbi Löw who creates a giant of clay which is brought to life by magical spells in order to help the Jewish community in time of persecution by the Emperor. In the first Golem film the statue is discovered in modern times, comes to life once more, and develops into a destructive monster when frustrated in its love for a young girl. It eventually dies by falling and shattering into pieces. Wegener played the Golem in both this and the later film of 1920, which he and Galeen set wholly in the historical period of the legend. This time the beserk monster is overcome by the innocence of a child. The sets were designed by the German architect, Hans Poelzig, who had worked for Reinhardt in the theatre.

The Golem, both as medieval legend and as a film, is a clear case of wishful thinking which oversteps itself because of its dependence upon " unlawful " black magic. In the face of persecution the Jews, through the magic of their Rabbi wearing a " wizard's hat " and calling upon the aid of Astaroth and spells which date back to Solomon, create an all-powerful monster. The " life " of the monster, which is covered with cabbalistic symbols, is activated by a Star of David screwed into his chest. Frustrated in his desire for the Rabbi's seductive daughter the monster turns against his creator, and is only stayed from destroying him when a fearless child appears to calm him and pluck the Star of David from his breast. Only pure innocence possesses the counter-magic to destroy the monstrous forces of evil.

Like all the German silent films which draw on magic and the supernatural, *The Golem* moves at a stately pace with stylized movements which border on slow motion. Settings and lighting are pictorialized to suggest a bizarre medievalism; the compositions of light and shade create a theatrical-cinematic atmosphere; the action is punctuated by a minimum of captions representing narrative links or dialogue. *The Golem* appears now beautiful rather than macabre, a kind of softened nightmare alleviated by the uniform beauty of its images and the unreality of its situations and characters.

Nosferatu (1922, directed by F. W. Murnau; adapted by Henrik Galeen from Bram Stoker's *Dracula;* camera, Fritz Arno Wagner, Gunther Krampf; design, Albin Grau) shares many characteristics with *The Golem,* though (as a result of Murnau's intense artistry) it is more genuinely horrific than either *Caligari* or *The Golem.* Its full title was *Nosferatu, eine Symphonie des Grauens* (Nosferatu, a Symphony of Terror). Its subject derives from the tradition of the vampire. Belief in vampires, a species of blood-sucking ghost, was (and maybe still is) widespread in Europe, and extended even to Asia; the restless spirit of a dead man or woman forces the body to rise from its grave and suck the blood of the living. Tradition has it that a vampire is destroyed by driving a stake through its heart as it lies in its coffin. Bram Stoker's celebrated story appeared in 1896, and the film was made out of copyright. (Hamilton Deane, the English actor-manager, was to dramatize the story in 1924 within copyright, while Universal bought the rights afresh when Bela Lugosi starred in the American *Dracula* of 1931, the first of the Dracula cycle which continues to this day). In the film, Nosferatu (Dracula) is a vampire isolated in a castle situated in a gloomy forest. He lies by day in a sarcophagus. At night he preys on the living world, bringing pestilence and death in his wake. Jonathan, the youthful clerk sent to the castle on business from Bremen, escapes death through the telepathic protection afforded him by Nina, his beautiful young wife, who remains in Bremen. Nosferatu is finally destroyed, like the Golem, by the innocent, unfearing love of Nina, who faces him fearlessly as the sunlight appears to destroy him.

Nosferatu moves slowly and deliberately, and once again it is the sheer beauty of the setting and camerawork which gives the film its dream-like illusion — the macabre Carpathian forest luminous in the moonlight (seen in negative), or the phosphorescent waters through which the deathship glides with no one left alive to pilot it, bringing Nosferatu to Bremen, and the shots of omnivorous plants which produce a nightmare out of actuality. Murnau used real locations, not studio sets, for his castle exteriors and landscapes, a practice unique at this time in a German film aiming at the unreal. Murnau and Wagner made nature supernatural. For his town scenes he used real buildings and streets, carefully chosen for the half hallucinatory appearance they could be given through the magic of the camera.

Murnau was pre-eminent among German directors for his imaginative use of images, and for his creative editing. *Nosferatu* remains one of the most impressive of the macabre films of the German silent cinema precisely because Murnau makes the horror an experience, not a by-product of expressionist décor and choreography. The vampire is a terrifying vision which approaches us inexorably, as in a nightmare, a hideous monster of overwhelming, preternatural proportions. In spite of its theatrical acting, *Nosferatu* remains a work of art *as a film*, not just a pleasing curiosity from the early cinema.

Kracauer classifies this as the first of the German 'tyrant' films, with a specific meaning of its own which goes beyond that of the normal vampire theme:

> The horrors *Nosferatu* spreads are caused by a vampire identified with pestilence. Does he embody the pestilence, or is its image evoked to characterize him? If he were simply the embodiment of destructive nature, Nina's interference with his activities would be nothing more than magic, meaningless in this context. Like Attila, Nosferatu is a "scourge of God", and only as such identifiable with the pestilence. He is a blood-thirsty, blood sucking tyrant figure looming in those regions where myths and fairy tales meet. It is highly significant that during this period German imagination, regardless of its starting-point, always gravitated towards such figures — as if under the compulsion of hate-love.

With *The Threepenny Opera* (1931, directed by G. W. Pabst;

script: Leo Lania, Bela Balasz, Ladislaus Vajda from the play by Berthold Brecht; camera, Fritz Arno Wagner; design, Andrei Andreiev) we move forward almost a decade, and into the early period of sound. Times are troubled again in Germany: the economy is once more in recession, unemployment is rising rapidly (4,350,000 in September 1931), and the Nazis have become in the 1930 election the second largest party in the Reichstag, with some 6.5 million votes. Brecht's Left-wing play had been produced in 1928 with great success in Berlin, staged at the Theater am Schiffbauerdam, where he was later to create an international reputation after the second world war with the Berliner Ensemble. Brecht had re-set Gay's eighteenth-century play with songs, *The Beggar's Opera,* in a London of the late nineteenth century in order to stress the decadence of the contemporary bourgeois world. The film was in some respects an unfortunate production, since Brecht failed to agree with Pabst on the interpretation given his work, in spite of the fact that some members of the original cast appeared in it, including Lotte Lenya as Jenny and Carola Neher as Polly, who were able to retain something of Brecht's intention in their rendering of those of Weill's songs which remained, with their diseuse diction and downbeat lilt. Pabst, however, stressed the romantic image of the underworld; most of Brecht's acid sarcasm was softened away and his social satire largely lost. Brecht was so exasperated that he sued the production company, Nero, while the film was still in production. He claimed that his political message had been entirely abandoned in the process of adaptation, in spite of the fact that his contract gave him the right to approve the script. Brecht lost his case, largely because he had, in the end, left the script to Pabst and his writers.

Perhaps Pabst was largely attracted to this play because it suggested to him something of the same, dark, romantic, slum atmosphere he had created in *The Joyless Street, Pandora's Box,* and *Diary of a Lost Girl.* As a result he either forgot, or purposely eliminated, the peculiarly harsh quality of burlesque in Brecht's uncompromising production for the theatre. The film belongs far more to Pabst than to Brecht.

Andrei Andreiev, who had been Pabst's designer for *Pandora's Box,* created a visual fantasia out of a dockside environment swathed in mist and shadow. The beggars' rags were heightened into a form of décor, while the Victorian brothel, dominated by large statues of half-naked Negresses, became the epitome of fin-de-siècle bourgeois decadence.

M (1931, directed by Fritz Lang; script, Thea von Harbou; camera, Fritz Arno Wagner; sets, Emil Hasler and Karl Vollbrecht) moves further in the direction of social and psychological realism, though remaining essentially a tragic melodrama. It confronts the audience with the inability of the psychopathic murderer of little girls to control his actions. The film derived from the facts of the case of the Düsseldorf child murderer, Kürten. M, the murderer, is also confronted by his own guilt; it is almost as if a doppelgänger takes control of him. A whole city is riven by his actions to the extent that the police and the underworld, opposing organizations, find themselves adopting parallel methods to hunt down the noxious alien in their midst. The murderer is finally rounded up by the underworld, not the police, tried by a " kangaroo " court, and threatened with lynch law until, in the final climax of his terror, the police intervene to " rescue " him.

This was Lang's first sound film.[1] His deeply moralistic approach to human concepts of justice are as apparent in this film as they are, for instance, in *Fury* and *You Only Live Once;* what is the difference between justice and revenge? The criminals will not accept a compulsive, uncontrolled killer in their midst; he is psychotic, and therefore outside their pale, their concept of a criminal code. Yet when they capture him, they behave just as compulsively as he does in their urge to kill him, especially when reinforced by the mothers of the dead girls. During the celebrated sequence which intercuts the meeting supervised by Lohmann, the police Superintendent, with that supervised by Schrenke, the criminal boss, Lohmann (a character who re-appears in *The Last Will of Dr Mabuse*) complains ironically of lack of cooperation from the public. Until the very end, the criminals are far more effective in their organization than the police, who spend most of their time in a state of bafflement.

Lang in *M* is still affected by the expressionistic imagery and shadowed pictorialism which haunts his silent films, scripted always as melodrama by his wife of the German period, Thea von Harbou, a

[1] A shortened version (92 minutes instead of the original 114) was later circulated in New York. A dubbed version in English was produced in England, largely with different actors, except for Lorre. In 1950 Joseph Losey directed a remake for Columbia.

successful writer of thrillers who had worked with him consistently since 1920. Visual symbols are used, for example the balloon caught in the telegraph wires, the rolling rubber ball, signs that the child victims are dead. But the element of actuality behind the formidable façade of melodrama points ahead to Lang's American films, which were to be far more realist in approach than his German films. Becker, the killer, is seen as the pathetic victim of his other, psychopathic self against which he vainly struggles. The film is imaginative in its use of sound; Lang is evidently determined to make the transition from silent film with the same, close-knit structural control as he had evolved in the 1920s. Voice or music are carefully used to bridge continuity, and Becker is given his musical motif, the tune from Grieg's *Peer Gynt*. Tension is greatly increased by careful use of the sound track wherever possible to complement or counterpoint the visuals. Peter Lorre's intense depiction of fear, though essentially a tour de force, is endowed with a sympathy, understanding and subtlety which raises it well above the needs of melodrama.

Nicholas Garnham has written of this film:

> The world he portrays is a Manichean one in which the forces of good and evil, equally matched, constantly fight for man's soul as the police and the underworld both relentlessly pursue M the murderer. Lang's favourite image for this dualism is the mirror. For it is significant that the murderer first sees the M on his back, the mark of Cain, in a mirror. M is also a letter whose mirror-image is the same as its real self. This mirroring is carried right through the structure of the film. For the conflict between good and evil within the murderer himself, the doppelgänger who haunts him, is itself a reflection of the conflict between crime and the law.

Lang's last German film, *The Last Will of Dr Mabuse* (1932) represented a demented criminal plotting to ensnare the world of sanity. For Lang this stood for Hitler, or so he has claimed. Goebbels banned it before its release in 1933, but offered Lang (in spite of the fact that his mother was Jewish) the opportunity to make films for Hitler. Lang fled to Paris that same night, abandoning all his possessions in Germany. His wife, who supported the Nazis, divorced him, and he had, like so many others who had helped to create the greater German cinema of the past decade, to make a new career for himself elsewhere. Lubitsch, a Jew, had long since left for Hollywood, while Freund had gone there in 1929. Murnau had died in a car accident in Hollywood in 1931. Among those who were forced to leave Germany in addition to Lang were Max Reinhardt, Dieterle, Veidt, Kortner, Lorre, Poelzig, Andreiev and Brecht. Wegener remained, as did Fritz Arno Wagner; Pabst, after a period in exile, returned to Austria (then part of the German Reich) on the eve of the war. German cinema, meanwhile, remained technically proficient but fundamentally uninspired. Goebbels was to develop it primarily as an instrument of entertainment, leaving hard-core propaganda largely as a specialist activity for the newsreel, the documentary and the documentary-feature supervised by his Ministry. Only Leni Riefenstahl, working directly for Hitler on *The Triumph of the Will* (1935) added something of the mystical qualities of the German silent cinema to her image of the Führer.

CREDITS:

Produced by	Universum-Film-Aktiengesellschaft (Ufa)
Directed by	Paul Wegener, with Henrik Galeen and Carl Boese
Scenario by	Henrik Galeen, adapted from Gustav Meyrink
Camera operators	Karl Freund, Guido Seeber
Designed by	Hans Poelzig
Costumes by	Rochus Gliese

CAST:

Rabbi Löw	Albert Steinrück
The Golem	Paul Wegener
Miriam	Lydia Salmonova
Famulus	Ernst Deutsch
Rabbi Jehuda	Hans Sturm
Tempeldiener	Max Kronert
Emperor Luhois	Otto Gebühr
Florian	Lothar Müthel
Rose girl	Greta Schröder

THE GOLEM

A night of stars and mysteries outlines in light some crippled buildings, their roofs put on their walls like the pointed hats on wizards. Seven haloed stars are set in the dark sky above the tallest tower, reaching narrowly to heaven. . . .

TITLE: *The learned Rabbi Löw reads in the stars that misfortune threatens the Jews.*

On the roof of the weird tower marked on each corner by a great stone, Rabbi Löw sits behind an early telescope, studying the constellations. He is bearded with long locks of hair. (*Still*)
Through the eye of the telescope, we sweep across the heavens.
The Rabbi looks down from his instrument on its pivot and pores over a book on alchemy. He is backed by smoke and a strange light.
In the Rabbi's study below, a glass retort bubbles on a flame. Watching it is the Rabbi's pale assistant, FAMULUS, who looks up from his experiment at a girl, MIRIAM, smiling and holding a lamp burning in her hand. Her shoulders are bare, her robe is long, her hair in black braids. The two are in a room made of stone blocks with a domed roof, like a rough-cast observatory. The girl walks sensuously past the fire and the assistant, then puts down the lamp on a table. FAMULUS gestures towards the roof above.
There the Rabbi looks up from his book, rises and walks across the roof towards a stairwell.
Down some curving stairs, the Rabbi descends until he is standing between MIRIAM and his assistant.

TITLE: *"I must speak with Rabbi Jehuda. Danger threatens our people."*

MIRIAM's face is full of pain. FAMULUS runs to the back of the tower room and returns with a tall pointed bent hat, shaped like the buildings. The Rabbi puts on his magician's hat and leaves.
Outside between the dark walls of the ghetto of the medieval city, the Rabbi hurries through the darkness with his assistant carrying a smoking torch.

By the light of twin candles, the old Rabbi JEHUDA is reading a large tome. Hearing a noise, he takes off his spectacles and puts up his hand to shield his weak eyes from the glare.
Rabbi Löw and his assistant are brought into the older Rabbi's room by a servant carrying a lantern.
The two Rabbis strike their hearts three times in ritual woe, then take each other by the hands, their faces full of foreboding. Rabbi Löw warns.

TITLE: *"Call all the elders of the community together to pray. The stars predict disaster."*

Old JEHUDA is worried and speaks his fears, as the assistant and the servant listen. Then he gives a command and all leave the room.

Now two small windows shine in the blackness and three torches move across the dark towards a gothic arch.
Labyrinthine passages are seen through the arches, as six men lead Jewish worshippers towards their prayers.
A Jew prays before the Menorah with a shawl over his head. He strikes his heart three times, lifts up his hands and bows forwards. Behind him, men kneel in the darkness and lift their heads into the light, then lean back so that their faces are upside down. They strike their hearts three times and prostrate themselves again.
On a rooftop, a black cat stalks the tiles in front of a crooked chimney.
The roofs of the houses curve and sidle under the stars.
The seven haloed stars over the Rabbi's tower shine bright, then dissolve into a mailed fist holding a written order:

> INSERT: *DECREED AGAINST THE JEWS: We can no longer neglect the complaints of the people against the Jews. They despise the holy ceremonies of Christ. They endanger the lives and property of their fellow-men. They work black magic. We decree that all Jews shall be expelled from the city and all adjoining land before the end of the month. IMPERATOR.*

Fade to the HOLY ROMAN EMPEROR's face as he is clearly shown seated in state at his court, wearing rich clothes and signing the decree with a gloved and jewelled hand. When he has finished signing, he picks up a large royal seal and presses it down on some wax.

The CHAMBERLAIN hands the decree to a courtier on his left, who puts it into a courier's round satchel, then hands it back to the CHAMBERLAIN, who gives the case to the EMPEROR.
Three young courtiers talk as they wait for nothing to do. The EMPEROR smiles and gestures towards the courtiers with the courier's satchel. They are aghast, but one with a feather in his hat runs forward to the EMPEROR, while the others watch his temerity. The EMPEROR speaks to the bold one.

TITLE: *"Knight Florian, deliver our decree to the Ghetto."*

As the EMPEROR smiles in front of his attendants, FLORIAN takes the satchel and turns to leave, smiling his satisfaction at his friends.

Fade to the hand of Rabbi Löw tracing out an alchemist's drawing of the figure of the GOLEM, a mythical giant with a five-pointed star of Judah on his breast, who may be summoned by the Jews in their hour of need. Hieroglyphs cover the parchment—instructions on how to make the giant. The hand turns over another page of parchment covered with astrological designs and crabbed writing. The Rabbi is planning.

TITLE: *"Venus enters the constellation of Libra! Now is the auspicious hour to summon the dead spirit Astaroth, and compel him to reveal the magic word. Then we can bring the Golem to life to save our people."*

The fingers trace out more of the diagrams, then dissolve to the Rabbi's face as he studies his book by his window. He puts up his hands and rocks back, then bows forwards to the wisdom of the book.

Fade to the knight FLORIAN as he rides on his white horse in front of a huge black wall pierced by an arched gate. On a watchtower, a bell rings and the watchman comes down some steep steps to look over the wall to see who is at the gate. He then hurries down.
FLORIAN is still horsed outside the walls.
The watchman hurries down masses of winding steps, until he reaches a barred window by the gate. There FLORIAN holds the sealed courier's satchel in one hand, the halter of his horse in the other hand, and a rose between his teeth. The watchman shakes his head,

then sees the EMPEROR's seal and opens the gate for the knight, who is smiling.
A doorkeeper pulls down the bar of the gate.
FLORIAN now stands by his horse with his hand on his hip and his legs crossed, the casual messenger of bad news. The gate opens and a man takes the horse's halter to lead it into the city. FLORIAN follows, the rose between his teeth.

In her chamber, MIRIAM combs her dark tresses. The walls are covered with patterns of flowers and weeping leaves.
In his study, Rabbi Löw looks up in pain from the parchment which he puts aside. He closes a large book, puts it in a recess, then crosses to the doors leading into the room and locks them. Restlessly, he moves in and out of the arches of the chamber. Round him, the glass beakers of his experiments. His passing takes him now into a dark small room with a triangular window, where he pulls aside a rug and opens a trapdoor. He climbs down through it into a secret corridor with lines on its wall ending in a triangular door, sealed with a metal strip ornamented with hieroglyphs. Rabbi Löw cuts through the seal with his knife and pushes the door open. In the secret room, the Rabbi passes a diagram of the GOLEM fixed to the wall and pulls down from an arched window a huge slab on twin cross-bars. Two other diagrams of the GOLEM are now seen near a lump of clay, roughly fashioned in the shape of a giant. Rabbi Löw now begins to work at the eyes of the monster, pushing at the clay and moulding the face of the GOLEM.

Fade to FLORIAN, as the watchman leads him and his horse down the steps and through the streets of the city. Between the heavy dark walls, people run about to watch him and wait on top of the arches of the massed buildings. The EMPEROR's messenger has come. In his study, the old Rabbi JEHUDA is ready at his table. A limping spry man comes in and taps him on his shoulder.

TITLE: *"A messenger from the Emperor is here."*

JEHUDA signals the man to bring in the stranger while he takes off his glasses, uncomprehending, and puts his hand over his tired eyes. Fade to FLORIAN, as the man brings him in to see JEHUDA. The courtier hands the Rabbi the imperial decree with a grand flourish,

then leans back against the middle arch of the room, crossing his ankles, one hand on his hip, gaily swinging the rose with his free hand and reading the decree over the old Jew's shoulder.
JEHUDA drops the scroll and puts his hands over his heart in shock. He moves beside FLORIAN and speaks to the knight, who is full of disdain.

TITLE: *"Come with me to the Chief Rabbi Löw, who is like a father to our whole community."*

As JEHUDA is scraping and bowing, FLORIAN nods. The old Rabbi reaches out to kiss the dandy knight's sleeve, but FLORIAN jerks away, and they leave together.
Fade to the Rabbi Löw kneading a mass of clay in his hands as he studies the diagrams. He turns and smears the clay on the GOLEM's face. His hands work at the features of the monster.
Fade to the ghetto street outside Löw's tower, where FLORIAN is walking with a crowd leading his horse.
MIRIAM is putting her hair up under a coif, when she hears the noise in the street, looks out of the window, and moves with joy to see the handsome knight below. (*Still*)
The walls rise, slant and beamed and high, above FLORIAN and his horse, as the ground swallows them up.
From the street, JEHUDA is made to look up by FLORIAN tapping his shoulder.
MIRIAM leans out of her window, looking down and smiling. FLORIAN looks up and waves his rose at her.
MIRIAM looks down in delight.
Beside the knight, JEHUDA gestures towards the door of the house. MIRIAM nods and draws her head back inside the window.
Below, the old Rabbi explains to FLORIAN who the girl is.
Inside Löw's study, MIRIAM runs over to the assistant FAMULUS and tells him of the arrival of the EMPEROR's messenger. As he runs off, she folds her arms and sighs.
In his secret room, the Rabbi Löw works on the GOLEM's clay face, now smooth and humanoid. He looks upwards, then moves over to the arched window. He places the slab over it, plunging the room into darkness. Then he opens the door of the room, letting in the light as he goes out. Finally he closes the door on the GOLEM in its black sepulchre.

Fade to Löw's study where the assistant ushers in the haughty Florian and the old Jehuda. When Löw comes in, he bows and takes the knight back through an arch to a dark recess, where there are some heavy curved chairs set under stalactites which grow out of shell-like niches. As Florian toys with his rose, the Chief Rabbi speaks.

Title: *"It was I who drew the Emperor's horoscope. I warned him of danger twice. Tell him now that I humbly ask for an audience with him."*

Florian smiles and nods while the two Rabbis speak together. Miriam comes in, holding a large goblet and a bowl of fruit, which she sets on a table before offering the goblet to the knight.
In answer to her smile, Florian grins toothily, showing the gap between his front teeth.
Miriam looks away, smiling, then lowers her lids in false shyness.
The two Rabbis look at each other, then off at the two young people.
Miriam now drinks out of the goblet herself before offering it to the knight, who slyly turns the goblet round to kiss the brim and drink out of the same place as she did. He gives his rose to the girl. She plays with it softly.

Fade again to the starry night sky with the seven stars haloed in the heavens, then dissolve to a star of David made of cracked clay, then dissolve to the powerful face and shoulders of the finished Golem, its eyes closed, crowned by a mass of clay hair. Löw stands with his hand on the standing monster's chest, propped against the wall of his secret room.

Title: *"The hour has come!"*

He looks up at the diagram, then bends to pull the Golem forward. He takes its weight on his shoulder, struggles, then pushes the clay monster back upright. His heart has been strained, so he massages it before leaving the room.
Famulus is heating a prong at the forge when the trapdoor opens behind him and Löw appears. The Rabbi's assistant drops the hot iron in terror, as his master comes up behind him and takes him by the shoulders and speaks.

Title: *"Guard this secret with your life."*

The assistant rolls his eyes as the Rabbi takes his hand and leads him over to the trapdoor.

TITLE: *Knight Florian brings the Emperor's answer.*

FLORIAN rides into the ghetto and stops between two rows of houses with gables hanging askew, aslant. He claps his hands and a man appears at a high window. He waves a sheet of parchment, and people run up to the EMPEROR's messenger on his horse.
In his secret room, Löw demonstrates the GOLEM to his assistant, pointing to the star of David on the monster's chest, then to the diagram on the wall. FAMULUS rolls his eyes with wonder and terror.
In the study, MIRIAM shows FLORIAN to a carved bench. As she tries to leave, he catches her hand and draws her down beside him. Their breathing quickens, their lips near, his hand touches her breast, her hands cover his before ending on his chest. Faint with desire, the pair lean back on the bench.
Fade to Löw and his assistant struggling with the body of the GOLEM up the steep corridor. The wrapped head of the monster is pushed through the trapdoor.
Back on the bench, FLORIAN keeps his hand over MIRIAM's heart as he whispers in her ear and she smiles.
Fade to FAMULUS unwrapping the head of the GOLEM. He and the Rabbi push the monster towards the arched doorway. (*Still*). Löw moves over to the triangular window to look out. He sees below . . .
The white horse being led up and down between two rows of people and the narrow walls of the ghetto.
Seeing everybody's attention safely elsewhere, Löw locks the doors of the room while his assistant closes the trapdoor.
Fade back to the couple on the carved bench with their arms round each other. Rabbi Löw comes on, his face full of worry. The couple spring up as he passes and FLORIAN gives him the parchment with an embarrassed flourish.
As MIRIAM backs away, her finger to her lips, the Rabbi reads the scroll:

INSERT: *In memory of your services we will grant you an audience. Come to the Festival at the Castle, and amuse us again with your magical arts.*

FLORIAN and the ecstatic MIRIAM glance at each other.

Rabbi Löw looks up from the scroll, smiling. He speaks to FLORIAN, who puts on his hat and walks grinning past MIRIAM. The Rabbi passes her and scowls and follows the knight out of the room. MIRIAM runs over to the window.
Outside the tower, FLORIAN appears with the Rabbi and takes the halter of his horse. The people watch below the tall buildings.
MIRIAM backs away from the window and cowers, her arm over her head, expecting punishment. When Löw comes back into the room, he lectures her as she shakes her head. He points towards the bench, but she still denies his charges. So he takes her wrists, forces her to kneel and grips her by the neck, threatening her.

TITLE: *"You shame me, but I will soon have a guardian for you."*

The Rabbi stops throttling the frightened MIRIAM, who presses her face against his legs in submission.
On a road over a bridge, FLORIAN rides his horse, outlined against the sky.

Löw's hand opens the leather cover of a book, intricately decorated. Inside, a drawing of the GOLEM with crabbed writing at its side. On the other page, a German text:

INSERT: *This figure, called the Golem, was made long ago by a magician of Thessaly. If you place the magic word in the amulet on its breast, it will live and breathe as long as it wears it.*

Fade from the open book to Löw and his assistant poring over it, then fade again to them as the assistant looks up in fear and the Rabbi tells him to be brave. Löw closes the book and picks up a hollow Star of David and a piece of paper. Then he opens another old tome and reads its text.

INSERT: *Astaroth guards the magic word which can give life even today. He who possesses the key of Solomon can force Astaroth to reveal the word, if he observes the due hour of the meeting of the planets.*

The Rabbi looks at his assistant as he closes the old book. He takes the Star of David and folds up the pieces of paper to fit the hollow inside the star.
On the chest of the GOLEM, there is a clay circle waiting for the star.

Löw moves towards the monster, while his frightened assistant lags behind, his hands over his face. Löw forces the hands of FAMULUS apart so that he must watch the Rabbi pointing to the circle on the GOLEM's chest.

Now the Rabbi wears his wizard's hat, ornamented with cabbalistic symbols and the Star of David. He has a wand in his hand, which he brings down, raises, brings down.

FAMULUS watches, rigid with terror.

Löw continues with his magic ceremony, drawing a circle about him with the wand. Fade to him, now standing within a ring of fire. He pulls his assistant into the charmed circle, and suddenly a clay Star of David appears at the end of his wand, while he waves thrice.

FAMULUS grips his master in fear.

Three lighted torches flare above the Rabbi and his assistant in their ring of flames. FAMULUS begins to faint and slide to the floor, while the Rabbi also weakens, sinks down, holding the clay star above him.

TITLE: *"Astaroth, Astaroth, appear, appear! Speak the word!"*

Löw's face is distorted as he holds up the clay star. A demon's head appears by the Rabbi and his assistant. It burns and floats, its forehead huge above its bulging white eyes, smoke curling from its black lips.

Löw cries out in fear.

From the mouth of Astaroth, the smoke writes the magic word: *AEMAET*.

Now the clay star blazes at the end of the Rabbi's wand and he throws it outside the circle of fire. Then he pulls off his wizard's hat and staggers round the ring of flames, trying to get out. Finally he collapses, his arms stretched wide, as the centre of the circle explodes in a flash of white light.

As the smoke clears, the Rabbi is seen crouching over his unconscious assistant.

Outside the tower, the smoke flies up to the sky from a small window.

Inside his room, Löw drags FAMULUS over to a bench, shakes him and wakens him. He points at the paper in his hand and the clay figure of the GOLEM. FAMULUS tries to stop his master, but Löw seizes the pen, dips it in ink and begins to write.

The thick quill writes out the word *AEMAET*.

The Rabbi finishes writing, then runs over to the GOLEM and signals FAMULUS to help him move the monster. The two of them stand the GOLEM in front of some crooked steps. The Rabbi puts the paper inside the hollow Star of David, then screws it into a socket inside the clay circle in the GOLEM's chest. Immediately, the eyelids of the GOLEM open, his clay head moves, as FAMULUS backs away.
The GOLEM's face is blank, its eyes open and white, the mask of clay hiding any form of intelligence.
The Rabbi looks at his creation.
The GOLEM turns, its mouth severe. It has ropes tied on its arms, narrow legs and heavy shoes.
The assistant crouches on the steps, ready to run.
The GOLEM looks at Löw, who backs away. Then it rocks, its eyes staring wide. It moves forwards, swinging its legs clumsily like lead weights on poles. As it reaches the Rabbi, Löw orders the monster to stop. It does stop. Then the Rabbi orders the GOLEM to walk away. It obeys him, knocking over the assistant who happens to be in its way. Then it halts on Löw's order.
Hesitant and fearful, Löw approaches his monster and pulls the Star of David out of its socket. The eyes of the GOLEM shut, it rocks on its feet and falls back against the wall. The Rabbi and his assistant look at the lifeless monster, then begin to praise the Lord.

Now the GOLEM is seen swinging an axe, then by a well, splitting logs. One blow is enough to cut a huge log in half.
Two men look down watching the GOLEM at work below their window.
Four children peep over the wall at the toiling monster.
The GOLEM moves with the logs, then looks upwards.
Its master, the Rabbi, is leaning out of his tower window.
The GOLEM stumps up to the well.
The Rabbi signals with his arm.
The GOLEM nods twice jerkily, unties the well rope and begins to pull up a bucket of water.
Inside his tower room, Löw turns to sit at his table by the window while MIRIAM rushes in to point out the monster at work.
The GOLEM pulls a bucket of water from the well.
In the room, MIRIAM is upset, but the Rabbi lays down the law.

TITLE: *"This is my new servant, Golem."*

MIRIAM looks fearful and glances out of the window.

TITLE: *The Golem's first appearance on the street.*

FAMULUS comes out of a small archway in a timbered wall, signalling the huge GOLEM to follow him with a large basket. The monster looks pleased at its first sight of the ghetto. Now it moves between the high walls, making two men flee for their lives. But some children run up to it and skip around it, while it swings its basket at them. Now the children run down some steps, while mothers pull their babies away from the passing monster and the Rabbi's assistant.

In an apothecary's shop, a man and a woman and a boy are working over a table scattered with herbs. The door is pushed open by the GOLEM, which knocks over a stool and stands by the counter. The three people in the shop are terrified.

The monster reaches into its basket for its shopping list and stiffly holds the list out in its gloved fist. Now FAMULUS runs into the shop to explain. As he does so, the GOLEM turns to glare at the hated assistant.

TITLE: *"This is the Rabbi's new servant. He cannot speak, but he will not hurt you. He will come to you every day, with a list of the articles we need."*

On the assistant's signal, the man and the woman begin to pull down the herbs from racks above.

Fade to FLORIAN, now standing by the city gate and arguing with the watchman. He puts a folded letter between his teeth so that he can bring up his purse and drop coins one by one over his shoulder into the watchman's open palm. Five coins complete the bribe. The watchman's hand takes the note, and FLORIAN grins his delight.

Fade to the Rabbi's laboratory, where FAMULUS is leading in the GOLEM, who is carrying the herbs and the basket and other loads. The assistant smiles and takes the herbs from the monsters, but it will not give up the basket. The assistant backs away, telling the GOLEM to put out its arm. It does so with a jerk, nearly knocking FAMULUS over; but now he can get the basket from the monster.

The assistant tries to get more work from the GOLEM. He taps down the monster's arm, then takes it over to the spit, where there is a

large bellows worked by a handle over the fire. FAMULUS demonstrates how to work the handle, which the GOLEM does with such vigour that the assistant has to leap from the flare of the flames fanned by the bellows.
Löw watches the comedy, considering.
The assistant runs from the room, as the GOLEM makes the fire spurt high.
FAMULUS runs up to the Rabbi, who walks over to the monster and raises his hand in a curt command. The GOLEM stops working the bellows and leaves the room at Löw's order. The Rabbi turns to his assistant.

TITLE: *"Today I go to show the Golem to the Emperor. Stay and guard my house."*

Löw moves across to speak to the GOLEM, which follows its master out, leaving the assistant behind.

Fade to a high tower and a wall, with MIRIAM entering, her scarf blowing in the wind, her arms held high. She walks over to another tower, more leaning than Pisa's, and meets the watchman there. He hands the folded letter to her and disappears, while she opens it, smiles to read it, folds it up and kisses the words of her lover.
Fade into a road over a bridge, where the Rabbi is leading the GOLEM towards the EMPEROR.

TITLE: *The Rose Festival.*

Four trumpeters stand on a balcony festooned with banners hanging from stag's horns. They blow their brass notes to north, east, south and west.
In the EMPEROR's hall, two rows of men with torches, two rows of girls in bright dresses dance and whirl to the music.
Above them, six musicians puff and blow wind instruments from a balcony.
The men dance with their torches held high.
The courtiers round the EMPEROR's throne link arms and sway to the music. A jester mocks the girl with the EMPEROR. FLORIAN runs out of the hall.
Two tall knights with feathered helmets stand on either side of an open heavy door, through which FLORIAN comes, closing it behind

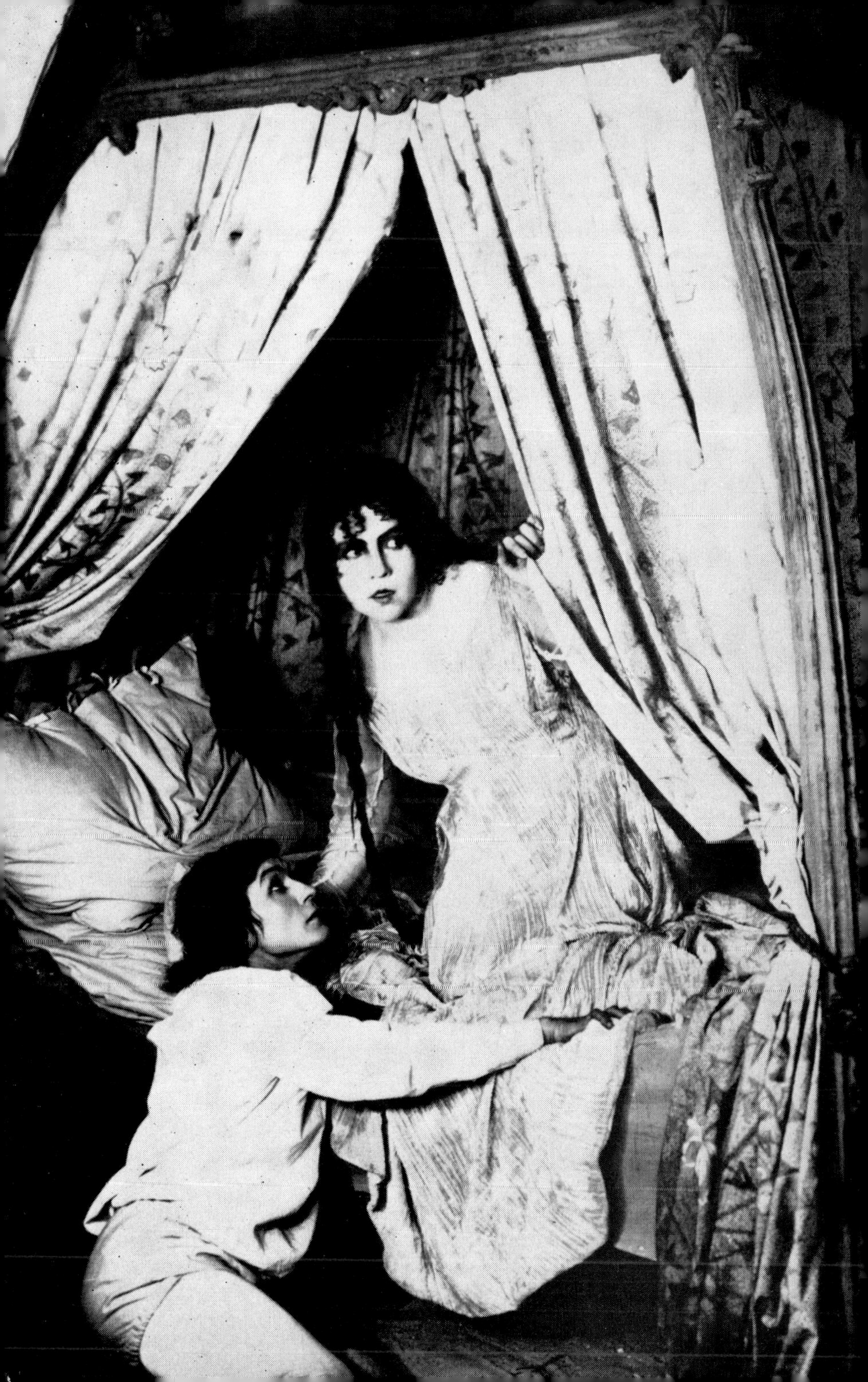

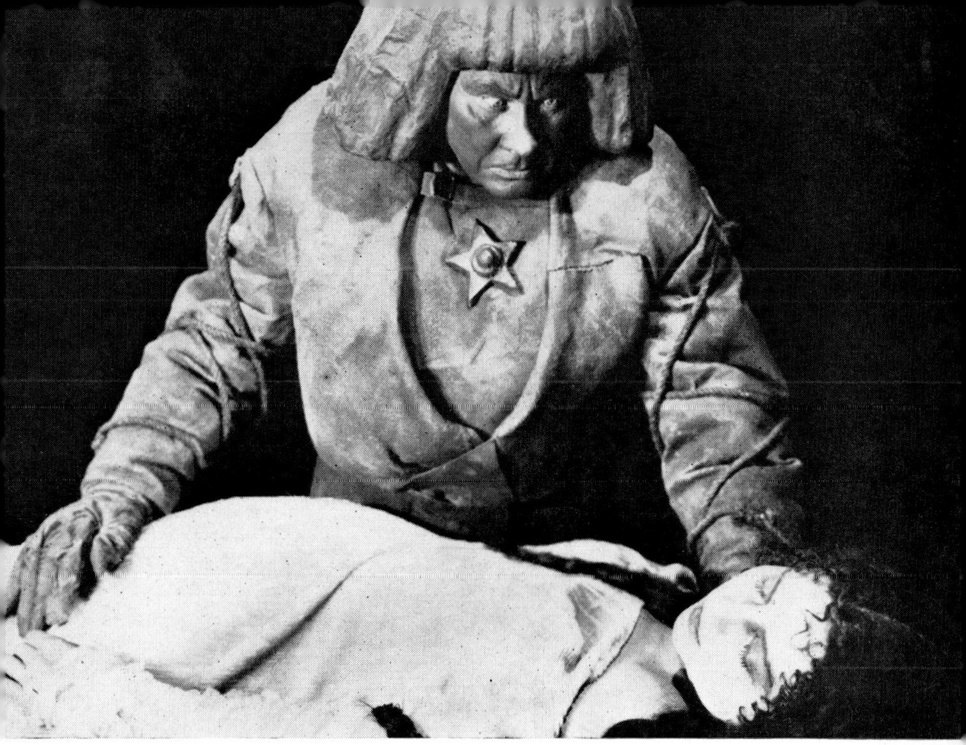

him before dashing off.
The dancing men still whirl with their torches.

Fade to MIRIAM, bare-shouldered under her turban, as she reads FLORIAN's letter.

INSERT: *"At the time chosen by the Emperor to see your father, I will leave the castle and come to you. I have bribed the watchman. Place a light in your window as a sign that you are waiting for me, Florian."*

MIRIAM's face is hot in the lamplight as she closes her eyes and puts her forehead to the letter.
Fade back to the dancers, as they part, holding their torches high.
The two knights at the heavy door stop the Rabbi and the GOLEM as they enter. Löw explains the reason for his coming and is allowed to enter. More knights cluster round the GOLEM, staring at it.
In the hall, Löw walks towards the EMPEROR. He looks strange in his dark cloak and pointed wizard's hat. He bows low before the EMPEROR and kisses his ring. The EMPEROR pats him, condescending, while the jester leers.
Two beautiful girls with jewelled circlets on their foreheads smile, then suddenly go white with fear to see:
The GOLEM, towering and blinking by the door.
Now the EMPEROR and his girl see the monster. The EMPEROR asks Löw about it and is impressed. The Rabbi raises his hand.
The GOLEM moves down the hall between the dancers, who fall back in fear.
One of the musicians stops playing and stares with a slack mouth, then taps the shoulder of another musician, whose mouth also drops open. The music from the balcony stops.
The EMPEROR's guests draw back in terror.
The GOLEM moves down the hall straight at the EMPEROR's throne.
Three girls shrink back, crouching on the floor.
The GOLEM comes to a halt before its creator and the EMPEROR.
Rabbi Löw explains.

TITLE: *"He is my creature, called Golem. I may not tell you more."*

As the Rabbi and the EMPEROR move away, girls surround the GOLEM like a plaything. (*Still*). Greatly daring, one girl touches its cheek. It snaps back at her and all the girls dart back. Now another girl shrugs and offers the monster a flower. It looks at the flower in its hand, then slowly reaches out to touch the girl's head in gratitude. But the girls dart away from its touch, and it stares after this beauty vanishing, lost. Its face is sad as it learns its own horror.

Fade to FLORIAN creeping back across the road bridge.

Fade back to the Rabbi, the EMPEROR and the GOLEM. The EMPEROR's girl elbows the monster, but it does not move. She stands, smiling her triumph at her lover, while he turns to put a hand on Löw's shoulder.

TITLE: *"What kind of miracle can you show us today, you strange magician?"*

As the EMPEROR folds his arms, the Rabbi becomes grave and raises his hands and his eyes towards heaven.

TITLE: *"I will show you the history of our people and our fathers. If you value your lives, no one must speak nor laugh."*

The EMPEROR smiles and shouts to the guests and waves his hand above his head. They toss flowers in the air and laugh their pleasure.

Fade to FLORIAN running into the dark arch of the doorway of Löw's tower. He stops to look upwards. MIRIAM appears in a white gown and pulls him inside. In a dark hall of the tower, a single lamp shines on MIRIAM pausing to sink into the knight's arms and kiss him. Then she leads him on into the darkness.
FAMULUS lies asleep at a table, the Rabbi's books open in front of him.

Fade back to the EMPEROR's court, where all are seated with their backs to us while Rabbi Löw stands on a platform. Behind him, stone branches weave in and around a niche in the wall. The Rabbi raises his hands. There is an explosion of white flame. Fiery particles shoot out and scare the EMPEROR's guests.
Now the Rabbi raises his hands again. There is a flare of light and as the guests wonder, we see two lines of people toiling across the desert.

Now superimposed over the EMPEROR's hall, we see the three Wise Kings, Mary on the donkey's back with the Christ child, and the wandering tribes of Israel.
Löw's eyes burn as he summons up the history of the Jews.
The people about the EMPEROR all watch intently.
In a group round a young man, a girl whispers. He puts a finger to his lips to hush her.
The musicians in the balcony stare downwards.
The GOLEM watches the magic show between two of the EMPEROR's knights.
Now MOSES appears superimposed over the imperial hall.
The jester giggles and nudges the EMPEROR's girl. Then he grimaces and makes her laugh. This makes the EMPEROR laugh. Following their master's lead, all the courtiers laugh as the jester waves them on to more derision.
MOSES walks towards the mocking guests, his staff threatening them.
Löw raises his hands in an incantation.
MOSES looms over the laughing courtiers.
Löw's face is fearful.
Now MOSES towers over the EMPEROR himself. He conjures up a lightning flash. Smoke fills the hall.
Seven frightened faces stare up like the haloed stars.
Above them, three ceiling beams fall down between the pillars of the hall.
Dust showers the milling mob of courtiers.
The beams slide further down between the pillars.
The courtiers panic, fight, choke in the dust.
The musicians cower on the balcony.
The beams crush still further down on the people.
The GOLEM stands at the door of the hall, its arms spread blocking the way out. Onc frightened girl kneels in front of it, begging its mercy; but the GOLEM shakes its head and bars the door. A beam falls off its shoulder and crashes down on a man. The rest shrink back.
Other beams fall about the frantic jester and the frightened courtiers, who begin to attack one another and fight their way out.
Rabbi Löw stays standing by the EMPEROR and his girl.
The courtiers attack each other to scramble out of holes in the

cracking walls and windows.
Now outside the hall, people are seen falling out of the windows between the great pillars which support the palace.
Löw stretches up his hands to heaven as more courtiers panic by the EMPEROR, who seizes the Rabbi and shakes him from his trance.

TITLE: *"Save me, and I will pardon your people."*

The Rabbi smiles faintly and reaches out his hand and cries out to his monster.
By the door, the GOLEM nods and moves from the main doorway.
As the Rabbi and the EMPEROR and the courtiers move away, the ceiling falls where they have been standing. They step their way over the prostrate wounded to where the GOLEM lurches up onto a stone platform and puts his shoulders and hands under some fallen beams. The monster strains mightily at the falling roof.
The beams part into a triangle of escape for the people crouching behind, including the Rabbi and the EMPEROR . . . (*Still*)

Fade to the road bridge, across which the Rabbi is returning with his monster.
Now FLORIAN is seen with his head on MIRIAM's breast as she lies back on her pillows, the two drapes of her bed in a triangle of escape behind her.

Now fade to a tall arched gate in the city wall, where Löw pulls the cord of the bell, while the GOLEM waits.
The watchman is asleep in the bell tower, while a bird is asleep on the bell itself. As the bell rings, the bird flies off and the watchman springs up, looks over the wall and rushes off down some steps.
The gate opens to let in the Rabbi and the GOLEM. The Rabbi tells the watchman the good news, his hand on the other's shoulder.

TITLE: *"We are saved! The Emperor has withdrawn his decree. Wake my sleeping brothers with the glad sound of the Schofa horn."*

The smiling watchman kisses Löw's sleeve, then leads him and the GOLEM into the city.

Fade to MIRIAM's bed, where she is asleep with FLORIAN on the floor beside her. She wakes in fear and rouses FLORIAN, who is also afraid. (*Still*). She rises from her bed in her long white nightgown, her black braids reaching nearly to her ankles. Her lover holds her gown and the curtains of the bed, then lets her free to go to the window. Below in the courtyard, Rabbi Löw and the GOLEM go towards their tower while the watchman runs back up the steps to sound the horn from the ghetto wall.

MIRIAM comes back fearfully from the window, takes FLORIAN'S hand, then locks the door of her bedroom.

The Rabbi leads his monster back into his study, takes off his hat and cloak, then turns to put his hand on the GOLEM'S shoulder. It stares at him with sudden hatred. Löw slowly takes back his hand. The GOLEM sneers, one white eye ablaze.

Löw slowly reaches for the Star of David on the monster's chest, but it holds its clay hand over its source of life.

The Rabbi backs away from his creation, then crouches over a table.

The GOLEM'S face convulses with fury, its teeth bared.

The Rabbi cowers at the table.

The monster raises its hand, ready to strike. It moves round behind the Rabbi, but it is too slow. Löw pulls out the Star of David from its chest and it drops its hand, rocks and falls back lifeless.

Now the Rabbi crouches down by his unmoving monster and puts his hand on its clay face.

From the ghetto wall, the watchman blows the Schofa horn.

A man pokes his head out of a small window.

As the horn sounds again, men talk from the windows. The horn sounds yet again. A woman appears at a little window, then a thin man in a doorway shorter than he is. He joins three other men dressed like himself in pointed hats and black gowns. Women gather around them and wave at the ghetto wall. The horn sounds again. There is general excitement, as the Jews come out into the streets. One man stands on a platform, waving his hands in the air, while the crowd surrounds him.

TITLE: "*Let us rejoice.*"

The crowd begins to dance, throw their hats away, shout.

The watchman sounds his horn yet again.

A group of men run down to help the old Rabbi JEHUDA to climb some steps.

Fade to FAMULUS, the Rabbi's assistant, as he wakes from his sleep and hurries to the window, then returns to his bed to put his coat on.
Fade to the Rabbi reading from his old books of magic with the clay figure of the GOLEM stretched out at his feet. His hands trace out the German text:

INSERT: *If you have brought the dead to life through magic, beware! When Uranus comes into the House of the Planets, Astaroth will take back his creature. Then the dead clay will scorn its Master and destroy him and all living things.*

The Rabbi looks down from his book at the lying monster.

TITLE: *"Your work, Golem, is done. Turn to lifeless clay again, before the powers of darkness take their revenge."*

Löw closes his book, rises and picks up a large wooden mallet, ready to smash the GOLEM to pieces. But FAMULUS runs in and stops him.

TITLE: *"Master, Jehuda waits below with the elders to escort you to the Synagogue for the Ceremony of Thanksgiving."*

Löw looks off with his assistant to see:
Twelve men carrying the Ark of the Covenant between them on long poles. They are surrounded by other men blowing the Schofa horns with people kneeling about them.

In her bedroom above, MIRIAM pushes FLORIAN back from the light into the shadows. They hold each other in fear and love, looking wildly for an escape. She counsels him.

TITLE: *"After all have gone, steal through that gate."*

MIRIAM points the direction to FLORIAN, then sinks back in his arms.

Rabbi Löw comes through a low arch to meet old JEHUDA and go with him into the street. FAMULUS watches the two men leave.
Out in the streets of the ghetto, the jammed people wave and shout between the tall crooked buildings.
Waving tall fans in the shape of palm-leaves, the people part to let the Ark of the Covenant pass along the narrow street.
FAMULUS watches the procession, smiling from Löw's doorway.

The procession moves on towards the Synagogue.
Fade to Miriam and her lover, crouched by the window of her room.
Fade back to Famulus, as the crowd moves off after the Ark. He runs after them, then runs back below the tower, struck by a happy thought.

Title: *"I will be the first to bring the glad news to Miriam."*

He runs into the doorway. Then he runs up to the door outside Miriam's room and bangs the metal ring on the wood to warn her.
Miriam runs to press herself against the bedroom door and listen. She holds out a hand to hush Florian.
Famulus shouts his excitement to her on the other side of the door. She shouts back, shaking her head.

Title: *"I am not ready. Go . . . And I will follow."*

She shouts, shaking her head with her eyes closed.
Famulus holds onto the ring on the door. He is gay and persuasive.

Title: *"No, I will wait and take you to the Synagogue."*

He grins and leans sighing back against the room wall.
Florian rushes across to speak with Miriam. She silences him with a hand across his mouth, but he whispers on.
The smile of Famulus outside the door begins to fade.
Inside the room, the lovers whisper before Miriam puts her hand again over Florian's mouth.
Famulus presses his ear against the locked door, then draws back, his eyes wild.
Inside the room, the lovers clutch each other, knowing they are discovered. (*Still*)
Famulus is mad with jealousy. He runs off in the Rabbi's study and searches for the Star of David. Once it is found, he bends to screw it into the lying Golem's chest. The monster rises, stiff and upright, to its feet. It sneers at the dazed Famulus. As it lurches towards him, he points off with both of his hands, and he shouts:

Title: *"There is a stranger in there who has brought shame upon us. Seize him!"*

As Famulus rages, so the Golem's wrath grows. It lurches forwards, making the Rabbi's assistant cower back. Then it marches to the

closed door and hammers the wood with its fist.
Inside the room, the lovers shrink together.
The GOLEM pounds on the door.
The couple cringe.
The GOLEM looks at the assistant, who mimes the action of smashing his arms through the wood.
The GOLEM crashes its fists straight through the door.
MIRIAM faints into her lover's arms.
The GOLEM pushes in the door as FAMULUS leans against the wall and grins. Then the monster moves to look into the room, while the Rabbi's assistant sidles into the doorway to watch the fun over the GOLEM's shoulder.
FLORIAN notices something at his feet, while MIRIAM lies swooning in his arms.
The GOLEM bares his teeth while the assistant shows his teeth in a grin.
FLORIAN leaves MIRIAM on the ground, then leans down to seize a dagger lying on the floor among the splintered panels from the wrecked door.
He leaps at the GOLEM and stabs it. The dagger breaks in his hand, and the monster cuffs him away.
The GOLEM lumbers over to MIRIAM and grabs her long braids. (*Still*)
FLORIAN pulls her away and attacks the GOLEM, which gives him a violent blow. FAMULUS turns smiling to the girl on the ground.
FLORIAN tries to escape down the steps through the hall. But the GOLEM pursues him, blocking his escape.
FLORIAN runs up the flight of curving stairs that leads to the roof.
FAMULUS grabs MIRIAM by the arm, but she rouses herself and begins to struggle. She breaks free and runs out, followed by her attacker.
On the top of the tower between the great stones at each corner, the tiny figure of FLORIAN appears, running from his doom. He crouches in the corner of the tower, the broken dagger in his hand.
The head of the ravening GOLEM appears through the small opening in the tower roof. It is as much clay as the tiles.
FLORIAN crouches, ready to defend himself.
The GOLEM is beserk.
It stalks the knight across the tower roof. It seizes him as he

struggles. It carries him to the edge of the drop. It throws him over.
From beneath the tower, we see the GOLEM staring downwards.
Now we look down on the broken body of FLORIAN, who has been smashed to death on the logs split by the monster in the shadow of the tower.
MIRIAM runs up the curving stairs to the tower roof. Behind her, the assistant.
She puts her head through the hole in the roof, then shrieks and shrinks back against FAMULUS, who is also cowering with terror.
The girl and the assistant now run out onto the roof. The GOLEM knocks the assistant down and seizes the girl.
It carries her down the winding stairs.
She lies fainting in the monster's arms. It lays her out on a table in the Rabbi's study, then puts its hands on her face and looks closely at her.
Slowly the GOLEM passes a huge clay hand over MIRIAM's throat, over her breasts, over her hip. (*Still*)
It stares down, its mouth slashed in a strange smile. It looks down curious, intent. Its eyes roll white in their sockets.
The assistant runs down the tower stairs, pauses, then runs on.
MIRIAM looks up, then faints again.
The GOLEM holds the girl's head in its hands, its face close to hers.
FAMULUS runs in, stops, reaches slowly for the Star of David on the monster's breast. But the GOLEM puts one huge hand over the talisman.
It pushes the assistant back with its free hand, while MIRIAM stirs on the table.
It lifts a huge fist.
MIRIAM shrieks from the table.
The GOLEM rages in front of the assistant, who puts up his hands like claws in front of his white face. Then he runs at the monster, which beats him to the ground and seizes a burning log from the fire. MIRIAM falls off the table in another faint. The monster threatens FAMULUS with the burning brand, then puts the flame to the bottom of the stairs. One of the Rabbi's chemical jars explodes and fire licks up about the steps.
The GOLEM rages through the blazing room. It seizes MIRIAM by her braids, drags her off.
Smoke billows out of the tower window.

The GOLEM stares at the flames. It picks up a blazing piece of wood and brandishes it, the girl's hair still knotted in its other hand.

Fade to candles burning over JEHUDA and Löw and a third Rabbi as they pray over their Holy Book in the Synagogue. Behind them, a host of hands reaching up like candle flames in the darkness. Through the bowing worshippers, FAMULUS forces his way until he is stopped. He speaks wildly, moves on.
Some old men in the Synagogue whisper and mutter.
The assistant is now speaking to his master and JEHUDA:

TITLE: *"Your house is on fire. The Golem is beserk."*

While FAMULUS speaks, the Rabbis bow to the altar.
The old men begin to push their way out.
The crowd now begins to jostle its way out, followed by the Rabbis.
The street outside Löw's tower is now jammed with the crowd.
Smoke pours out of the tower window.
The GOLEM stands in a fiery arch, the braids of the girl knotted round its fist. It lurches on, dragging her behind it.
Below the tower, the crowd watches, as the roof catches ablaze.
FAMULUS runs on with Löw and JEHUDA and some of the crowd behind him. They stop to stare at more broken bodies lying on the stairs below the fiery arch. A raving man is caught by Löw and his assistant.

TITLE: *"The demon has carried Miriam away. It is destroying everything."*

The raving man looks up to see with the others:
White smoke pouring from the dark walls.
We look down now from the high roofs onto the packed crowd milling in the street below. Smoke drifts through the air.
The Jews sink to their knees on the stairs, imploring their Chief Rabbi Löw.

TITLE: *"Rabbi, save us, or we shall all be destroyed!"*

The Rabbi nods, then climbs the steps between the people and stands framed by the arch in front of the smoke. He bids all kneel, then goes on himself into the inferno, his arms raised above his head.

The GOLEM is now dragging MIRIAM by the hair across a field of stones in front of a huge wall, held up by buttresses of boulders.
Flames blaze from an arch in the burning ghetto.
Löw appears in front of his burning tower, his arms held high.
A thatched roof is ripped by flame.
The people kneel and pray between the burning buildings.
The Rabbi prays to heaven amid the clouds of smoke.
Thick smoke billows from the tower, fills the street.
The people rise and fall in their prayers.
The timbers blaze above them.
Smoke blots out the praying Jews.
The Rabbi is also lost in the smoke.
His tower falls in a pillar of fire.
The whole ghetto smokes like Gomorrah.
The Rabbi moves his arms in circles, begging his God.
The GOLEM drags MIRIAM over to a smooth rock in front of a ridged wall. It lays her out on this sacrificial altar.
It bends over her, then looks about itself wildly, then bends to look at the girl again. She does not move. It does not understand. It shakes its head, lumbers away.
The Rabbi finishes his prayers, then leaves through a dark arch in front of the pointed roofs of the town.
MIRIAM opens her eyes weakly, then faints again on her rock.
High on the ridged wall, Löw appears. He looks down and sees MIRIAM. He runs down some curving steps and embraces her. He pulls her up to him, strokes her face.
The people rise and fall in prayer, as JEHUDA and other Jews move through the crowd, embracing each other, joyful. JEHUDA speaks:

TITLE: *"Let us show our gratitude to the great Rabbi Löw."*

Led by the Rabbis, the crowd moves between the high walls, shouting and running.
Fade to Löw and MIRIAM on the stone, as FAMULUS comes up to them.

TITLE: *"Rabbi Löw, the people have come to thank you for saving them."*

The Rabbi rises and takes his leave, while the assistant sits by the girl and takes her hand. As she looks away in shame, he speaks:

TITLE: *"The Rabbi's tower has fallen and the stranger is buried in its ruins. No one knows nor suspects. I shall be silent for ever. Will you pardon me?"*

MIRIAM turns and buries her head in the assistant's neck.

By the great city gates, the GOLEM appears. It stares from side to side, then moves on. It stops by the gates to look through a small window. It sees outside the walls:
Pretty children in wispy dresses playing in the sun. One lifts another up to put flowers on the top of a statue of a child on a column.
Now the children dance in a circle outside the great gates.
The GOLEM pushes at the gates.
The children stop their play to watch and listen.
The GOLEM strains at the gates. The beam holding the doors together breaks in two. The monster opens the gates in the bright sunlight outside the ghetto. (*Still*)
The children are frightened. They turn and run away, their dresses floating, flowers in their hair.
One small child stays where it is, and bursts into tears.
Slowly the GOLEM comes out of the gate.
The monster stares and smiles gently.
A small girl sits on the ground, looking curiously back. She has one shoulder bare.
The GOLEM lumbers over to stand in front of the little girl, who rises to look at the monster. She offers it an apple. (*Still*). The GOLEM picks her up, holds her against its chest.
The little girl puts the apple into the GOLEM's mouth.
It smiles and looks around. She drops the apple, plays with the Star of David on the monster's chest.
Easily, simply, her fingers take out the Star, drop it on the ground.
The GOLEM lets the little girl fall, rocks, crashes down.
The little girl stands at the feet of the lifeless monster. She jumps over its huge shoes of clay and runs to its clay head. She waves to the other children, then runs off.

Fade to the crowd, pressing forwards to see Rabbi Löw with the wizard's hats of the pointed ghetto roofs askew behind. Löw raises his head from the blessing of the old Rabbi JEHUDA, then asks the question all wish to ask.

TITLE: *"But where is the Golem?"*

The crowd begins to split up to start the search.
The little girl leads on the other children to play with the fallen GOLEM. They swarm all over the huge body of the monster, poking it, feeling the clay. The little girl shows them the Star of David.
The talisman is passed through the children's hands.
Then the Star is tossed in the air, thrown away, lost.
Inside the ghetto, the watchman rushes up to Rabbi Löw.

TITLE: *"The gate has been broken open! The Golem is by there!"*

He leads Löw and the crowd off.
The children now sit on the GOLEM's body in rows. Their hands are full of flowers; flowery its body.
Now from the gate of the city, the Rabbi and the dark crowd come.
The children rise and run away from the monster, while Löw and the Jews surround the fallen GOLEM in a half-circle of black figures.
Löw raises his hands and face yet again to God.

TITLE: *"Praise Jehovah, for He has shown His love for His people three times today."*

Löw drops his hands and the crowd kneels in the half-circle and all along the line of people stretching back to the great gates of the city. The Rabbi motions some men to rise.
Ten of them pick up the GOLEM. Its body is stiff and heavy as clay.
They carry it back towards the gates.
From outside the curving walls of the medieval city, we see the body of the GOLEM carried in below the watch tower. The gates close on the procession. On the black walls a white clay Star of David appears, and then it becomes a white star in the darkness of the heavens.

CREDITS:

Produced by	Prana-Film
Directed by	Friedrich Wilhelm Murnau
Scenario by	Henrik Galeen, adapted from Bram Stoker's *Dracula*
Camera operators	Fritz Arno Wagner, Gunther Krampf
Designed by	Albin Grau

CAST:

Count Dracula, or Nosferatu, the vampire	Max Schreck
Renfield	Alexander Granach
Jonathon Harker	Gustav von Wangenheim
Nina	Greta Schröder
Westenra	G. H. Schell
Ruth	Ruth Landshoff
the Professor	John Gottowt
the Town Doctor	Gustav Botz
Captain of the "Demeter"	Max Nemetz
the First Mate	Wolfgang Heinz

NOSFERATU

TITLE: *From the diary of* JOHANN CAVALLIUS, *able historian of his native city of Bremen:* NOSFERATU! *That name alone can chill the blood!* NOSFERATU! *Was it he who brought the plague to Bremen in 1838?"*

TITLE: *"I have long sought the causes of that terrible epidemic, and found at its origin and its climax the innocent figures of Jonathon Harker and his young wife, Nina."*

Behind the spire of a cathedral we see a number of high, flat-front German residences.

A young man stands at mirror on left, tying his tie. He turns with a sudden brilliant smile, pulls vest down, then turns back abruptly.

He steps to the window and stoops to peer over the sill; bright light streams through the window.

JONATHON's pretty wife dangles a ball on a string (or flower) before a cat, which paws it playfully; she is surrounded by bouquets of flowers.

The young man is seen cutting flowers in a brightly sunlit garden.

His wife sits sewing.

The husband opens the door and comes in coyly with his hands behind his back; he bends forward.

His wife looks up and smiles tenderly at him.

Husband comes forward, bending over and smiling, before going out of the room.

Then the husband, holding the flowers behind his back, suddenly rushes towards his wife, who runs with open arms toward him.

The husband and wife fall into each other's arms, whirl round once, kiss firmly three times, then the husband slowly hands his wife the bouquet.

The wife turns away slightly, holding the bouquet lovingly; she caresses it with her hands and turns back to face her husband with a touched expression.

He raises his hands to his wife's head and caresses her.

JONATHON is walking along a street through alternate shadow and sunlight. An older man hails him, and JONATHON stops and speaks to him.

TITLE: *"Wait, young man. You can't escape destiny by running away . . ."*

JONATHON smiles, shakes the older man's hand and walks quickly away from him; the older man smiles, shakes his head, and moves away more slowly.

TITLE: *"The agent Renfield was a strange man, and there were unpleasant rumours about him."*

A shrivelled, decrepit old man is sitting on a high stool. He is bald, with bushy white eyebrows and a band of hair around the back of his head. He is wearing light-coloured trousers under a dark tail-coat. This is RENFIELD.

He turns more towards us, holding a paper.

His hands hold up a white paper against a black background; the paper is covered with indecipherable hieroglyphics.

RENFIELD reads intently and gleefully, the paper held close to his face; when he has finished reading he looks up thoughtfully; he holds his head slightly on one side, mouth open, squinting intently.

JONATHON is at work in his office, which is cluttered with books and folders; he turns and moves towards us.

He comes through the door into RENFIELD's office and walks up to RENFIELD, who has now folded his letter up; RENFIELD smiles and flashes his bad teeth at JONATHON.

TITLE: *"Here is an important letter from Transylvania. Count Dracula wishes to buy a house in our city."*

RENFIELD's evil face leers at JONATHON's innocent, open countenance.

TITLE: *"It's a good opportunity for you, Harker. The Count is rich, and free with his money."*

RENFIELD whispers into JONATHON's ear.

TITLE: *"You will have a marvellous journey. And, young as you are, what matter if it costs you some pain—or even a little blood? . . ."*

JONATHON laughs, while RENFIELD cackles wildly, causing JONATHON to withdraw slightly; his face is obscured by the shadow of the other man.
JONATHON looks rather alarmed, then becomes reassured again and smiles at RENFIELD. The latter gently propels JONATHON towards the map, takes out the letter again, and unfolds it.
RENFIELD's hands are seen turning the letter over, then holding it quite still.
A crafty expression comes into RENFIELD's eyes.
JONATHON points to an area on a map.
He turns to face in RENFIELD's direction.
At the same time RENFIELD turns to face JONATHON, who is coming eagerly from the map; RENFIELD folds the letter up again and points out of the window.
We are looking at an ancient house through panes of glass; it is six or seven storeys high, with arched windows open; it exudes a sombre, death-like atmosphere.
RENFIELD looks at JONATHON, then gestures towards the window; JONATHON looks vaguely alarmed.

TITLE: *"The house facing yours . . . That should suit him."*

RENFIELD suddenly grasps JONATHON's shoulders.

TITLE: *"Leave at once, my young friend. And don't be frightened if people speak of Transylvania as the land of phantoms. . . ."*

RENFIELD and JONATHON break into loud laughter.

JONATHON's wife is gazing out of a window, then she turns toward door and adjusts her shawl. The door bursts open and JONATHON enters quickly and throws himself at her feet.
JONATHON and his wife gaze affectionately at each other.

TITLE: *"I may be away for several months, Nina. Renfield is sending me to some lost corner of the Carpathians . . ."*

JONATHON utters his message quickly, briefly kisses his wife on the forehead and then runs from the room.
JONATHON rushes out of the room, then suddenly stops and goes back to get his hat. His wife remains standing dejectedly alone.

JONATHON is busily packing saddle bags. Suddenly he pauses in his packing as though he realizes he has forgotten something. He walks over to a bureau, takes a book down, then comes back and tucks it in his bag.
His wife enters the room, staring gloomily; she moves in JONATHON's direction.
JONATHON bends to kiss his wife, trying to gaze into her down-turned face.
JONATHON finally puts his arms around the neck of his wife and they move away from us.

TITLE: *"Harker left Nina with his good friends, Westenra and his wife Lucy."*

We see the brightly illuminated facade of a house; a curving staircase leads to the doorway, and there is a flower garden in front of the house.
JONATHON and NINA take their farewell in front of the house; another couple emerges from the house to watch them; JONATHON begins to come down the stairs.

TITLE: *"Don't worry, Nina. Nothing will happen to me."*

WESTENRA and JONATHON shake hands, while LUCY tries to comfort NINA in her distress.
JONATHON turns away and walks down the stairs and away through the garden.
His wife looks up, grief-stricken, and she calls out.
JONATHON stops at the foot of the steps; NINA rushes down them and they embrace again. LUCY comes down the stairs to comfort NINA.
We see a stableman standing with a horse by a fountain; around are a number of half-timbered houses. JONATHON appears, mounts the horse and rides away.

TITLE: *"From relay to relay, through the dust raised by the stages, Harker hurried on."*

Gaunt mountains rise beyond a plain which is sparsely covered with trees. The landscape gives a vivid impression of bleakness.
Four horses pull a coach up to the shaded entrance of a small inn;

there is a rider on the back of left front horse; the driver rises from his seat and starts to take bags from the top of the coach.
JONATHON steps out of the shadow of the coach, while the innkeeper steps towards the coach and picks up the bags; they enter the inn together.
The innkeeper ushers JONATHON into the main room of the inn.
JONATHON is wearing a full travelling cape and a cap with a front brim.
The innkeeper dusts a seat of a chair with his apron before JONATHON sits down on it. A girl brings him a glass of beer. He reaches forward to take it.
JONATHON drinks his beer rapidly, looks down, then up again and breaks into gay laughter; he gaily pounds on the table and calls out.

TITLE: *"Dinner, quickly! I should be at Count Dracula's castle."*

Four peaceful-looking peasants register alarm; one man rises with a horror-struck expression on his face.
The innkeeper and serving-girl look worriedly at JONATHON.
JONATHON laughs loudly, stops suddenly, then turns to look back over his shoulder.
Innkeeper walks slowly in JONATHON's direction shaking his head and holding his hand to his throat.
He walks right up to JONATHON.
He bends close to JONATHON, points outside and whispers something to him.

TITLE: *"You must not leave now! The evil spirits become all-powerful after dark!"*

The innkeeper takes JONATHON's hand and shakes it.
He finishes shaking JONATHON's hand, then turns and walks away.

A jackal or similar creature approaches down a path through the woods.
The horses jump about in fright, then break loose.
The animal runs down the path and disappears.

We are in JONATHON's bedchamber: a girl comes in and turns back the bedclothes; JONATHON throws his hat on the bed, and the girl

picks it up and hangs it on the wall. JONATHON has almost removed his coat when the girl stops to look and he grins at her. She hurries out and JONATHON goes to hang his coat up and turns to look through the window.
The horses can be seen galloping across the landscape.
The jackal-like animal turns and looks towards us.
Four peasant women huddle together and hide their eyes; one crosses herself piously.
The jackal disappears behind some rocks.
JONATHON shudders, rubs his arms, then slams the window shut
and walks back towards the centre of his room, now lit in ghostly glow by a candle.
JONATHON picks up his candle, and walks away from us.
He carefully sets the candle down on his table, sits on the bed and picks up a book.
Matching action, closer shot of JONATHON with book.

INSERT: in Gothic script: *The Book of the Vampires.*

JONATHON avidly turns a page of the book.

INSERT: *And it was in 1443 that the first Nosferatu was born.*
INSERT: *That name rings like the cry of a bird of prey. Never speak it aloud. . . .*

JONATHON suddenly seems overcome by fatigue and yawns; he throws the book aside by his pillow.
Then he gets up off his bed and kicks his boots off.
A ray of light shines in through a crack in the window, falling on JONATHON's face and lighting it up. He wakes up, stretches his arms and starts to get out of bed.
He leaps from his bed, pulls open his window, and stretches again energetically.
A group of horses appear over the horizon in front of the trees, driven by a band of peasants.
JONATHON stretches again, then notices the book he has been trying to read and picks it up again.

INSERT: *Men do not always recognize the dangers that beasts can sense at certain times.*

JONATHON laughs and throws the book contemptuously down again.

Then, preparing for his morning wash, he pulls the sleeves of his nightgown off his arms, and ties them around his waist, then he quickly immerses his face in a pan of cold water.

A coach is standing in front of the inn; the two drivers are also there, surrounded by several women.
JONATHON climbs in the coach on the far side. The front driver mounts his horse and the coach finally pulls away from the inn.
The coach approaches down a lane, on either side of which are dark and sinister-looking shrubs.
The mountains can now be seen rising beyond a stream in the foreground; then on the right of the screen we see the horses pass, pulling the coach behind them.

TITLE: *"Hurry! The sun will soon be setting!"*

JONATHON sticks his head out of the coach window.
A bank of heavy clouds begins to obscure the sun.
The coach horses gallop wildly across a wooden bridge.
The coach appears, moving over a rocky prominence and coming down towards us.
JONATHON jumps quickly out of the coach and gestures angrily in another direction; the driver on the coach appears to have no intention of following JONATHON's instructions.

TITLE: *"We will go no further, sir. Not for a fortune!"*

The driver turns away from JONATHON, who moves away.
JONATHON walks round to the front of the horses.
He comes round to speak to the rider on the front horse.

TITLE: *"We will go no further. Here begins the land of phantoms."*

JONATHON laughs mockingly, then walks back towards the coach.
JONATHON walks away as the driver throws down his bags from the coach and drives away. JONATHON walks down rocky slope to left.
JONATHON walks away over the wooden bridge.

TITLE: *"And when he had crossed the bridge, the phantoms came to meet him."*

We see a castle with a strange tower springing from it, almost like a natural pinnacle on a cliff.

A coach draped in black cloth jerks weirdly along the road; the horse and driver are likewise draped in black.

JONATHON appears walking along an open lane; suddenly he stops as the black draped coach appears, jerks forward and halts before him.

JONATHON looks bewilderedly in the direction of the coach.

A crushed hat with a narrow feather casts a shadow over the driver's eyes, and his cape is drawn up to his face. He points towards the coach with his whip.

JONATHON looks on, very uncertain.

He finally makes up his mind and climbs into the black-draped coach; the coachman draws back to crack his whip.

The horses start to gallop very quickly, almost immediately; they wheel around in an arc to the left and the coach rattles off back up the road.

The window curtains of the coach move with the shaking; JONATHON sticks his head out through them into bright white light. He holds his hat on and gasps for breath, as though suddenly finding himself among alien elements, then hurriedly withdraws into the coach.

The coach rattles up the hill away from us.

The coach shows up as a black mass in negative images, while the trees through which it is passing are a ghostly white.

The horses struggle up the hill, only visible over the rise; they seem to be moving back and forth, then suddenly they top the hill and race forward and flash past our field of view.

The coach suddenly skids to a halt and JONATHON gets out and looks around in surprise.

The driver stares malevolently from between his cape and hat, then points sharply with his whip in another direction.

We see the top of a tower in which there is a single low window.

JONATHON looks upward in the direction of the tower then hoists his bag up on to his shoulder.

He secures his bag on his shoulder, then moves alongside the horses.

He walks rapidly up a steep slope and onto the drawbridge of the castle; the paint and bricks have fallen away from the wall in places, making it look rotten and decrepit.

JONATHON suddenly spins round to gape over his right shoulder.

The coach rushes away swiftly into the distance, its sinister black outline disappearing round an outcrop of bushes.

Jonathon turns back to face the doors; as he steps forward towards them the right one mysteriously swings open; Jonathon, alarmed, makes an involuntary movement backwards, then, seeming to take courage, moves forward purposefully again.
The terrible figure of Nosferatu begins to emerge from between a dark arch and a light arch. (*Still*)
Jonathon climbs up into the courtyard of a medieval castle. The doors swing close behind him and he spins round to face them. He pauses, then turns to climb on up the hill.
The tall thin figure of Nosferatu waits, slightly bowed. (*Still*). He stands in silhouette against an archway, through which the small dark figure of Jonathon now appears. He pauses when he sees the alarming sight awaiting him. Then he comes forward towards Nosferatu: when he gets close enough to observe the singular appearance of his host, he stops and removes his hat. Nosferatu makes a strange, almost unhuman movement with a long tapering hand, flicking it up to his brow and down again. Jonathon replaces his hat.
Jonathon stares incredulously at his host, who stands with his hands folded and a black cloth hat on; he has shadowed staring eyes, a large hooked nose, protruding from an emaciated face. He flashes angrily at Jonathon.

Title: *"You are late, young man. It is almost midnight. My servants have all retired."*

Nosferatu gestures towards a dark archway, then takes one or two steps in that direction. Jonathon begins to follow tentatively, Nosferatu turns and walks towards the archway; they disappear together into the blackness.

Jonathon and Nosferatu are seated together at a table; the floor is made of chequered tiles.
Jonathon cuts his food and starts to eat.
Nosferatu sits in a high straight-backed chair, peering intently at a piece of paper which he holds very close to his face.
Jonathon reaches for the bread and a knife; he holds the bread clumsily against his chest, then begins cutting it, holding the knife in his right hand and moving it towards him.
Nosferatu stares over the edge of his paper, on which are strange musical hieroglyphics; his eyes are almost lost in shadow beneath

his bushy brows.
The skeleton on top of a clock strikes a glass chime: it is midnight.
JONATHON suddenly gasps and looks up in alarm.
We see the skeleton clock striking again.
JONATHON looks down at the bread in his hands.
The knife and bread are suddenly snatched away by JONATHON's hand; his left thumb is cut and the blood has begun to well up.
JONATHON laughs sheepishly and starts to wipe the blood up with his napkin; NOSFERATU seeing the blood, gestures for him to wait; he rises and starts to move menacingly towards JONATHON.

TITLE: *"Blood! Your precious blood!"*

NOSFERATU seizes JONATHON's hand, pulls it to his mouth and begins sucking the blood. JONATHON jerks his hand away and looks at NOSFERATU, horrified. He starts to back away from NOSFERATU, who follows very deliberately: the hunter is stalking his prey.
JONATHON backs away as far as a flight of steps; NOSFERATU is moving ever closer to him.
NOSFERATU moves closer and closer to JONATHON; the threat is still present, then the atmosphere relaxes slightly.

TITLE: *"Let us chat together a moment, my friend. There are still several hours until dawn, and I have the whole day to sleep."*

JONATHON backs away towards a chair; NOSFERATU gestures for him to sit down and JONATHON collapses helplessly into the chair.

TITLE: *"As the sun rose, Harker felt himself freed from the oppression of the night."*

It is clearly dawn, but JONATHON is still slumped in his chair. He wakes up with a great start, looks towards the smoke-blackened fireplace, yawns, stretches, looks towards another part of the room.
In the far corner of the hall is the table with two chairs; there is food on the table.
JONATHON gets to his feet, looks at his injured thumb, then he feels his throat. Finding something which puzzles him, he stoops to his bag and takes out a mirror, holds it up and looks at his throat.
Looking into the mirror, we see JONATHON's fingers go to his throat, on which there are two small dots. JONATHON's jaw drops, making

his mouth appear in the mirror. His lips twist into a strange smile. JONATHON replaces his mirror in his bag, sticks his hands in his pockets and yawns.
An impressive display of foodstuffs is laid out on the table.
JONATHON lopes towards the table.
JONATHON looks eagerly at the food, sits down in NOSFERATU'S chair and begins to eat.

JONATHON walks left up a flight of steps onto a platform under an arched pavilion; he moves over to the platform railing.
JONATHON steps up to the railing and leans against a pillar smiling; then he takes out some writing paper and begins to write a letter.

INSERT: *Nina, my beloved—Don't be unhappy. Though I am away, I love you. This is a strange country, amazing.*

Then JONATHON snatches up his paper and swipes at something that flies above his head but which we cannot see, then he smiles and goes back to his writing.

INSERT: *After my first night in this castle, I found two large bites on my neck. From mosquitoes? From spiders? I don't know . . .*

JONATHON feels his neck again at the spot where the dots are; he rubs it tenderly, then goes back to writing his letter.

INSERT: *I have had some frightful dreams, but they were only dreams. You mustn't worry about me.*

JONATHON continues writing his letter.

A horseman rides by at the foot of the hill down which JONATHON is looking from the castle.
JONATHON runs into the main archway of the castle and seems to call out in the direction of the horseman.
The horseman hears JONATHON'S shout and comes to a halt.
JONATHON waves his letter above his head and shouts again.
The horseman begins to ride in the direction of JONATHON.
JONATHON runs to meet the horseman; he hands him the letter, then steps back as the horseman rides away.
A bank of clouds, shot through with patches of light, gradually grows dark.

TITLE: *"As twilight came on, the empty castle became alive with menacing shadows."*

NOSFERATU is sitting looking at some papers; JONATHON stands by him. Then JONATHON reaches for his bag to take some papers out of it.
A small round picture is lying by the bag.
JONATHON lays the papers in front of NOSFERATU, who sits staring at the table.
We see the picture again.
NOSFERATU suddenly scoops the picture off the table, holding it in his long tapering hand very stiffly; he stares at the picture, looks sideways up at JONATHON, then stares again at the picture, holding it very close to his face.
NOSFERATU examines the picture very closely and points at it with his long tapering fingers, then looks towards JONATHON.

TITLE: *"Is this your wife? What a lovely throat!"*

NOSFERATU coolly drops the picture back into the hand of the horror-struck JONATHON, who hurriedly thrusts it in his inside coat pocket; NOSFERATU takes up a quill and speaks.

TITLE: *"That old mansion seems quite satisfactory. We shall be neighbours."*

NOSFERATU scribbles his signature and gives the papers back to JONATHON. The latter takes them and hurriedly crams them in his bag, still looking very alarmed after NOSFERATU's attraction to the picture of his wife.
JONATHON, now alone, is admiring the picture of his wife; he kisses it, then bends to put it back in his bag.
JONATHON finishes placing the picture back in the bag; as he does so he comes across the book about vampires. He takes it out slowly and starts reading it.

INSERT: *Nosferatu drinks the blood of the young, the blood necessary to his own existence.*

JONATHON bends close to the candle to read the book better.

INSERT: *One can recognize the mark of the vampire by the trace of his fangs on the victim's throat.*

The skeleton figure on the clock strikes midnight on the glass chime. JONATHON suddenly jumps up and hides the book behind him, and moves to another part of the room.

JONATHON walks to an arched door, opens it slightly, looks through, but jumps back involuntarily.

At the end of a dark hallway stands the terrifyingly cadaverous figure of NOSFERATU, eyes gleaming.

We move closer to the figure of NOSFERATU, who is now seen to be standing in a patch of light.

JONATHON in his terror, tries to close the door and fasten it, but there is no latch. He looks about him, beside himself with fear, then creeps away, keeping close to the wall.

JONATHON runs across a dim bedchamber.

JONATHON moves across the bedchamber towards his bed.

He sinks down on it and leans back.

An arched door swings mysteriously open, and a lighted patch of chequered floor shows beyond.

JONATHON suddenly throws his head rigidly to the left, eyes wide open and staring. He breathes in short, sharp gasps.

NOSFERATU appears in the doorway, somehow becoming larger and larger until he fills the doorway completely; he moves slowly forward through the archway, arms hanging low at his sides and head bowed.

JONATHON is absolutely terrified by the sight of the figure advancing towards him; he turns his face away from the sight and pulls the sheet over his head.

NOSFERATU continues his slow and deliberate progress into the room.

NINA is sitting up in bed, which is lit by a candle; around her black drapes hang down. She looks around her with staring eyes.

A gowned man is sitting at a desk, writing and smoking a very long pipe.

NINA rises from her bed and walks across her bedchamber on tiptoes. She passes through glass doors out on to a little balcony, which is lit by bright moonlight.

TITLE: *"That same night in Bremen, in a somnambulistic dream . . ."*

The man is attracted by something to one side; he puts his pipe down and goes out of the room.
Looking through the glass and the curtains we see NINA walking, apparently asleep, along the top of the balcony railing, arms outstretched before her.
A man sees NINA through the glass and curtains, and suddenly leans forward, calling out.

TITLE: *"Nina?"*

He rushes out on to the balcony and manages to catch her, just as she collapses from the rail.
An old woman opens the door slightly and peeps through the crack.
The man holding NINA turns to give an order to the old woman.

TITLE: *"The doctor, quickly."*

The woman backs hastily out of the door.

A circular pool of light illuminates the figure of JONATHON as he lies asleep in bed. The shadows of the hands and head of NOSFERATU creep up across his victim.

NINA, in bed, suddenly springs upright, staring in front of her very wildly; the man and his wife, with a doctor, are standing behind her, alarmed expressions on their faces. NINA shifts further down towards the foot of the bed and throws her arms forward, crying out.

TITLE: *'Jonathon! Jonathon! Hear me!"*

The shadow of NOSFERATU is still hanging over the recumbent figure of JONATHON; then suddenly the shadow begins to withdraw.
NOSFERATU turns round from the bed to show his pointed ears, mis-shapen skull, hollow eyes, fangs, bushy brows; he is wearing a bulky coat which fits high up around the back of his neck.

NINA is sitting up in bed, panting heavily; she still holds her hands extended in front of her.

NOSFERATU turns further to move away from JONATHON'S bed.
He seems to step up close to us, then walks away through an arch,

down some steps and out into the hall; the door shuts behind his tall menacing figure.

The doctor rushes over to NINA's bed to calm the now hysterical girl; he tells her to lie back on her bed.
Then a man taps the doctor on the shoulder and speaks to him.

TITLE: *"A sudden fever."*

The people in the room go to NINA's bed and bend anxiously over it.

TITLE: *"The doctor attributed Nina's trances to some unknown disease. Since then I have learned that she had sensed the menace of Nosferatu that very night. And Harker, far away, had heard her cry of warning."*

A bank of clouds is lit up by the early morning light.
The sunlight falls across JONATHON's recumbent form, as he lies on his bed. The consciousness of the light makes him wake up suddenly. He feels anxiously at his throat, then stands up and thrusts his clenched fist to his forehead.
Then, in a brusque movement of anguish, he tears his fist away from his forehead and runs around foot of bed, then halts suddenly.
JONATHON steps over to an arched door and pulls it hurriedly open. He walks through the doorway, then down a lighted hall; he turns right at the end. (*Still*)
JONATHON descends a flight of stairs, keeping close to a rough stone wall.
JONATHON rushes up to a pair of heavy iron-bound doors; he tugs desperately at them and finally succeeds in getting them open. He runs out into a dark passage beyond.
JONATHON slowly comes down a flight of steps into a dank-looking chamber; on the right is a wooden sarcophagus. JONATHON goes up to it, steps up on to the pedestal, and gazes down over the sarcophagus.
The face of NOSFERATU can be seen staring up ghoulishly through the rotting boards.
JONATHON leaps away in shock and fright, then runs to the coffin.
JONATHON throws the lid back off the coffin, to reveal NOSFERATU lying inside, with long white hands crossed. JONATHON steps haltingly away, starts to run and falls on the steps.

Jonathon starts to crawl up the stairs in his desperation to escape from what he has just seen; he finally manages to stumble to his feet and stagger out of the room.

The morning sun shows wanly through a line of tall, narrow trees. Jonathon lies on the floor of his room, seemingly almost unconscious. Then he begins to pull himself to his feet; he staggers over to the window and starts to open the shutter.
He opens the shutter and looks out, then suddenly stares, as his attention is caught by something unusual below.
Looking down into the courtyard from Jonathon's point of view; Nosferatu is placing a coffin on a horse-drawn wagon, on which two coffins have already been placed.
Jonathon looks down in horror, clinging to the window.
By now, Nosferatu is putting a sixth coffin, open, on top of five others. He climbs up on to the wagon and lies down in the coffin. The lid of the coffin flies shut, and the horses pull the wagon out through the narrow gate of the courtyard.
Jonathon draws back into the chamber.
As he turns from the window, he falls to the floor, thrusting his clenched fist to his brow.
Jonathon leans momentarily at the foot of the bed, then rushes to the window and gazes down, seemingly gauging its height from the ground. Then he runs back to the bed, hurls his bedding and pillow across the room, seizes a sheet and begins to tear it into strips.
Jonathon, now wearing his hat and cape, slides down a rope of sheets.
Jonathon slides into sight down the sheets and hangs still for a moment.
He drops down on to the grass at the foot of a rocky facade.

A large raft is being swept along in the rushing waters of a turbulent river.

Title: *"The men little suspected what terrible cargo they were carrying down the valley."*

There are two men on the raft; a number of coffins are piled up between them.

A man is leaning over a bed, in which Jonathon is lying.

The man gets up from his bending position and turns to speak to a woman.

TITLE: *"Some peasants brought him here last evening. He still has a high fever."*

The doctor looks down again towards the form in the bed.
JONATHON sits up in bed, supported by the man and the woman; he gestures weakly but desperately.

TITLE: *"Coffins . . . Coffins filled with earth."*

JONATHON clings to the woman in fear; she begins to lower him back to the bed.
She finally lets JONATHON fall into a recumbent position, and remains standing by him.

A group of workmen are loading NOSFERATU's coffins on to a ship.
Two workmen are looking down official-looking sheets of paper as though looking for a listing of the coffins. Failing to find it, they call laughingly to another man.
A number of workmen come up to the coffin, and begin trying to open the top.
When the lid has finally been thrown open, the foreman of the workers bends over to look in the coffin, which appears to be full of earth.
Foreman gives a signal to the workmen who turn the coffin upside down to empty it.
As they pull the coffin away, we see that the earth around is swarming with rats.
The foreman waves the papers and walks away with the other workmen, but one remains staring at the rats.
The rats crawl by the workman's foot, then one suddenly bites the foot which is immediately lifted out of sight.
The workman dances about holding his foot; he picks up a shovel and beats at the rats several times, then starts dancing about again.

TITLE: *'Nosferatu was en route; and with him disaster approached Bremen. At the same time, Dr. van Helsing was giving a course on the secrets of nature and their strange correspondences to human life."*

Title: *"The professor told his students about the existence of a carnivorous plant."*

A brightly-lit lecture room: the professor is standing on a podium; by him is a stand with a glass case on it. Five students are standing round the podium gazing at the case.
Scientific film: a fly is captured by a Venus flytrap.
The professor looks mischievously over his glasses; he is eccentrically dressed in a skull cap and flowered robe.

Title: *"Astonishing, isn't it, gentlemen? That plant is the vampire of the vegetable kingdom."*

The professor looks down over his students, a satisfied smile on his face.

Title: *"Nosferatu held Renfield under his influence from afar."*

A lunatic asylum: a bewhiskered man is sitting at a table; behind him is an arch, and beyond that a curtained rectangle. He is busily counting pills when his attention is attracted by a dark-suited attendant who appears from beneath the archway.

Title: *"That patient who was brought in yesterday has gone out of his mind!"*

Doctor removes his glasses and follows the attendant out of the room.
Doctor enters a large cell, where Renfield is crouching on the bed.
Renfield grins stupidly and snatches in the air as if catching insects with his left hand. Then he places the fingertips of his right hand in his mouth and starts to suck.

Title: *"Blood! . . . Blood! . . ."*

Renfield stares cannily toward the others who are out of sight.
The supervisor and the attendant look warily in the direction of Renfield.
Renfield again snatches at the air with one hand, sucks at the other; then he begins to grin sinisterly and moves slowly across the room with his left hand extended in front of him.
The supervisor and attendant watch Renfield's progress.
Renfield moves slowly towards the two astonished observers, his

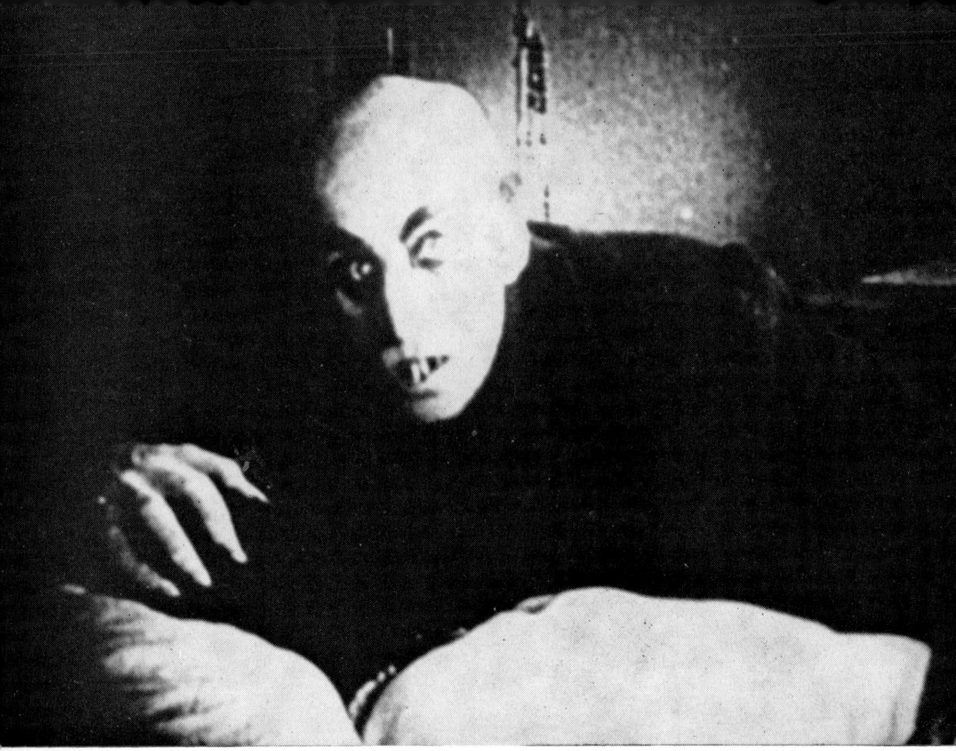

hand held above his head, then suddenly makes a determined leap for the throat of the supervisor. The attendant grabs Renfield and wrestles him down on to the bed, holding his arms behind him.

The professor bends over a small tank, long thin glass wand in hand. A number of students lean towards him.

Title: "*And now, gentlemen, here is another type of vampire; a polyp with claws . . .*"

A small round creature attacks a long thin one.
We see the students following the professor's demonstration attentively.

Title: "*. . . transparent, without substance, almost a phantom.*"

We see a number of transparent organisms in enlargement.
The professor, looking very serious, drops the tip of his wand downwards.

An attendant is standing over Renfield, who points upwards with his free arm; he grins as he speaks.
We see a white spider against a dark background, busily enticing a victim into a web.
The supervisor walks over to Renfield and points at him while speaking to the attendant, then he turns to leave while the attendant begins to bind Renfield with a rope.

Title: "*Nina was often seen alone among the dunes, watching and waiting for her husband's return.*"

Nina sits down on a bench among dunes which are covered with leaning crosses. She gazes out wistfully towards the sea.
The sea is rolling in towards the shore; it looks dark in the distance, becoming distinctly lighter as it gets closer.
Nina is still sitting among the dunes; she is dressed completely in black.
The sea shines as it rolls in towards the shore.
A scene of great tranquillity: the sand topped by grass against a sky of slow-moving white clouds. A couple appear over the dunes and wave to Nina.

NINA turns round to look in their direction.
The man and the woman run down the dunes towards where NINA is sitting.
The woman is dressed in white; she runs towards NINA. The woman is carrying a letter and NINA impatiently makes her open it.
NINA waits breathlessly, while the woman is opening the letter.

INSERT: *I have had some frightful dreams, but they were only dreams. You mustn't worry about me.*
INSERT: *I am leaving immediately to return to Bremen—and to you.*

Clutching the letter, NINA rises from her seat.
She stands still for a moment, clutching the letter, then runs away behind the bench and disappears.

JONATHON, now dressed as though for a journey, is sitting on a bed.
Eventually he gets up, but has to be steadied by a nurse.
JONATHON stares away left, then suddenly turns his head to look towards us.
He turns to thank his nurse, then staggers out of the room.
The nurse sadly shakes her head as JONATHON — a wreck of a man — staggers away.

A ship at sea, becoming gradually larger.

JONATHON leads his horse down a steep and overgrown hillside.

The bleak ship sails ever more swiftly across our field of vision.

An attendant is sweeping up in RENFIELD's room.
There is a paper sticking out of the attendant's hip pocket; RENFIELD sees it and slyly removes it from the pocket and hides it behind his back.
Attendant sweeps out of RENFIELD's cell.
RENFIELD eagerly opens the paper.

INSERT newspaper with the central feature printed in heavy black: *NEW PLAGUE BAFFLES SCIENCE—A mysterious epidemic of the plague has broken out in eastern Europe and in the port cities of the Black Sea, attacking principally the young and vigorous. Cause of the two bloody marks on the neck of each victim baffles the medical profession.*

RENFIELD drops the paper, puts his hands on his knees, rubs them up and down on the front of his shins, grinning more and more broadly.

We see the heavy grey rigging of the ship as it sails diagonally across our field of vision.
The wake of the ship hisses by.

JONATHON rides his horse through a running stream in rocky terrain.

The ship sailing.
We are now on the ship: the mate comes out of hatch and walks away the length of ship and down into the aft hatch.
The mate comes through the hatch and down the steps into the captain's cabin.
The captain is taking a drink; the light from a porthole shines through his whiskers.
The mate looks in the captain's direction.

TITLE: *"Aboard the Demeter, first one man was stricken, then all."*

Captain comes down a number of steps from his table, then goes up the steps leading from the cabin, followed by the mate.
A sick man is lying in a hammock in a hold; he turns his head away quickly as the captain enters down steps. The smoke from his pipe glows whitely in the stairwell.
The captain speaks roughly to the man in the hammock then starts to leave. Meanwhile, the mate gives the man a flask from which he drinks eagerly.
The man continues drinking as the captain goes up the steps; the mate settles the man down in his hammock, folds his arms, covers him up and follows the captain up the steps.
The man lies still for a moment, then suddenly his attention seems to be attracted by something and he sits bolt upright.
Suddenly we see NOSFERATU sitting on top of a coffin, then his image fades away just as quickly. (*Still*)
The man spins to lean against the left hand side of the hammock, facing the coffins.

JONATHON is leading his horse through a darkly shadowed and wooded grove.

TITLE: *"One evening, at sundown, the captain and his first mate buried the last man of the crew."*

The captain and the mate finish tying a body in a sack; the mate looks fearfully over his shoulder; then the two men lift the heavy sack up on to the ship's rail.
The men throw the body into the sea over the side of the ship.
The men remain leaning for a time on the ship's railing; then the mate stoops and determinedly picks up a hand axe.

TITLE: *"I'm going below. I want to have a look in the hold."*

The mate looks grimly in the direction of the hold.
The mate moves slowly away towards the hold, while the captain turns back from the rail.
Mate descends into the dark hold and marches determinedly towards the coffins.
He smashes his axe into one.
The mate moves on to the next coffin, axe in hand.
Suddenly the hold is alive with rats which quickly pour out of the broken boards of the coffin.
The mate goes to the next coffin and smashes his axe into it, then draws back in horror, axe raised.
The lid of the coffin flies off and NOSFERATU rises absolutely stiff, pivoting upward from the feet and standing erect.
The mate's face registers his sudden terror; he drops his axe and raises his hands pathetically, in hopeless defence.
Mate turns and runs to get out of the hatch; NOSFERATU's right hand begins to rise.
Captain is at the ship's wheel.
Mate rushes out of the hatch, eyes rolling with fear.
Captain cranes his neck to see what the mate is doing.
Mate falls back over a barrel in his terror, then backs up to the ship's rail.
Captain throws his arms up in warning.
But he is too late; the mate falls backward into the sea.
Captain lets his arm drop despairingly: then he turns and seizes a

rope and proceeds to tie himself to the wheel.
NOSFERATU appears ominously above a hatch.
Captain finishes tying himself to the wheel.
NOSFERATU continues to edge his way in the direction of the captain.
(*Stills*)
The captain looks panic-stricken as the sinister form of NOSFERATU continues its progress towards him.

TITLE: *Despite all sorts of obstacles, Harker pushed on towards Bremen. Meanwhile, driven by the fatal breath of the vampire, the vessel moved rapidly towards the Baltic.*

The ship's prow moves up and down, concealing then revealing the horizon.

NINA, dressed in a white gown, is standing against a glass door, looking out into the darkness.
We see the setting sun half-obscured by a cloud formation.
A light breeze blows NINA's gown about her.
A stagecoach is driven past a farmhouse.
NINA turns and walks on tiptoes to a railing, where she stretches her arms out.

The prow of the ship plunges swiftly up and down.

Surf comes crashing up on to the beach.
The curtains are blowing about in LUCY's bedchamber; she gets up, puts her shawl on and leaves the room.
LUCY runs to NINA, who is standing on tiptoe, arms raised above her head.
NINA stares towards us, then begins to smile slightly.

TITLE: *"He's coming. I must go to meet him . . ."*

NINA moves away, her face brushed by the leaves of a tree; LUCY follows.

The stagecoach comes to a halt in front of a cottage with a large gnarled tree; JONATHON climbs down from the coach and takes hold of his bag.

The sea, bright in the moonlight, surges forward towards the shore. NINA runs through the garden of a large house.

We see the rigging of a ship.

RENFIELD, mad with excitement, runs to put his stool on the bed and climbs eagerly on it to look through the window.

The phantom ship sails swiftly up a river.

Renfield shifts about to look through the window; strong light floods through the bars.

TITLE: *"The Master is coming! . . . The Master is here!"*

Renfield grins with satisfaction and turns to climb down from the window.
He then replaces it on the floor. He tosses his head, animal-like, then leaps onto his bed and crouches on his knees like a dog.

We return to NOSFERATU's ship again.
The canvas on the top of the hatch suddenly rolls itself up to reveal the hatch. Then, sinisterly, the top of the hatch itself is gradually pushed open; then NOSFERATU appears in the hatch, one claw-like hand holding the edge.

The attendant enters RENFIELD's cell and casually lights his pipe from the lantern; seeing the attendant inattentive, RENFIELD jumps on him and throws him to the floor, then runs from the room.

TITLE: *"I have long tried to understand why Nosferatu travelled with the earth-filled coffins. Recently I discovered that to preserve their diabolic power, vampires must sleep during the day in the same unhallowed ground in which they had been buried."*

NOSFERATU's ship can be seen on the other side of a large Gothic arch; NOSFERATU passes with his coffin, then glides right, carrying it horizontally; it floats forward, too large for a man to carry.
A rat appears over the edge of the hatch, then another, followed by swarm upon swarm of rats.

JONATHON walks by a row of low houses.

NOSFERATU walks out from under a large tree in front of a large building with one Gothic door. He walks with his coffin to the middle of a street, stops, looks both ways, then turns and walks away.

JONATHON runs along by the front, many-windowed, wall of a house; he stops and calls out.
NINA runs out of the front door, almost collapsing with emotion as she sees JONATHON. He runs to catch her and clasps her in passionate embrace.

NOSFERATU carries his coffin into the same courtyard where JONATHON had mounted to begin his journey; he stops in the shade of a tree, looks about, then turns and moves away.

JONATHON is still clasping his fainting wife to him; slowly she recovers as JONATHON kneels on the sofa by her.

NOSFERATU stands looking at JONATHON's house; he gradually moves towards it and stops in front of the wall.
NOSFERATU in profile; odd protuberances on skull, hair in front of ears, but the effect in daylight is not very alarming.

JONATHON and NINA hug each other closely.

NOSFERATU turns and looks up, smiling subtly.
NOSFERATU breaks into a creeping run, carrying his coffin.

JONATHON and NINA are still in each other's arms.

TITLE: *"Jonathon! Thank God you are safe! Now I feel that I too have been saved . . ."*

The couple continue their embrace.

The rotted and crumbling house with many arched windows: NOSFERATU appears standing in a small pointed boat, holding his coffin horizontal; the boat glides slowly across a stream with no visible

means of propulsion. (*Still*)
NOSFERATU carries in his coffin, looming ominously. He stops in front of a wooden door with curved top and looks up.
We look up the threatening brick facade of the house; the window apertures gape emptily and many of the wooden shutters hang loose.
NOSFERATU steps towards a wooden door carrying his coffin; as the coffin end approaches the door, NOSFERATU fades out.

A number of men are gathered at a landing stage; a gangplank is laid up to the side of the ship; a group of customs officials go up the gangplank and board the ship.
The captain is slumped on the wheel, eyes staring glassily. A number of tiny marks are distinctly visible on his throat. More people climb up on to the ship.
WESTENRA, bearded and dressed in a cape, goes up to the figure of the captain at the wheel, lifts up his head, which suddenly falls back. The sailors come in and begin to untie the captain from the wheel.
One of the seamen, very shaken, comes down the gangplank towards the others waiting on the quay.
He comes down the gangplank and joins his colleagues waiting on the quay.

TITLE: *"We couldn't find a single living soul on board!"*

The seaman goes back on board, while the men on the landing stage look at each other.
A man dressed in a cape comes down into the captain's cabin; light reflected from the sea moves back and forth on the ceiling of the cabin.
The men on the quay stand watching as some workers carry the body of the captain down the gangplank and away along the quay; all but one of the officials turn to follow the body.
The man with a cape finds the log book in the captain's cabin, and carries it over towards a lighter part of the cabin and starts to read a page.

INSERT: *Ship's Log — Varma to Bremen — 29 April 1838 . . . Passed the Dardanelles — East Wind — Carrying 5 passengers, mate, crew of 7 and myself, the Captain.*

The man shakes his head solemnly, looks back towards the captain's quarters where light dances on the ceiling, turns to the steps, slams the book shut and climbs the stairs.
He walks down the gangplank from the ship, still carrying the log book. Another man hands him his hat and walking-stick, then he walks away, shaking his head.
We are looking down from a balcony, of which the rail is just visible; a group of men are clustered around a body at lower right. There is a ship on a table and a painting of a ship in a stormy sea on the wall; a triton can be seen in silhouette on the right.
A man kneels, looking at the throat of a body; other men stand around in a group. WESTENRA enters and shakes the hand of the kneeling man and seats himself in the centre of the circle, by the head of the body; he opens the log book and begins to read.
We see WESTENRA reading from the log book.

INSERT: *6 May 1838 — Rounded Cape of Lustegran — One of my men, the strongest, is sick — Crew is restless, uneasy. . . . 7 May 1838. Mate reported stowaway hiding below decks — will investigate . . .*

WESTENRA reads out the log to the listening group.
The asylum supervisor shakes his head gravely.
The group of men listen keenly as WESTENRA reads.

INSERT: *18 May 1838 — Passed Gibraltar — Panic on board — Three men dead already — Mate out of his mind — Rats in the hold — I fear for the plague . . .*

The doctor rises and takes hold of the log book himself.
The doctor reads, then he turns and speaks to the other members of the group.

TITLE: "*The plague is here! Stay in your houses!*"

We are looking from a distant balcony as the doctor concludes his announcement; some break and run, one man takes out his handkerchief and puts it to his face; the doctor is the last to leave the room, taking his hat and stick and leaving the body on the floor.

A lone figure is seen walking down the middle of a narrow street; the shadows of the houses stretch towards the centre of the street.

A drummer beats a warning drum.
An old man sticks his head out of an arched window.
A young child appears at a window, opens it and climbs out on to the sill. The child rolls a ball along the sill.
The drummer stops his drum roll, takes out a rolled proclamation from his pocket and starts to unroll it.
A window opens and an old man and woman lean out to see what the commotion is all about.
The drummer reads from the proclamation.

INSERT: *NOTICE — To halt the spread of the plague, the Burgomaster of Bremen forbids the citizens of this city to bring their sick to the . . .*
Dissolve to INSERT: *. . . hospitals until further notice.*

A man's head is drawn back through the window, which closes behind him.
A pair of hands stretches through the window to pull the child back from the sill. The window swings closed.
The old couple also withdraw into their room and swiftly shut the window.
The drummer rolls up the proclamation, sticks it in the front of his jacket, takes his drumsticks which are passed through a loop on his chest and begins to beat the drum again.
Drummer walks away down an empty street.
A man in a dark top hat solemnly chalks a cross on a dark door. He finishes chalking his cross, then walks on to the next door where he does the same, then he walks past some windows, opens one and speaks to somebody.
A coffin is carried out of a doorway by four men, as the man in the top hat appears. (*Still*)
The coffin-bearers move in front of the houses; the man with the chalk closes a door and marks it with a cross; he marks a cross on the next door, walks past a number of windows to the next door and marks that with a cross.

TITLE: *"Nina has promised her husband never to open The Book of Vampires, but she found herself unable to resist the temptation."*

NINA leans on the arm of a chair, half-hiding the book and looking furtively around her, then her head falls back again on the back of her chair as if in agony. Then her face moves closer to the book.

INSERT: *The Book of the Vampires.*
INSERT: *One can recognize the mark of the vampire by the trace of his fangs on the victim's throat.*
INSERT: *Only a woman can break his frightful spell — a woman pure in heart — who will offer her blood freely to Nosferatu and . . .*
Dissolve to INSERT: *. . . will keep the vampire by her side until after the cock has crowed.*

NINA stares forward, very moved by what she has read.
JONATHON runs in and snatches the book away from NINA.
NINA gets up from her chair and presses against JONATHON, then turns and points out of the window.
We see the decayed house of NOSFERATU, with its blank window apertures.
NINA points out of the window, then turns to look at JONATHON.

TITLE: *"Look! Every night, in front of me . . ."*

NINA presses against JONATHON and hides her face in his chest.
JONATHON steps up to a window, then suddenly turns his back to it. He shakes his head negatively with a frantic smile.
NINA looks down and presses her fists into her face.
JONATHON looks towards his wife with a very pained expression.
NINA walks away slowly, holding her face in her hands. JONATHON turns to face the window, then starts back, turns and throws himself on the bed.

A fog-shrouded street: a man lights a large lantern, then steps over to a rope which hangs by a well. He pulls on the rope which lifts the large lantern into the air.

TITLE: *"The townspeople lived in mortal terror. Who was sick or dying? Who will be stricken tomorrow? . . ."*

WESTENRA sits down by his wife, who is lying down; he takes hold of her hands.
The wife convulsively grabs at her husband, then falls back again.
WESTENRA gets to his feet.

TITLE: *"Don't be frightened. I will get the professor."*

WESTENRA rushes out of the room.
A sudden gust blows the curtains inwards, causing the candle to flicker and go out.
Wife leaps out of her bed and runs across the room.
She pulls desperately on a bell cord.
We see a servant sleeping oblivious in bed.
The wife begins to sob desperately and falls to the floor.

NINA gazes out through the window of her bedchamber.

A procession of men carrying coffins passes down an otherwise empty street. Each coffin is carried by two men.

NINA turns from her window and collapses on to an ottoman; she clutches at her breast.
Then NINA suddenly sees the vampire book again: she picks it up in spite of herself and starts to read.

INSERT: *Only a woman can break his frightful spell — a woman pure in heart — who will offer her blood to Nosferatu and . . .*
Dissolve to INSERT: *. . . will keep the vampire by her side until after the cock has crowed.*

NINA looks up staring, horrified by what she senses she must do.

An old white-haired woman and some younger men are talking between buildings with black vertical walls.
The woman talks very earnestly to the young men, who listen with very concerned expressions on their faces.
The woman and young men look fearfully in another direction.
Two ancient white-haired women talk excitedly to each other.

TITLE: *"They saw him escape. He strangled his keeper."*

The women turn to look down the street.
RENFIELD runs round a corner at far end of street, pursued by an angry crowd; he runs forward down the street, then suddenly turns left about half-way down the block.
A lone figure runs down a street.

Other people come into sight and they are stopped by the lone figure who points upwards.
High above the street, RENFIELD is seen sitting on the gable roof of a house; he hurls a stone down towards the crowd below.
The people in the crowd start to pick up stones and throw them up at RENFIELD.
RENFIELD cackles madly and ducks his head back and forth; his collar is pulled up around his neck making him resemble his secret mentor, NOSFERATU.
A wild, pushing and shoving crowd is beginning to fill the street; more stones are flung upwards.
Finding himself pelted by more and more stones, RENFIELD leaps away over the rest of the roof.
As RENFIELD moves, the crowd also moves down the street.
RENFIELD slides down to the edge of the roof, climbs onto a small metal pipe, dangles momentarily, then drops down into a courtyard and scuttles furtively away.

NINA is sitting in a chair sewing, looking very thoughtful.
Over her shoulder we see a sampler reading "Ich Liebe Dich."
NINA pauses, looks up pensively, sighs, then continues her sewing.

RENFIELD lopes furtively through an archway.
He crouches for a moment before dashing across a road; the crowd of pursuers appears almost immediately to give chase.
RENFIELD crouches behind a stump, peeping out from time to time and grinning broadly.
His pursuers appear confused and point wildly in different directions, before separating.
RENFIELD laughs behind his stump, then jumps up and dances away into the darkness.
A figure stands in silhouette against a flat skyline.
The boy in a cap leads the pursuers through some trees, waving for them to follow.
The pursuers rush towards the figure on the skyline, which turns out to be a scarecrow. They wrench it up and dash away, whirling it in the air.

NOSFERATU stands close to a window, glaring malevolently.

NINA, dressed in a white nightdress, is lying asleep in bed. Suddenly she sits upright, a look of horror on her face.
NOSFERATU continues to stare out of the window.
NINA holds her hand to her left breast; her head sways backward; she starts to get out of bed.
NINA climbs out of her bed and we now see that JONATHON is lying asleep in an armchair: NINA stretches out her arms in front of her as though she is sleepwalking. She begins to move towards the window.
NOSFERATU suddenly stares hard at one of his long tapering hands which begins to unflex and open wide.
NINA momentarily takes her hands away from the window knobs, and leans to one side of the window, gazing lovingly in the direction of her husband.
JONATHON sleeps on, his features lit by a bedside light.
NINA stands by the window gazing fondly at JONATHON.
NOSFERATU stands poised, almost excited, by the broken window; his eyes open wide in anticipation.
NINA hides for a moment behind the edge of the window, then steps decisively to it again and grasps the knobs. She throws the windows wide open and stands in the casement with arms held wide.
NOSFERATU turns left, still looking out of the window. He raises his claw-like hands, then moves back behind the wall.
NINA's head jerks backwards as she stands holding on to the windows.
JONATHON slumbers oblivious in his armchair.
Huge wooden doors with curved tops pop open in four stages to reveal NOSFERATU standing behind them with claws at the ready.
NINA spins away from the window, claps her hands over her eyes, staggers, leans against the foot of the bed, breathing heavily.
NOSFERATU stands poised in his doorway. (*Still*)
NINA goes over to JONATHON and desperately shakes his arm. As he awakens, she begins to faint. Seeing his wife falling, JONATHON leaps to her side and helps her over towards the bed.
He lowers her to the bed. She, suddenly, stretches up her arms and grasps JONATHON.

TITLE: *"The professor! Call the professor!"*

She falls back in a dead faint, while JONATHON, shocked, rushes from the room.

Jonathon appears, dashing out of the front of the house; he runs down the street.

Nina rises from her bed, walks slowly to the window and gazes out again.

We see Nosferatu's derelict house across the street.

Nina continues to gaze through the window, apparently in horrified fascination.

The shadow of Nosferatu, hunched, with claw-like hands at the ready, appears in the stairwell. (*Still*)

Nina spins round in terror, like an automaton, clings to the window behind her. Her eyes dilate with horror as she looks at what is coming from the stairs.

The shadow of Nosferatu, hands extended, moves across the wall.

Nina, first almost sorrowful, then terrified, raises her hand to her breast and begins to back away.

Nina backs to the bed, then pulls herself up on to it, still clasping her breast.

Nina's face expresses a horrible fascination and attraction, as the shadow of Nosferatu's hand creeps up across the white of her dress until it rests over her heart. Suddenly the shadow of the hand grips into a fist; Nina's face is thrown back in a convulsion of pain, and then her expression relaxes.

Jonathon shakes the professor, who is lying asleep in a chair; he crouches by him, and finally the professor gets to his feet, listens carefully to Jonathon, then hastily begins to dress.

In the dim light of Nina's room, Nosferatu's head can just be seen close to Nina's throat.

An attendant comes into the room of the asylum supervisor, tells him something; they both run out of the room through an archway.

Nosferatu stands still, drinking at Nina's throat.

A cock crows in the dawn light.

Nosferatu raises his face slowly and deliberately from the throat of his victim and turns to look towards the window. (*Still*)

Renfield leaps up, panic-stricken, from his cell bed, raises his arms and cries out.

Title: "*Master! Master! Beware!*"

He stands for a moment, hands above his head.

Jonathon hurries out through the garden of his house; the professor pauses for a moment, then hurries after him.

Renfield hangs onto the bars in the window and begins to pull himself up the wall by them. Then a number of attendants rush into the room and pull him back on to the bed.

We look through the window of Nina's bedroom towards the rotting house opposite; a straight band of sunlight moves rapidly down its façade.
Nosferatu rises slowly to his full height; he turns slowly towards the window; holds his left hand to his chest as he staggers to get away from the light coming through the window.
Nosferatu stumbles, as the bright beams of the sun streaming in the window strike him. His right hand goes across to shield his face; he turns about, faces left, and then his image begins to disappear. (*Still*). White smoke rises from a sunlit patch on the bedroom floor.

Tightly bound, Renfield sits up on his bed against the wall in his dimly lit cell; he raises his face, then looks sorrowfully down.

Title: *"The Master is dead!"*

Renfield's head slumps forward.
Nina comes to her senses, sits slowly up in bed, looks about the room. A faint smile of recognition passes over her face, and she raises her hands in front of her.

Title: *"Jonathon!"*

Nina sits with her hands up, smiling.
Jonathon runs up the steps at the front of his house; the professor follows him.
Nina is slowly falling backward as Jonathon rushes in and takes hold of her. She speaks a few tender words to him, then goes limp; he lays her back, then buries his face on her chest.
The professor stands by the doorway, remaining still, as he sees the figure of Jonathon lying sprawled over his wife on the bed.
The professor remains by the door.

TITLE: *"And at that moment, as if by a miracle, the sick no longer died, and the stifling shadow of the vampire vanished with the morning sun."*

The blasted ruins of the castle of DRACULA stand silhouetted on a hilltop.

TITLE: *THE END.*

M

CREDITS:

Produced by	Nero Film A.G.
Directed by	Fritz Lang
Scenario and dialogue by	Thea von Harbou
after an article by	Egon Jacobson
In collaboration with	Paul Falkenberg, Adolf Jansen and Karl Vash
Murderer's theme by	Edward Grieg: extract from 'Peer Gynt'
Director of photography	Fritz Arno Wagner
Camera operator	Karl Vash
Chief editor	Paul Falkenberg
Designed by	Emil Hasler and Karl Vollbrecht
Film shot during	Six weeks in 1931
Original duration	114 minutes
Duration as seen	99 minutes
Process	Black and white (normal screen)

CAST:

Hans Beckert, the murderer	Peter Lorre
Inspector Lohmann	Otto Wernicke
Schränker, head of the underworld	Gustaf Gründgens
Mrs. Beckmann	Ellen Widmann
Elsie Beckmann	Inge Landgut
Chief of police	Ernst Stahl-Nachbaur
The Minister	Franz Stein
Inspector Groeber	Theodor Loos
The burglar	Fritz Gnass
The safe-breaker	Fritz Odemar
The pick-pocket	Paul Kemp
The con-man	Theo Lingen
The blind beggar	Georg John
The night watchman	Karl Platen
The Inspector's secretary	Gerhard Bienert
The landlady of the 'Crocodile Club'	Rosa Valetti
A prostitute	Hertha von Walther
The lawyer	Rudolf Blümner

with: Almas, Balhaus, Behal Carell, Dahmen, Döblin, Eckof, Else Ehser, Elzer, Faber, Ilse Fürstenberg, Gelingk, Goldstein, Goltz, Heinrich Gotho, Gretler, Hadank, Hartberg, Hempel, Hocker, Hoermann, Isenta, Karchow, Kepich, Hermann Krehan, Kurth Leeser, Rose Lichtenstein, Lotte Löbinger, Lohde, Loretto, Maschek, Matthis, Mederow, Margarete Melzer, Trude Moos, Netto, Neumann, Nied, Maja Norden, Edgar Pauly, Klaus Pohl, Polland, Rebane, Paul Rehkopf, Reihsig, Rhaden, Ritter, Sablotzky, Sascha, Agnes Schulz-Lichterfeld, Leonhard Steckel, Stroux, Swinborne, Trutz, Otto Waldis, Walth, Wanka, Wannemann, Wulf, Ziener and members of the underworld, police or people of the town

M

Close-up of a large white M on a black screen. At the end, over the black screen, the titles unroll and a child's voice is heard singing.

Shot from above of a group of children standing in a circle, playing a game. In the centre of the circle a little girl passes from one to another, chanting.

LITTLE GIRL: *Just you wait a little while,*
The evil man in black will come.
With his little chopper,
He will chop you up.

The LITTLE GIRL stops in front of one of her playmates and gestures to her to leave the circle.

LITTLE GIRL: *You're out.*

The child leaves the circle and the game continues.

LITTLE GIRL: *Just you wait a little while,*
The evil man in black will come.
With his little chopper,
He will chop you up.

During the song, the camera pans off to show two coal-bunkers in the courtyard of a block of flats. The camera climbs the face of the tenement block to show an outside balcony with washing hanging out to dry. A pregnant woman appears, carrying a basket of laundry; she leans over the balcony and shouts down to the children.

WOMAN: *Will you stop singing that awful song* . . .The singing continues off . . . *Can't you hear?* . . . Mutters to herself . . . *Always that awful song.*

She disappears and the song continues.

LITTLE GIRL: *Just you wait a little while,*
The evil man in black will come.
With his little chopper . . .

Cut to the narrow staircase of the tenement block. Shot from above, we see the front door of one of the flats.

In front of the door, the WOMAN with the basket of laundry

rings the bell. The camera tracks in as the door opens and a tired, haggard, middle-aged woman appears. It is MRS. BECKMANN. Behind her, we see a kitchen. The WOMAN hands the basket to MRS. BECKMANN and wearily wipes her brow. During the following dialogue, a rapid series of cuts takes place between the two women.

WOMAN sighing: *Oh, dear!*

MRS. BECKMANN: *What's the matter?*

WOMAN: *I'm always telling those kids to stop singing that terrible murderer's song . . . and they do nothing but sing it at the top of their voices all day . . .* A pause. *As if we hadn't heard enough of that murderer.*

MRS. BECKMANN: *Oh, leave them alone. As long as they're singing, at least we know they're still there.*

WOMAN: *Yes, I suppose you're right.*

She shrugs her shoulders and shuffles away.

Camera pans with MRS. BECKMANN, as she shuts the door and puts the basket of washing in a corner of the kitchen. Pan with her to reveal a poor but clean kitchen. MRS. BECKMANN bends over a bowl of water and continues with her washing. Medium close-up of her. A cuckoo-clock strikes. As MRS. BECKMANN looks up, the camera follows her eyes to a close-up of the cuckoo-clock, which shows midday. The ringing of a church bell mingles with the cuckoos. Cut back to MRS. BECKMANN, who straightens up, drying her hands.

In the street, a group of parents is waiting on the pavement outside the main entrance to the local school. Cars pass. The bell stops ringing as the children come out; one little girl waves and goes off in a different direction to her friends. It is ELSIE BECKMANN; she has a satchel on her back and carries a string bag with a ball in it. When she comes to cross the road she steps off the kerb without looking, a car hoots at her and she steps back onto the kerb. A policeman stops the traffic and escorts her across. In the kitchen, MRS. BECKMANN is laying the table. In the street, ELSIE runs along the pavement of a busy road, bouncing her ball. She stops by a circular pillar of the sort used as a billboard and starts throwing her ball against it. The camera follows the ball and tracks in to show one of the posters:

10,000 Marks Reward

WHO IS THE MURDERER?

Since Monday, 11th June this year, the following have disappeared: the school-children Klaus Klawitsky and his sister Klara, who live at 470 Müller Street. Various evidence leads us to believe that the children were victims of a similar crime to that committed last autumn against the Doering sisters.

As the ball continues to bounce against the poster, the shadow of a man in a hat falls across the pillar: it is the shadow of the murderer.

MURDERER off: *What a pretty ball.* The shadow bends down. *What's your name?*

ELSIE off: *Elsie Beckmann.*

In the kitchen, MRS. BECKMANN is peeling potatoes and putting them into a tureen. Quick cut to the clock. It is 12.20. Cut back to MRS. BECKMANN, who puts the lid on the tureen. She hears footsteps, goes to the door, opens it and looks up the stairs. Two little girls are going up.

MRS. BECKMANN: *Elsie didn't come with you?*

1ST LITTLE GIRL: *No.*

2ND LITTLE GIRL simultaneously: *No, she didn't come with us.*

Cut back to MRS. BECKMANN who watches from the doorway, as the girls go on up the stairs; then she leans over the bannisters. The camera tilts straight down the empty staircase well. Cut back to MRS. BECKMANN who goes back into her flat.

Shot from high above, as a beggar is seen walking along the pavement of a busy street. Camera tracks in slightly to show the card hung round the beggar's neck, which reads BLIND. He stops at a corner to sell balloons. A paper windmill is stuck in his battered hat. The MURDERER and ELSIE stand beside him examining the balloons. The MURDERER whistles loudly and off-key, the first bars of a tune from Grieg's 'Peer Gynt.' He buys a balloon in the shape of a huge doll and hands it to ELSIE who thanks him with a little curtsey.

ELSIE: *Thank you very much.*

Cut back to the kitchen, where MRS. BECKMANN is putting the tureen into a steaming saucepan. The bell rings. Pan with her, as she rushes to open the door. On the doorstep stands the PAPERMAN.

PAPERMAN: *Good morning . . . A thrilling new chapter, Mrs. Beck-*

mann! He hands her the paper. *Passionate, moving, sensational . . .*
MRS. BECKMANN very wearily: *Good — thank you.* A pause. *Oh . . . just a moment Mr. Gehrke.*

She takes the paper and moves away. Camera stays on the PAPERMAN.

MRS. BECKMANN off: *Tell me, Mr. Gehrke . . .*
PAPERMAN: *Yes?*
MRS. BECKMANN off: *Have you seen Elsie?*
PAPERMAN: *Didn't she just come up the stairs?*

MRS. BECKMANN comes back to the door to pay the PAPERMAN. Shot of the two of them.

MRS. BECKMANN: *No, she's not back yet.*
PAPERMAN: *Well, she won't be long now.* He touches the peak of his cap and turns to go. *Good-bye, Mrs. Beckmann.*
MRS. BECKMANN: *Good-bye, Mr. Gehrke.*

She hesitates for a moment, then goes onto the landing and leans once again over the bannisters. The camera tilts straight down the empty staircase well.

MRS. BECKMANN off, her voice echoing: *Elsie! Elsie!*

Cut back to MRS. BECKMANN who, looking worried, goes back to her flat and closes the door. Camera follows.

Close-up of the cuckoo-clock which shows 1.15; the cuckoo strikes once. Long shot of the room: MRS. BECKMANN opens the window and leans out, calling anxiously.

MRS. BECKMANN: *Elsie! Elsie!*

Cut to a tilt straight down the empty staircase well.

MRS. BECKMANN off: *Elsie!*

Cut to the loft of the block of flats, empty except for some washing hanging in the shadows.

MRS. BECKMANN off: *Elsie!*

Medium close-up, shot slightly from above, of Elsie's empty chair at the kitchen table: her clean plate, her spoon, and her folded serviette.

MRS. BECKMANN still calling off: *Elsie! Elsie!*

Medium close-up of a patch of scrubby ground. Out of the undergrowth, rolls ELSIE's ball. It stops in the middle of frame. The big, doll-shaped balloon, floats up and catches momentarily in some telegraph wires, until the wind shakes it free and carries it away.

MRS. BECKMANN off: *Elsie!*

Fade to black.

High shot from above of a street. Close-up of a car parked at the kerb. A PAPERSELLER rushes by waving the latest edition.

PAPERSELLER: *Extra! Extra! Extra!*

A passer-by stops him and buys a paper.

High shot from above of a different street. A PAPERSELLER can be seen, surrounded by a crowd.

PAPERSELLER: *Extra! Extra! New crime! Who is the murderer? Who! Who is the murderer?*

Inside his room, the MURDERER is seated at the windowsill, his back to the camera, writing. He has a cigarette in his left hand and is still whistling the tune from 'Peer Gynt.' Through the double windows, can be seen some fruit and other food. The camera tilts down on him and tracks in until we can see what he is writing. The handwriting is childish.

'Since the police haven't published my first letter, I am writing today straight to the NEWSPAPERS. Keep up your investigations. Everything will happen just as I have predicted. But I havn't yet FINISHED.'

Close-up of a police poster. We have time to read:

10,000 Marks Reward

WHO IS THE MURDERER?

Then the camera tracks back to show a crowd gathered round the poster. General hubbub.

VOICES OF CROWD: *Good God, off we go again . . . It's terrible! 10,000 Marks . . . The lettering is too small, we can't read it all! . . . Hey, read it out loud, you, there in front . . . Yes, read it . . . out loud . . .* Reading: *'The unknown murderer' . . . Let him read. Oh, hey! . . . Quiet! . . . Shut up! . . .* Reading: *'The terror in our town has found a new' . . . Oh, that's enough . . . Stop it! . . .* Reading: *'victim' . . . Louder, we can't hear a thing.*

The sound of the crowd mixes to the voice of a RADIO ANNOUNCER.

RADIO ANNOUNCER: *Certain evidence leads us to believe that the murderer is the same as the one who has already killed eight children in our town. We must once more draw your attention to the fact.*

Shot from above, we see a group of middle-class men sitting round a café table, smoking and drinking. One of them, an

Old Man, reads aloud from a newspaper. His voice takes over from the Radio Announcer. In the middle of the table, stands a little embroidered flag, the insignia of the club to which these gentlemen belong.

Old Man reading: '*That the first duty of every mother, of every father, is to warn their children of the danger which always threatens them. Moreover, because the danger is often hidden under an attractive disguise: some sweets, a toy, fruit, can be the murderer's weapons.*'

The Other Men: *Very true. Of course.*

The Old Man stops reading to take a gulp of beer. His neighbour, a fat civil servant in a stiff collar, impatiently stuffs a huge cigar into a cigar-holder.

Man with Cigar Holder: *Go on* . . . Nervously . . . *Come on now, read on.*

Old Man: *Right, right* . . . reading . . . '*The anxiety of the general public is all the greater, because police enquiries . . .*'

Cut to two of the other men at the table. Close-up of a bald man wearing pince-nez; beside him, a little to one side, a fat man twirls a glass of wine in his hand. Over this shot, the voice of the Old Man continues reading.

Old Man off: '*. . . have not yet finished. But the police find themselves faced by an almost impossible problem.*'

The Bald Man nudges his neighbour and they whisper to one another.

The Bald Man points his cigar at the man opposite him. The Old Man continues to read.

Old Man off: '*The guilty man has left no trace. Who is the murderer?* '

Cut to the man oposite listening attentively. On his cigar-holder, we see the design of a naked woman. Occasionally, the head of the Old Man appears in the left of frame.

Old Man continues: '*What is he like? Where is he hiding? No one knows. And, yet, he is one of us. Your neighbour could be the murderer.*'

He lowers the paper. Cut to the Bald Man and his small companion who stares with contempt at the Man with Cigar-Holder. On the table, the newspaper ' Tempo ', with the headline: ' 10,000 Marks reward '. The Bald Man grabs his glass of beer.

BALD MAN: *Yes, that's right.*

High shot of the whole group from above.

MAN WITH CIGAR-HOLDER: *Why do you look at me, when you say that?*

BALD MAN: *You know very well.*

MAN WITH CIGAR-HOLDER: *What do I know very well?*

Medium close-up of the BALD MAN behind his glass of beer; he leans forward and stares at his companion through his pince-nez.

BALD MAN: *All right . . . think a bit. You'll find out.*

Camera cuts between them as they speak.

MAN WITH CIGAR-HOLDER: *What are you insinuating?*

BALD MAN: *That I saw you going up the stairs, behind the little girl from the fourth floor.*

MAN WITH CIGAR-HOLDER jumps up, shouting angrily: *What? You're mad, you swine!*

BALD MAN also jumps up, shouting: *Who's a swine? Me? Me? Or the man who chases little girls?*

In the excitement, he loses his pince-nez. Shot from above of the whole group.

MAN WITH CIGAR-HOLDER mad with rage: *Bastard! Swine!*

BALD MAN in the same state: *Murderer . . . murderer!*

As the MAN WITH CIGAR-HOLDER tries to punch his opponent two friends and a waiter intervene. There is general confusion.

OLD MAN: *But, gentlemen! . . . Gentlemen! Gentlemen!*

MAN WITH CIGAR-HOLDER: *You . . . me? Both of us!* They are separated. *I'll see you in court.*

BALD MAN: *I'll see* you *in court.*

WAITER intervening: *Now then, gentlemen . . . calm down.*

ANOTHER CLIENT: *I didn't mean to . . .*

The HEAD WAITER, a CLIENT and the three friends go out. The SMALL MAN has been watching the row with fiendish glee. The BALD MAN continues to shout at his departing enemy.

BALD MAN: *Slanderer . . . ruining my reputation.*

Cut to a long shot of a bedroom in a comfortable bourgeois flat. The drawers of a chest have been pulled out and the contents scattered everywhere. Through the door we see a sitting-room.

A VOICE: *What a slanderer! What an awful man!*

A woman appears at the doorway, in tears.

THE VOICE continues: *And the police listened to him! . . . They're searching my house!*

A POLICEMAN and THE HUSBAND come through the door into the sitting room.

THE WOMAN weeping: *What shame! . . . Oh, what shame!*

THE HUSBAND: *Searching an honest man's flat, because of an anonymous letter. It's . . . it's . . .*

POLICEMAN calmly: *Mr. Jäger, calm down. We're only doing our duty.*

THE HUSBAND: *When we never have a minute's peace? Frightened about the children . . .*

POLICEMAN: *Look here. For that very reason, the police must follow every lead . . . Any man in the street . . .* cut to a man in the street *. . . could be the guilty man.*

It is evening. In the street, a little man of about sixty, wearing a bowler hat and spectacles with round, metal rims stops under a street lamp to read his paper. A LITTLE GIRL comes up to him, pushing a scooter.

LITTLE GIRL: *Could you tell me what time it is, please?*

OLD MAN very friendly: *Yes, my child . . .* He takes out his watch.

A few yards away, in front of a furniture shop, two shoppers, laden with parcels, look on. A WORKMAN with huge wide shoulders, wearing a cap, comes out of the shop.

Camera cuts back to the LITTLE GIRL, who stands with her back to the camera, with the OLD MAN in the bowler hat facing her. In the background, the big WORKMAN approaches, menacingly. The OLD MAN puts his watch away and bends down to the LITTLE GIRL.

OLD MAN: *Now, my child, you must go home . . . Where do you live?*

As the LITTLE GIRL goes off on her scooter, the WORKMAN interrupts.

WORKMAN: *What business is it of yours, where the kid lives?*

OLD MAN looking up terrified: *Excuse me?*

Medium close-up shot from above of the OLD MAN looking up anxiously, through his pebbled-glasses, with great, round, scared eyes.

Shot from below of the WORKMAN, who, enormous, rises on his toes.

WORKMAN: *What did you want with the kid?*

OLD MAN startled: *But . . . but . . . nothing at all! And you, what do you want with me?*

The WORKMAN seizes his arm. Some people stop and gather round.

WORKMAN seizing the OLD MAN: *Just you wait and see.*

OLD MAN struggling: *Let go . . . Let me go. It's a . . . a . . . an impertinence!*

FIRST PASSER-BY: *What's going on?*

OLD MAN to PASSER-BY: *It's an outrage!*

SECOND PASSER-BY: *What does he want, the one in specs?*

WORKMAN to OLD MAN: *Don't get on your high horse.*

WORKMAN to SECOND PASSER-BY: *First, he accosts children . . .*

ANOTHER BYSTANDER: *Punch his face in!*

WORKMAN continuing: *. . . and then, he comes on all high and mighty.*

OLD MAN struggling: *Let me go, can't you? I didn't start the conversation with the child.*

WORKMAN: *You wanted to get off with her, didn't you?*

PASSER-BY violently: *Yes . . . and then kill her like all the others . . . eh?* Everyone joins in and starts shouting.

CROWD: *It's the murderer! . . . It's him! . . . Hold onto him. Call the police . . . Of course, no cops when you need them . . . Oh constable . . . constable . . .*

Everyone hangs onto the OLD MAN. (*Still*).

Shot from above of the stairs of a double-decker bus; the crowd can be seen jostling and calling for a policeman.

CROWD: *Constable . . . constable.*

The CONDUCTOR comes down the stairs pushing people out of the way.

CONDUCTOR: *Move along, please . . . move along now . . . stop blocking the way.*

Behind the CONDUCTOR, comes a POLICEMAN, leading a THIEF.

THE THIEF insultingly: *You're good at catching pickpockets, that's all you know how to do . . . You'd do better to go after the child murderer.*

A dense crowd presses against the bus.

VARIOUS VOICES: *What? The child murderer? The murderer . . . That's him . . . the murderer!*

POLICEMAN: *Move along now.* To the THIEF: *Come on now . . . get a move on.*

Hysterical cries rise from the crowd. Fists are raised. The POLICEMAN and his prisoner have difficulty forcing their way through. Dissolve.

Close-up of the headlines of a daily paper, 'Tempo': 'THE MURDERER WRITES TO THE PAPERS'. Underneath, the MURDERER's letter is reproduced.

'Since the police haven't published my first letter, I am writing today straight to the NEWSPAPERS. Keep up your investigations. Everything will happen just as I have predicted. But I haven't yet FINISHED.'

A hand nervously holding a monocle spreads out the paper. It is the MINISTER; he sits at his desk, in his office, the newspaper spread out before him. He is speaking into a white telephone, emphasising his points with wooden gestures.

MINISTER: *It's an unheard-of scandal . . . What a deplorable effect this will have on public opinion, Inspector. It is a serious error, very serious.*

Cut to the Office of the Chief of Police. The CHIEF OF POLICE, an elegant man, is seated at his desk. In one hand, he waves a pen; in the other, he holds the telephone.

CHIEF OF POLICE: *But, Minister, we've no power to prevent the murderer from writing to anyone he wants to!*

The MINISTER's reply is inaudible. The CHIEF OF POLICE is passed some letters to sign, by his secretary. As he is leaving, the CHIEF OF POLICE signs to him to note a meeting in his engagement book. The SECRETARY does so and leaves.

CHIEF OF POLICE into the telephone: *The guilty man is a mental case. He must get pleasure out of seeing his actions reported in the papers. We immediately got in touch with the editor to obtain the original letter. The laboratory is already busy on it.*

Large close-up of a set of finger-prints in the Police laboratory. It is the dossier of a certain Richard Ernst, known as 'Four-Fingered Ernst.' Pan across the dossier to show the prints of the left hand, next to the right.

CHIEF OF POLICE off: *Of course, it is almost impossible to find usable finger-prints on a postcard that has been through so many hands.*

Close-up of a hand moving a magnifying glass across a dossier.

CHIEF OF POLICE off: *But we must try everything . . .*

In another room in the police laboratory, a finger-print is projected onto a large screen. Silhouetted against it a police research assistant compares the projection with the dossier, with the aid of a magnifying glass.

CHIEF OF POLICE off: *. . . to find in our archives a clue or a trail that will lead us nearer a solution.*

Cut to the office of the police archives where an employee is pacing up and down dictating a report.

Back in his room, the MURDERER looks at himself in the mirror and makes terrible faces, spreading his lips and lifting his eyebrows with his fingers. (*Still*).

Close-up of the MINISTER, on the telephone in his office.

THE MINISTER: *Yes, yes, Inspector . . . certainly. I don't doubt your keenness . . . the efforts of your men . . . But, all the same . . . the result.* Annoyed. *We must have results . . . results.*

The sound of The MINISTER's voice continues as we cut to the CHIEF OF POLICE's office. He puts down the receiver which continues to crackle '*results . . . results.*' He drums his fingers nervously on his desk, then picks up the receiver. During the following conversation the CHIEF OF POLICE's voice continues as images illustrate what he is saying.

CHIEF OF POLICE: *Minister, my men are only getting twelve hours' sleep a week. . . .*

A police-station at night. Several tired policemen slump on benches. As two come in off their beats another two get up and go out.

CHIEF OF POLICE: *. . . as well as searches on the spot, Minister.*

High shot from above of suburban gardens. Plain-clothes men are seen searching everywhere. In the background are two photographers. A flash-gun goes off. Behind a hedge one of the policemen finds a ball of paper.

CHIEF OF POLICE off: *. . . We find, for instance, behind a hedge in a thicket a little tissue-paper bag . . .*

Close-up of a pair of tweezers carefully lifting the paper bag on which can be read the word SWEETS.

CHIEF OF POLICE off: . . . *clearly it held cheap sweets . . . In a corner we found tiny crumbs of acid drops and some grains of coloured sugar. Within a radius of twelve kilometres, we have . . .*

Close-up of a map of Berlin. The gardens where the bag was discovered are circled and dated '21-6'. A compass draws a second larger circle dated '22-6'; the same compass starts a third circle.

CHIEF OF POLICE off: . . . *searched in all the sweet-shops, cake-shops, to find out where the bag came from . . . In vain . . . every day we widen the area of the search . . .*

At the counter of a sweet-shop, a detective questions a sales-girl who shakes her head.

CHIEF OF POLICE off: . . . *but, of course, no one remembers anything . . . or, at least not clearly enough . . .*

At a sweet and ice-cream kiosk, a detective questions a sales-man, without success.

CHIEF OF POLICE: . . . *In spite of all these negative replies we are keeping up the search, stepping more and more into an area of uncertainty . . .*

At a grocer's, a detective questions a grocer and his wife, without success.

CHIEF OF POLICE: . . . *without much hope of finding any solution. Our men . . .*

Cut to the MINISTER's office. Medium close-up of him crashing his palm violently against his desk, his other hand holding the telephone.

MINISTER furious: *What good is that to me? Inspector, I know you're not sleeping . . . but those are the facts: an unknown murderer terrorizes the town . . . a town of four million people . . . And . . . and . . . the police,* your *police, are failing.*

Medium close-up of the CHIEF OF POLICE at his desk. He is annoyed by what the MINISTER has just said.

CHIEF OF POLICE irritated: *Minister, you don't really seem to appreciate the incredible difficulties which face us.*

In an office at Police HQ a DETECTIVE questions two witnesses. One is large and fat; he wears a little beard and pince-nez. The other witness is stunted. In the background is a typist.

1ST WITNESS indignantly to 2ND WITNESS: *You don't know anything.*

2ND WITNESS leaping from his chair: *More than you, sir.*

DETECTIVE: *But, gentlemen, gentlemen . . . Could you at least come to some agreement on what colour bonnet the little girl was wearing, who you saw talking to an unknown man this morning?*

1ST WITNESS: *But, of course, Inspector, the bonnet was red.*

2ND WITNESS: *Inspector, the bonnet was green.*

1ST WITNESS rising: *It was a red bonnet.*

2ND WITNESS: *It was a green bonnet.*

Camera cuts between them, the shots getting closer and closer.

1ST WITNESS shouting: *Red.*

2ND WITNESS shouting: *Green.*

Camera cuts in even closer.

1ST WITNESS in an absolute fury: *Red.*

2ND WITNESS in as great a fury: *Green.*

The WITNESSES try to shout one another down. The DETECTIVE looks on amazed. Intercut extreme close-up of both WITNESSES.

1ST WITNESS: *Red.*

2ND WITNESS: *Green.*

1ST WITNESS: *Red.*

2ND WITNESS: *Green.*

1ST WITNESS: *Red.*

2ND WITNESS: *Green.*

The typist gets up. Group shot.

DETECTIVE: *Stop, stop! . . . It's hopeless. Thank you, gentlemen.*

1ST WITNESS: *Of course, Inspector, if you are prepared to listen to a socialist . . .*

Cut back to the office of the CHIEF OF POLICE, who is on the telephone again.

CHIEF OF POLICE: *The police have followed up, by today, more than fifteen hundred clues in this case. The dossiers we have collected fill sixty thick volumes. We have put all our men onto it . . .*

Camera cuts to a medium close-up of several policemen beating through the undergrowth of a wood. The voice of the CHIEF OF POLICE continues over the following scenes.

CHIEF OF POLICE off: *. . . to systematically comb all the areas around the town . . . Every thicket, every piece of undergrowth, every clearing is carefully examined, because behind each bush . . .*

Medium close-up of several policemen searching a wooded pit.

CHIEF OF POLICE off: . . . *in every hole, we might find something that would put us at last on the right track . . .*

Medium shot of a police dog as he picks up a scent and follows it to the edge of a lake, barking. A policeman follows him, holding him on a long leash. Other handlers and their dogs appear.

CHIEF OF POLICE off: . . . *We have sent out police dogs. The best trackers have been put onto the weak scents we have found . . . without any result. Since this murderer's first crime . . .*

Long shot of detectives checking the papers of down-and-outs in a scruffy dormitory of a doss-house, where rows of beds face one another and old clothing hangs from the walls.

CHIEF OF POLICE off: . . . *the police have inspected all the doss-houses every night and checked the identity of every vagrant. Of course, these steps don't increase the popularity of the police, nor do they calm the nerves of the general public . . .*

A smoky railway station. Detectives are checking everyone's papers.

CHIEF OF POLICE off: . . . *Nevertheless, we are keeping up our watch on all railway stations. But these checks are no more successful than our nightly raids . . .*

A deserted street at night lit by street lamps. A plain-clothes policeman is accosted by a tart, but he goes on his way. Further on, under a street lamp, another girl talks with a client.

CHIEF OF POLICE off: . . . *of the various underworld hangouts.*

Shot from above we see a dark street still wet from recent rain. A couple disappear into a seedy hotel. A detective, beneath a street lamp opposite, looks on.

Shot from above in a wider angle, the headlights of a car light up the walls. Some men leap from the car while it is still moving and station themselves rapidly in various doorways. Their footsteps continue to echo over this and the following shots.

Three detectives are waiting in one doorway. One of them looks at his watch and gestures at the others. They move out of sight.

Shot from above we see the street with the seedy hotel. Three detectives can be seen coming out of a near-by doorway; one of them gives a signal: a whistle blows.

Shot from above we see two lorries full of men drive up.

Policemen jump from cars. Motor-cycle policemen wait on their machines by the kerb. In the distance a group of plain-clothes men arrive, followed by uniformed men drawn up in two ranks. (*Still*). Cut to a shot looking down over the roofs at a line of uniformed policemen and a group of detectives.

A young prostitute rushes into a sordid basement bar down the spiral staircase which leads from the street. It is an underworld hangout. A stuffed crocodile hangs from the ceiling and there is an old piano on the right.

PROSTITUTE: *Cops!* (*Still*).

Without wasting a second, the clients, criminals and whores, rush for the exit, scrambling over the tables and chairs. Seen from the exit, the landlady lowers a grille which shuts her off behind the bar. Everyone rushes for the stairs.

General chaos and confusion, seen in a high-angle shot looking down the empty staircase. The young prostitute appears first, followed by a thief who gives a sudden start and, furious, turns back. Others pass him to be turned back in their turn.

Police whistle. Car horns. A line of policemen, advancing steadily, pushes the fleeing crowd back down into the room.

Cut to the street: two plain-clothes men lead away a prostitute.

POLICEMAN'S VOICE: *Police. Get back there.*

YOUNG PROSTITUTE'S VOICE among other cries: *Let me go, you bastard. Let me go. Eh, Inspector, let me go.*

A policeman descends the stairs carrying the YOUNG PROSTITUTE in his arms. The camera tracks with them and stops at the bottom of the stairs, beneath the arch of the entrance.

YOUNG PROSTITUTE: *Let me go, won't you? . . . you beast, let me go, let me go.*

THIEF: *Let the girl alone, filthy copper.*

General hubbub rising to a crescendo.

POLICE: *Silence . . . silence!*

The camera looks towards the stairs over the heads of the crowd, where a sergeant appears.

THE CROWD: *Ah, the head cop.* Laughter.

With a gesture the SERGEANT commands silence.

SERGEANT: *Quiet.*

A VOICE: *That would suit you, wouldn't it?*

The camera tilts down the stairs in the dim light of the cellar with the crowd of thieves and whores in the background; in the foreground, the dark silhouette of the SERGEANT.

SERGEANT: *Police orders. Nobody leaves this place . . . Get your papers ready.*

Cries of protest and whistles from around the room. The SERGEANT stands in the entrance flanked on either side by police. An inspector comes down the stairs with one of his men. It is INSPECTOR LOHMANN. He stops on the bottom step, his face still in darkness.

A VOICE: *Let's see you, let's see you!*

LOHMANN cheerfully: *Come on now, children. Let's not do anything silly.*

A THIEF raising his hat: *It's fatty Lohmann.*

A VOICE chanting: *Loh-mann, Loh-mann, Loh-mann.*

ANOTHER VOICE: *Pop Lohmann!*

Several wave their hats.

EVERYONE in chorus: *Loh-mann! Loh-mann! Loh-mann!*

The chanting ends in whistles. INSPECTOR LOHMANN comes down the last step and enters the light. He is a strong looking man, about forty. He gives the impression of shrewd efficiency.

LOHMANN: *Quiet!*

A VOICE: *Get out!*

LOHMANN: *You'll wear yourself out.*

A WOMAN'S VOICE hysterically: *It would be better if you caught the child murderer.*

ANOTHER WOMAN'S VOICE: *Yes . . . much better!* Whistles.

LOHMANN: *Quiet! Be reasonable!*

He steps forward. Several policeman follow him.

LOHMANN: *Spread out . . . spread out all of you. All of you . . . spread out. Come on, come on now. Get your papers out.*

More detectives come down the stairs.

A VOICE: *I haven't got any.*

LOHMANN off: *Show me your papers.*

A GIRL off, begging: *Let me go, please, Inspector.*

One of the criminals is hiding at the back of the cloakroom. He tries to get out through a skylight, but suddenly starts back. Shot from below, through the grille of the skylight which gives onto the street: a policeman stands outside. The thief resignedly turns away.

In the ladies' toilet, a policeman enters, hesitates, then pulls back a curtain. A thief, embarrassed, comes out of his hiding place.

In the main cellar. LOHMANN and two of his men are installed behind two tables. In front of him stands a young prostitute. Uniformed police form a corridor leading to the exit. In the background, the various occupants of the club are standing about.

LOHMANN: *Have you got any papers?*

THE GIRL: *But, Inspector, I can't go around everywhere with the date of my birth on me. That's asking too much.*

LOHMANN indifferent: *Let's not beat around the bush, darling.*

Reverse shot of LOHMANN and one of his assistants; between them facing the camera, THE GIRL stands beside an enormous thug, with a black eye, wearing a cap, a fag-end in his mouth, hands in pockets. A row of police lines the wall.

THE GIRL indignantly: *That's really asking too much, Inspector.*

LOHMANN severely: *Alex**.

THE GIRL: *Look here, it's disgusting.*

She goes off to the right. Pushed by the others, the THUG steps forward. He takes out a wallet and, very sure of himself, hands his papers to LOHMANN. Medium close-up of LOHMANN as he flicks through the papers. Sceptically, he examines their owner. Reverse shot of a policeman as he searches the THUG. LOHMANN whistles the song: '*Where did you get your beautiful blue eyes?*' and looks at the THUG with an understanding look. Behind them, a group of thieves surrounded by police. The policeman finishes searching and goes out. The THUG puts his hands back in his pockets and looks at LOHMANN triumphantly. Medium close-up of LOHMANN. He smiles and holds the papers up to the light.

LOHMANN commiserating: *Poor workmanship, old boy.* Camera cuts quickly to the THUG, surprised; he takes his cigarette butt out of his mouth. *You've been had.* A pause. He signals to a policeman. *Alex.*

The THUG furiously throws his butt to the floor.

THIEF insolently: *Better luck next time, Willi.*

THUG: *Oh . . . you . . . shut your face.*

---

* Alex is short for Alexanderplatz, the headquarters of the Berlin police.

LOHMANN: *Next.*

A greasy Mediterranean type steps forward, very smooth. He is wearing a sumptuous fur-collared overcoat. Taking off his bowler, he greets LOHMANN obsequiously and presents his papers.

ANOTHER THIEF admiringly: *Fancy boy.*

Another whistles. INSPECTOR LOHMANN looks at the papers and gives them back. The MAN raises his hat again and prepares to leave. The camera tracks with him. Suddenly LOHMANN catches him with the handle of his walking stick and pulls him back.

THE MAN astonished: *What's the matter?*

A THIEF: *Pop Lohmann has got him.*

SEVERAL VOICES: *He's got him.*

LOHMANN takes a newspaper out of the MAN's pocket and unfolds it. Shot of the front page of the newspaper dated 21st November, 1930. An illustrated article has been circled in pencil. It reads: 'Unsolved burglary at a furrier's shop.' LOHMANN puts down the paper.

LOHMANN: *Well . . . I think I had better take you down to headquarters.*

THE MAN horrified: *But after all, my . . . my papers are in order.*

While he protests, his papers are taken from him.

LOHMANN: *Next.*

The next to come forward is a little fat man, cheerful and very friendly.

LITTLE FAT MAN passing the smooth crook: *No luck, eh?*

He comes up to the INSPECTOR, and clumsily takes off his hat.

LOHMANN: *Next.* Holding out his hand. *Papers.*

LITTLE FAT MAN in a friendly tone: *I haven't got any.*

LOHMANN: *Alex.*

LITTLE FAT MAN shrugging his shoulders: *No luck.* He leaves.

LOHMANN: *Next . . . come on, let's carry on.*

Two policemen search a corner of the room. They look under the tables, tip up the chairs and go through the pockets of the coats in the cloakroom. One finds a revolver, the other a leather brief-case. Close-up of the brief-case as it is opened: inside a complete housebreaking kit.

Things that have been confiscated are piled up, a jemmy, a saw, revolver bullets, etc. A hand adds the empty briefcase to the pile. The camera pans over the spread-out weapons towards the

LANDLADY, who stands behind her bar talking to a SERGEANT, who takes out a cigarette. Medium shot of them both.

LANDLADY: *This is ruining our business, Sergeant . . .Every night there's interference. No one can have ten minutes in peace any more. Give us a chance!*

She goes to the back of the bar and pours herself a drink. Close-up of the SERGEANT lighting his cigarette at a gas lamp.

SERGEANT: *It's no joke for us either, out every night.*

LANDLADY in medium close-up: *Of course . . . but you're driving away my clientèle . . . And the fellow you're looking for isn't here.* She drinks. *You can't imagine how furious everyone is about this guy who's causing a raid every night. Especially the girls . . . okay, they walk the streets . . . but, believe me, each one is a little bit of a mother.*

The SERGEANT leans on the bar surrounded by clouds of cigarette smoke, seen slightly from below.

LANDLADY off: *I know a lot of crooks . . .* Cut back to her . . . *who grow quite tender when they see kids playing. If they catch that bastard . . .* She makes a short, sharp gesture . . . *they'll wring his neck.* Close-up of them both. *Believe me.*

Another policeman comes up and salutes the SERGEANT.

POLICEMAN: *Ready to go, Sergeant?*

The SERGEANT touches the peak of his cap and leaves with the policeman.

SERGEANT: *Good night.*

The LANDLADY watches them leave with a gesture of disgust. Medium close-up of a man in plus-fours standing by the window of a comfortably furnished middle-class room; he is looking at the street through binoculars. He is a PICK-POCKET. Quick tilt down to the street as two police lorries drive past, full of crooks. INSPECTOR LOHMANN follows in an open car. Cut back to the PICK-POCKET still looking through his binoculars.

PICK-POCKET: *So it's ' The Crocodile ' tonight.* He lowers the binoculars. *Two loads for the nick.*

He turns round. On the sofa, smoking a cigarette, sits a tall, thin man. He is a CON-MAN, dressed impeccably but a little pretentiously. He wears a dark jacket, a waistcoat and light trousers, and he has a thin moustache. Lounging beside him, a BURGLAR, tough but not very bright. He is also smoking. The

CON-MAN gets up impatiently.

CON-MAN: *What's keeping Schränker?*

Medium close-up and very slight tilt up to show the profile of a man with a moustache. He is a SAFE-BREAKER. He is seated at the table in the centre of the room, playing cards.

SAFE-BREAKER: *Isn't it three o'clock yet?*

PICK-POCKET: *I'll find out.*

He puts down the binoculars and walks from the window to the telephone in the middle of the room. Camera pans with him. He dials a number.

PICK-POCKET: *Hello . . . The exact time, please, Miss.* He sits on the edge of the table. *Two minutes to three. Thank you.*

He hangs up and, from various pockets, takes out a series of watches. He compares the time they show and places them on the table. Pan right onto the CON-MAN, who has sat down beside him and is playing cards.

PICK-POCKET setting one of the watches: *Two minutes to three.*

CON-MAN disgusted: *There are more police on the streets than tarts.*

Medium close-up of the BURGLAR in an armchair, a bag under his arm. In the foreground, in front of him, a small low table, with an ashtray on it overflowing with dog-ends.

BURGLAR: *Wherever you spit . . . nothing but cops.*

The SAFE-BREAKER, chewing on his cigarette holder, comes up to the table. He wears a white waistcoat and a white bow-tie. The camera tracks back: a 1900 style chandelier comes into shot.

PICK-POCKET: *Even when you're with a doll, they don't leave you in peace . . . And they've gone nuts too . . . All they can think about is that murderer . . .* To the SAFE-BREAKER . . . *Mine . . . she's got a little six-year old girl, and, every night, I have to waste time searching under the bed and in the cupboards to make sure the murderer isn't hiding there.*

The CON-MAN spreads three cards out on the table. The SAFE-BREAKER indicates a card with the look of an expert. The CON-MAN turns it up. It is an ace. The PICK-POCKET takes out a handkerchief and spreads it out beside the watches.

PICK-POCKET: *You can't even get on with your job. Everywhere you come across the police. There's no privacy any more . . . I'm fed up.*

The camera tracks back to show the SAFE-BREAKER walking

round the table, looking at the time as he passes.

CON-MAN bored: *Tell us something new.*

He puts the cards in his pocket. The PICK-POCKET arranges his watches in the handkerchief and slips them into his pocket. The SAFE-BREAKER sits down again.

CON-MAN: *What's keeping Schränker?*

PICK-POCKET: *Maybe he's been caught.*

BURGLAR laughing: *Not him.* He rejoins the others. *He did a bank job in London and Scotland Yard set a trap for him . . . there he was, hands up, back to the wall, millions of cops all round . . . and two seconds later there were two bodies on the ground and he'd scarpered!*

The BURGLAR has sat down, his bag on his knee. The SAFE-BREAKER lights another cigarette from the stub of the first.

SAFE-BREAKER with respect: *The best man between Berlin and San Francisco.*

BURGLAR: *They've been looking for him for six years and they haven't caught him.*

PICK-POCKET ironically: *Haven't caught him . . . Dogs kill wolves.*

SAFE-BREAKER: *Shut up.*

The PICK-POCKET tries to calm the SAFE-BREAKER. They are all nervous and worried, and smoke heavily. The CON-MAN looks at the time again.

CON-MAN: *The suspense is killing. He's usually bang on time.*

On these last words, the door bell rings four times. Relieved, they look at one another.

PICK-POCKET: *God be praised!*

BURGLAR: *At last!*

The door opens. SCHRANKER appears in leather overcoat, bowler hat and carrying a walking stick. He immediately shuts the door, but doesn't come into the room.

ALL: *Good afternoon . . . You've got here at last. Good afternoon.*

SCHRANKER: *Are you mad? Close the curtains.*

Cut to the window showing the curtains half-drawn. Next to it is the table where the SAFE-BREAKER is sitting. The PICK-POCKET creeps along the wall to the window to avoid being seen from the street. From above we see the PICK-POCKET returning to his place at the table in the middle of the room. SCHRANKER comes over to him and takes off his hat, putting it on the table with his stick.

SCHRANKER: *Gentlemen, the meeting can now begin.* He takes off his overcoat to reveal a chalk-stripe suit, dark tie and black leather gloves. He sits down to preside over the meeting. *According to the regulations, I confirm with pleasure that the leadership of every organisation in our Union is represented.* He grasps his stick. *I assume that you all have full powers . . .*

Medium close-up of the SAFE-BREAKER, who nods. Pan to the PICK-POCKET, who is cracking a nut; he nods too, then to the CON-MAN who, while lighting a cigarette, also nods. Finally, the BURGLAR, still bent over the bag, also gives his assent.

SCHRANKER off: *. . . authorizing you to vote for your members. Good . . . let's not be held up by procedure.* Reverse shot of the whole group. *We all know why we are here.* Vehemently. *Someone who is not a member of the Union is messing up our affairs. The new measures taken by the police, the daily raids in our areas to find this child murderer, interfere with our business activities in a quite unbearable way. We can put up no longer with the endless pressure from the police, in every hotel, café, or flat.*

SAFE-BREAKER: *Quite right.*

PICK-POCKET: *Here, here!*

SCHRANKER: *This state of affairs must not be allowed to continue. We'll have to put things right again or we'll be destroyed.*

Medium close-up of the BURGLAR, who stubs out his cigarette. As SCHRANKER continues to talk, the BURGLAR takes out another cigarette and strikes a match. Now and again SCHRANKER's gloved hand, playing with his stick, passes across frame.

SCHRANKER off: *The funds of our organisation are exhausted. Unless I make use of the funds put aside to support the wives of our colleagues who are being looked after by the state, I just don't know where I'll find the funds needed for the preparation and execution of our various projects. What is more, our reputation is suffering.* Big close-up of SCHRANKER. *. . . The cops are looking for the murderer in our ranks, gentlemen . . . When I come up against a cop while carrying on my business, he knows the risk he runs . . . and I do, as well. If one of us dies . . . okay . . . that's a risk one must take. It can happen: but we are not on the same level as this man they're looking for now.*

From behind SCHRANKER and over his head can be seen the rest of the group. SCHRANKER has underlined his last words with a wide gesture.

SAFE-BREAKER: *Exactly.*

SCHRANKER: *There is an abyss between him and us.*

BURGLAR: *Of course.*

PICK-POCKET at the same time: *No comparison.*

SCHRANKER off: *We are doing our job. . . .* Close-up of him . . . *because we have a living to make. But this monster has no right to live. He must dis . . . app . . . ear. He must be exterminated, without pity . . . without scruples.* Camera cuts to a high shot of SCHRANKER facing the group. *Gentlemen, our members must be able to carry on their business normally, without being handicapped by the growing nervousness of the police. I'm appealing to you . . .* He invites comments; on his gesture, the camera cuts to the . . .

CHIEF OF POLICE who continues SCHRANKER'S same gesture. A meeting is also in progress at his office, and seen from above, policemen and high-ranking detective inspectors are sitting at a long conference table. It is littered with brandy glasses and coffee cups and the air is full of cigar-smoke. The CHIEF OF POLICE is standing at the head of the table, furthest from camera.

CHIEF OF POLICE: *. . . for advice.*

He sits down and a police officer rises. Beside him a bespectacled man in plain clothes listens attentively.

THE OFFICER in a military tone: *I suggest a closer watch on identity cards, a systematic search of the whole town, police raids.* The bespectacled man looks dubious. *More numerous raids, and certainly tougher ones.* He sits down.

Cut back to the underworld meeting, the CON-MAN gets up. He faces camera, beside him the BURGLAR. To the left, in the foreground is the PICK-POCKET.

CON-MAN: *Spies . . . We need spies in the ranks of the police to give us plenty of warning of new measures.*

BURGLAR: *The girls must take a little more notice of the cops. We're always getting into trouble because one of the girls has grassed to her cop boyfriend.* The PICK-POCKET agrees; the CON-MAN sits down satisfied. *Now, it's up to the girls to grass for us!*

The SAFE-BREAKER rises on the right, in the foreground is the PICK-POCKET.

SAFE-BREAKER: *What we must do . . . And after all, we've all got contacts . . . What we must do is make a statement to the Press ourselves, tell them that* we, *the Organization, members of the Union* — we *condemn the bastard just as much! We ought to make it known that the police should quit looking for him in the underworld.*

Camera cuts back to the Police meeting where an elderly bespectacled detective, with a small beard and a stiff collar, is speaking. Another detective sits on his right; on his left, a police-officer with a monocle.

ELDERLY DETECTIVE: *I'm sure it's a man who looks like a peaceful little family man, who wouldn't harm a fly, except when he has his fits, of course!* Medium close-up of LOHMANN, who listens with interest, as the ELDERLY DETECTIVE continues off . . . *Perhaps in his normal state, he even plays marbles with the concierge's children.* LOHMANN nods agreement . . . *Or perhaps plays cards with his wife.* Cut back to the ELDERLY DETECTIVE. *Without this appearance of, let's say inoffensiveness in private life, it would be impossible to believe that murderers like Grossmann or Haarmann were able to live for years in large, busy blocks of flats without their neighbours suspecting them in the slightest.*

An OFFICER with a moustache, smoking a pipe, agrees; beside him a plain-clothes man takes notes.

THE OFFICER: *That's what we must get across to the public. They must help.*

Close-up of LOHMANN, clearly annoyed, rising to his feet.

LOHMANN: *Don't talk to me about help from the general public. It disgusts me just to hear them talk.* He bows towards the CHIEF OF POLICE. *Excuse me, Chief* . . . Camera cuts quickly to the CHIEF who, smiling, makes a gesture accepting the apology . . . *Excuse me, but that is the truth.* Cut back to LOHMANN. *Good God! Has help from the public brought us one useful clue?* Furiously, he stubs out his cigar. *Just a pile of letters full of the most incredible accusations!*

Camera cuts quickly to two INSPECTORS at the end of the table.

FIRST INSPECTOR: *Quite true.*

LOHMANN: *Calls to the police as soon as a dustman crosses a yard.*

SECOND INSPECTOR: *Exactly.*

LOHMANN: *But when we want really accurate information . . . they can't remember anything, they have seen nothing. That's help from the public for you.*

LOHMANN leaves his place. Medium close-up of the CHIEF OF POLICE.

CHIEF OF POLICE smiling: *I think you exaggerate a little, Lohmann.*

Cut back to the underworld meeting, great clouds of smoke drift over the table. They are all deep in thought. The PICK-POCKET breaks the silence.

PICK-POCKET: *I've an idea! There's a magician, no, a tele . . . telepa . . . or is it radiologist? Anyway, I don't know what you call them . . . one of those guys who finds handkerchiefs and wallets that have been hidden.*

Camera cuts back to a uniformed OFFICER speaking at the Police meeting. The last words from the PICK-POCKET overlay what he is saying.

OFFICER: *I also think the reward isn't high enough.*

His neighbour, an INSPECTOR, gestures in disagreement and gets up.

OFFICER: *Chief . . . we must offer a real fortune for catching the murderer.*

The INSPECTOR pushes his chair up to the table.

INSPECTOR irritably, as he leaves: *None of this is getting us anywhere.*

Camera cuts back to show the crooks' meeting, slightly from above. Clouds of cigarette smoke hang round the fringed lampshade.

SAFE-BREAKER: *That won't do any good.*

CON-MAN: *Well, what do you suggest?*

The BURGLAR gets up, moves round behind his armchair and leans on the back of it.

BURGLAR: *All the same we can't just wait until the police make up their minds to arrest this fellow.*

An INSPECTOR with long disorderly white hair leans over the back of his chair towards the CHIEF OF POLICE, continuing the movement of the BURGLAR as the camera cuts back to the police meeting. The POLICEMAN with the monocle sits on his left; on his right in the foreground, another INSPECTOR sits.

THE INSPECTOR: *The difficulty of solving this type of crime is increased by the fact that the wrongdoer and the victim are only connected by a chance meeting. An instantaneous impulse is the killer's only motive.*

THE CHIEF OF POLICE impressed: *Hmm . . . Hmm.*

THE INSPECTOR: *We find the victim; we identify him; we find out when he was last seen . . . And then, and then, nothing more. The children disappear.*

Cut back to a group shot of the underworld meeting where the SAFE-BREAKER is standing on the left. In the background, the rest are seated round the table. The BURGLAR is perched on the back of his chair.

SAFE-BREAKER: *The police have been looking for this murderer for eight months now. Now it's got to the point where they'll only catch him by luck.*

BURGLAR: *We can't wait for that . . .*

CON-MAN: *We'll be ruined before then.*

SAFE-BREAKER: *What are we going to do then?*

Cut back to a high group shot of the police meeting. The room is misty with thick clouds of smoke. The meeting has come to a full stop and some of the officers have got up and are pacing around the room.

Camera cuts again to the same high group shot of the underworld meeting, where the PICK-POCKET has made a huge question mark with the shells of his nuts on the table. The SAFE-BREAKER and the BURGLAR both pace restlessly up and down. (*Still*).

Cut back to a high shot from above of the police conference table. We can see that most people have left their places and are wandering around the room.

Cut back to the underworld meeting, only the PICK-POCKET and SCHRANKER are seated. The CON-MAN stands by the table, and the SAFE-BREAKER has moved into the background by the window.

SCHRANKER decisively: *We'll have to catch him ourselves.*

The others gather round him.

ALL: *Yes . . . we must. This is what we must do.*

LOHMANN's voice is heard over as the camera cuts back to show abandoned chairs round the conference table with most of the delegates wandering up and down. But gradually their attention is drawn by what LOHMANN is saying, and one or two nod their heads in agreement.

LOHMANN off: *There is still one possible way. The guilty man or the possible suspects must already have a record somewhere. Such a person, deeply disturbed, must already have fallen foul of the law. We've got to contact every clinic, every prison, every lunatic asylum.* Noise of general agreement. *We'll have to make enquiries about everyone who has been freed as harmless but who has the same pathological condition as the killer.*

Camera cuts to a close-up, followed by an extreme close-up of SCHRANKER's black-gloved hand placed over a map of the town.

SCHRANKER off: *Every square yard must be permanently watched. From now on no child must take a step without us being warned.*

CON-MAN: *Okay, but how do we do it?*

SAFE-BREAKER: *Yes . . . how?*

SCHRANKER off: *There must be people . . .* The group is seen silhouetted in shadow on the wall, SCHRANKER's shadow in the centre *. . . who can go anywhere without being noticed . . . who can follow anyone on the streets without arousing suspicion . . . who can follow the children right to their front doors without any trouble. In fact, people no one would suspect of being guilty.*

THE OTHERS off: *But who? . . . Who? People like that don't exist . . . Who could do it? . . . Who? . . . Who?*

SCHRANKER pauses and then rises so that his shadow on the wall swells up.

SCHRANKER off: *The beggars. The beggars' union.*

In the foreground at the Beggars' Market, the camera pans onto a notice which reads: NO MORE CREDIT. The camera pans, then tracks towards a table where two beggars are laying out bits of bread and slices of sausage. The tracking continues and ends in a close-up of their hands with the bread and sausage.

1ST BEGGAR off: *Sausage going up.*

2ND BEGGAR off: *God, this cheese smells good.*

Pan across to another table where a game of cards is in progress. Only the players' hands and the cards are visible.

3RD BEGGAR off: *That finishes you.*

Pan up to show a grizzled tramp, who has brought in a live chicken. He finishes a glass of wine. Camera tracks on past a grille in front of a cloakroom and comes to rest on another tramp, snoring. Beside him, two others take the fillings out of sandwiches.

4TH BEGGAR: *Stop snoring! You'll wake the lice.*

The camera tracks in towards the counter where the fat Boss of the Beggars' Market takes a steaming sausage out of a pot and takes a bite. Then he counts a packet of sandwiches one of them has brought him.

THE Boss counting: *Two, four, six, eight, ten, twelve, fourteen, sixteen, eighteen, twenty, twenty-two, twenty-four, twenty-six . . .*

As he continues, the camera rises towards a huge blackboard fixed to the wall behind him. On it is written 'PRICES FOR THE EVENING OF THE 16th,' and then a list of every sort of sandwich, classified according to filling and the quality of the bread. The Boss gets up on a stool and alters certain prices, murmuring to himself.

Boss: *Sandwiches: Friday, bad day for cold meat . . . No go.*

The voice continues, as the camera pans up to the floor above where there is a strange sort of office. A vulture's skeleton is on the left in the foreground. At the back of the room, beggars form a queue. Camera tracks through the window towards the office where two men from the Beggar's Union are working. One is studying a map of the town, the other is writing names into a huge register.

1ST MAN: *Now we must deal with the back-yards.*

2ND MAN: *Yes, from number one to number forty-eight.*

Camera tracks towards SCHRANKER who leans against the wall watching the work. Pan towards a door with a glass panel on which can be read: *ACCOUNTS. Please give your name to the outside office.*

In the corridor, as in the office, beggars wait behind a small barrier.

2ND MAN off: *Next.*

The pan continues, as the barrier is raised and a beggar comes up, taking off his cap. Shot of the TWO MEN, the BEGGAR standing in front of them, his back to the camera; he is given a small slip of paper. The 2ND MAN keeps a carbon copy of it.

2ND MAN: *You are responsible for the courtyards of every block of flats from 1 to 81 High Street.*

BEGGAR: *Right.*

The BEGGAR goes out. Another comes up.

2ND MAN: *Next.*

Insert of a street map marked with the places where the child-

M

M
dein mörder
sieht dich
an

M

M

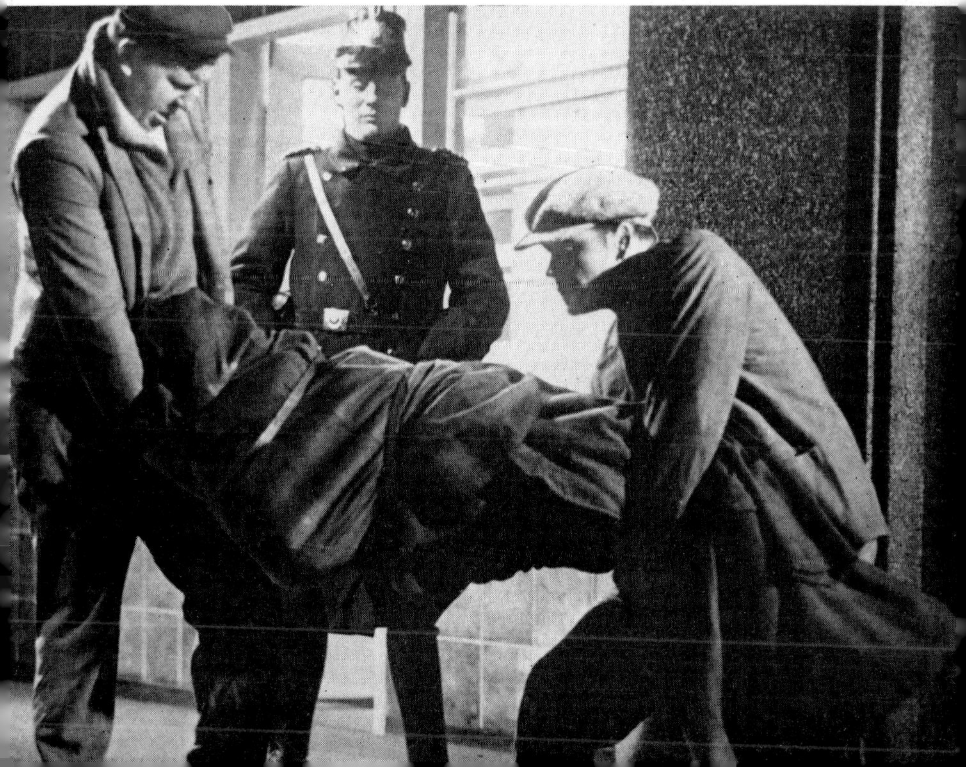

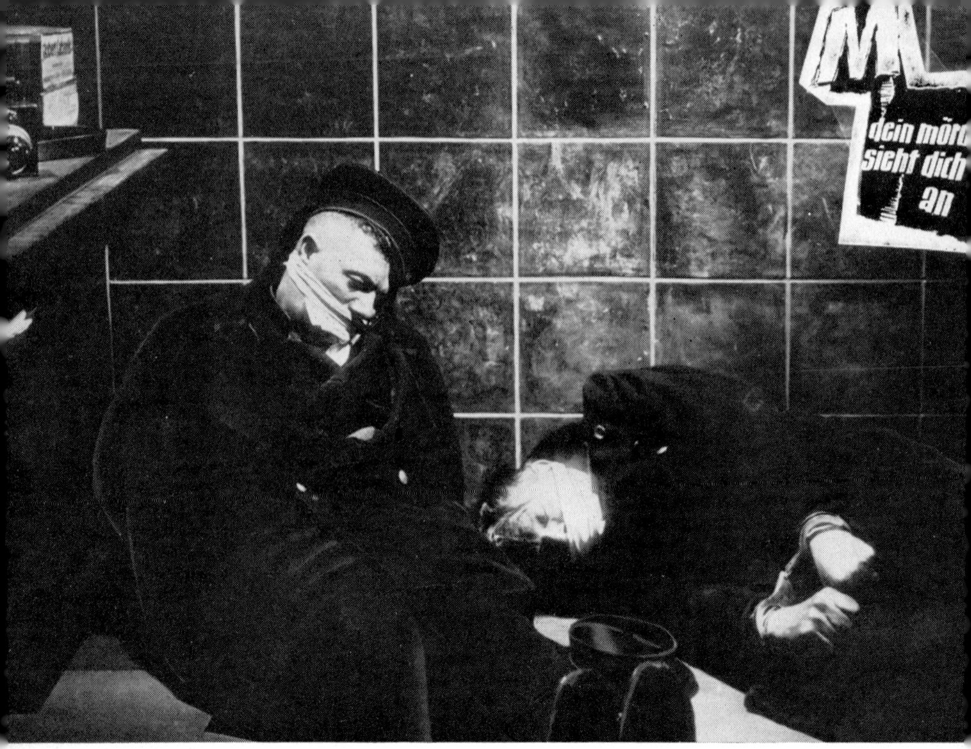
M
sieht dich
an

M

M
dein mörder sieht dich an

M
dein mörder
sieht dich
an

M
dein mörder
sieht dich
an
NERO

ren have disappeared and been murdered. Close-up of the 1st Man's pencil which follows one of the streets.

1st Man off: *89 to 196 High Street . . . Fine.*

Camera cuts back to a medium shot of the office. One tramp stands with his back to the camera and two more join him. The 2nd Man notes down the first one's particulars.

2nd Man writing: *89 to 196 High Street . . . What's your union number?*

Tramp after some thought: *Three, seven, ninety-five. Emil Dustermann.*

Large close-up of a hand writing the name and number in the register.

2nd Man: *Three . . . seven . . . ninety-five . . . Emil Dustermann . . .*

The hand tears a slip from the register. Shot from above of a line of Beggars with Dustermann in the foreground: he has a wooden leg and leans on a stick . . .

2nd Man: *There you are, Emil.* He gives him the paper. *Maybe, you'll win the fifteen thousand.*

Dustermann tapping his leg: *Touch wood.*

Camera cuts to another part of the market where an assorted collection of second-hand goods and junk is on display. A line of metal grilles form a cash desk, and there are violins and accordions spread out on a long table. In the background there are several barrel organs, and on a shelf a stack of old shoes and boots. A constant murmur of voices reaches us from other parts of the market. The junk dealer is demonstrating one of the barrel organs to a beggar, but it is very out of key and only plays a few wheezy notes.

Medium close-up of the Blind Beggar, who sold a balloon to the Murderer. He is sitting at a nearby table drinking a beer, balloons floating above him. Putting down his glass, he covers his ears. Immediately, the excruciating noise from the barrel organ stops; but as he lowers his hands, it starts up again. After a while another organ starts to play a polka. The Blind Man is delighted and conducts an imaginary orchestra.

The music continues over as the camera cuts to a high shot of the courtyard of a tenement block. It is early evening and the setting sun casts long shadows across the tarmac. In the gloom a few children stand in twos and threes watching the Beggar playing a barrel organ, and coins are thrown from windows above. Medium close-up of the barrel organ. The music stops and the last coin rolls along the ground.

THE BEGGAR off: *Thank you, ladies and gentlemen, thank you.*

Camera cuts to another street, where a beggar's legs are seen from above. The BEGGAR is seated on the kerb, his hat upturned beside him. A man and a little girl pass, but only their legs are visible. The little girl throws a coin into the hat.

Medium close-up of the BEGGAR wearing dark glasses and a notice round his neck saying 'BLIND'. A German sheepdog sits beside him.

BEGGAR: *Thank you.*

The two shadows of the passers-by draw away. The BEGGAR lifts his glasses and takes a sly look after them, and the dog turns its head in the same direction. From the BEGGAR's point-of-view, we see the man and the little girl walking off arm-in-arm. Camera follows them, past a poster advertising 'West-front 1918'. The man goes with the little girl as far as the entrance to a school. He kisses her and leaves here there. Beside the school entrance, another BEGGAR, with two white pigeons, is on the look out. Camera cuts to two little girls looking into the window of a sweet shop. EMIL DUSTERMANN stands beside the window.

Next we see into the window of a toy shop, where a windmill and a fairground roundabout are turning. Two children stop to watch while their nurse continues her walk. Other children join the first two, and there is a legless beggar, squatting on a little cart, looking on.

In his office, INSPECTOR LOHMANN is sitting at his desk, smoking a cigar and reading a letter. Insert of the typewritten letter in the machine: '*When searching their homes, we must above all look for any clue by which we could establish where the murderer's letter to the papers originated. If there is an old wooden table on which the letter could have been written, if there is a red pencil or any tiny pieces from sharpening such a pencil, or writing paper of the same type. The inquiries must be made as discreetly as possible.*'

LOHMANN's hand comes into shot holding a pen. He underlines the words '*old wooden table*' and corrects a typing error.

LOHMANN muttering off: *Idiot.* He also underlines the words '*red pencil*'. There is a knock on the door. *Come in.*

The whole office comes into frame as LOHMANN signs the letter. An ASSISTANT comes in and passes him a file.

THE ASSISTANT: *Here's the list of mental patients who have been let out as cured or harmless in the last five years.*

Insert of the file as LOHMANN sorts through it. It contains reports from 'Dr. Goll's Psychiatric Institute,' from 'Professor Emil Lebbowitz's private clinic for mental patients,' from 'The Protestant Hospital of Nazareth,' from 'The Elizabeth Clinic,' from 'St. Hedwig's Hospital,' etc.

ASSISTANT off: *Reports from every institute, private and public.* LOHMANN picks up another file . . . *And that's a list of their present addresses.*

LOHMANN opens the file and flicks through it.

Camera cuts to the MURDERER, coming out into the street from a lower middle-class rooming house and moving away to the left. LOHMANN'S ASSISTANT immediately appears from the right. He hesitates an instant, then throws down his cigarette and goes in.

Close-up of a name plate above a bell. It reads: ELIZABETH WINKLER.

In the entrance hall, a close-up of the ASSISTANT'S hand as he ruffles through a notebook full of addresses. All except the last three have been crossed out. His finger stops at HANS BECKERT, c/o E. WINKLER, Gleder St. 15, 2nd Floor.

Dissolve to the ASSISTANT standing by a door on the landing. He rings and puts his notebook away. A small frightened old lady answers the door. A large key-ring is fixed to her apron. The ASSISTANT greets her. Shot of them both.

MRS. WINKLER very softly: *Morning.*

ASSISTANT: *Does a Mr. Beckert live here?*

MRS. WINKLER: *What?*

ASSISTANT louder: *Does Mr. Beckert live here?*

MRS. WINKLER: *I'm afraid I can't hear you . . . I'm a bit hard of hearing.*

ASSISTANT to one side: *As if I didn't know.* Shouting. *Does a Mr. Beckert live here?*

MRS. WINKLER a little worried: *Oh. Mr. Beckert? Yes . . . yes, of course. Yes, Mr. Beckert lives here. I'm afraid he has just gone out.*

ASSISTANT: *Pity . . . I wanted to see him.*

MRS. WINKLER very softly: *Oh yes.* She shrugs her shoulders.

ASSISTANT loudly: *I'm from the Income Tax people.*

MRS. WINKLER startled: *Oh, good God! The tax people? Yes . . . yes. Would you like . . . would you like to wait?*

She gestures to him to come in. He bows.

ASSISTANT: *Yes, thank you.*

MRS. WINKLER: *Not at all, please take a seat.*

She goes out. The ASSISTANT puts his hat on the round central table and sits down. As soon as the door is closed, he jumps up to examine the room, but he hears MRS. WINKLER coming back and only just has time to sit down again. She hands him a newspaper.

MRS. WINKLER: *Perhaps you'd like something to read?*

ASSISTANT loudly: *Thank you. You're most kind.*

MRS. WINKLER: *Not at all.*

He takes the paper. Close-up of the front page of the 'General Anzeiger' for 24th November, 1930.

ASSISTANT off: *Tell me, Mrs. Winkler, does Mr. Beckert take this paper?*

The ASSISTANT sits in an armchair, his back to the camera. MRS. WINKLER, already at the door, turns round.

MRS. WINKLER astonished: *Mr. Beckert?* She laughs. *No, he always borrows mine.*

ASSISTANT: *Ah, thank you.*

MRS. WINKLER nods and leaves the room. As soon as she has closed the door again, the ASSISTANT gets up and looks at the table where he put his hat. He throws the hat onto a chair and carefully raises the cloth. From high overhead we see him bending over the table and scratching the wood with his finger nails.

Cut to a medium close-up of a fruit-seller's barrow in the street, piled high with apples, oranges and bananas. From a strut hang some superb pineapples. The MURDERER is standing behind the barrow dolefully eating an apple, at the same time gesturing to the fruit-seller to put another in the bag being filled for him.

Back in the MURDERER'S room still seen from above, the

ASSISTANT finishes his inspection; disappointed by the negative search, he slowly replaces the cloth. Camera cuts to a slight low shot of the ASSISTANT beside the table. Above his head, hangs a Tiffany-style glass lampshade, and beyond him a large pottery stove stands against the wall. As the ASSISTANT carefully surveys the room, camera pans across from the bedside table to the double windows. There is a bowl of fruit and other foodstuffs stored in the space between them. We recognise the same wide windowseat where the MURDERER wrote his letter to the press. Pan continues until it reaches the ASSISTANT again. He is leaning over a wicker waste-paper basket from which he extracts an empty cigarette packet, a publicity hand-out for cigars and a postcard, which he lifts up and studies carefully.

Cut to the street: the MURDERER is eating an apple and looking at a window display in a cutlery and silverware shop. We see him from inside through the glass, his face framed in the reflection of a diamond-shaped display of knives. The reflections of other cutlery form geometric patterns around him.

Camera cuts back to show the street behind him and his view of the shop window: the knives are arranged round a diamond-shaped mirror on the screen at the back of the window.

Close-up of the MURDERER munching his apple. Suddenly he stops chewing. Reflected in the mirror he can see a little girl leaning against the railings on the other side of the street, the image framed with knives. The MURDERER stands transfixed, staring at her. He wipes his mouth with the back of his hand, eyes bulging. The little girl leans nonchalantly on the railings, obviously waiting for someone. The MURDERER's arms fall limply to his side, he gasps for breath and his eyes close as he sways forward against the shop front. Then the fit subsides and he recovers slightly. Seen in reflection, the little girl leaves the railings and goes out of sight. The MURDERER wheels round and follows her with his eyes. He lowers his head and sets off slowly, whistling the ' Peer Gynt ' theme.

In the MURDERER's room, the ASSISTANT picks up an empty sweet carton from the bedside table, examines it and makes a note. Camera cuts back to the same street to a view of a bookshop window, where a cardboard circle with a spiral design turns endlessly while a huge arrow shoots endlessly up and down. The little girl stares fascinated by the continual motion, until she turns away distracted by something else. The 'Peer Gynt' theme accompanies her, whistled piercingly, as camera follows her as she wanders on past other shop windows. Suddenly she turns delightedly and flings her arms round a smart young woman who has come into shot from the right. The whistling stops abruptly. The woman and the little girl walk off, arms round each other. Camera follows them along the pavement as they pass the MURDERER who ducks into the doorway of the bookshop, back to camera, pretending to look at some books displayed there. He looks round furtively and eventually steps out into the street to watch them go, his eyes drooping and his mouth partly open. He puts his hands together on his chest, nervously scratching them. Behind him the arrow continues to fly up and down, appearing to pierce the revolving spiral at every descent. The MURDERER scratches the back of his hand nervously.

The camera follows the MURDERER as he turns into a café with tables outside, screened from the street by a trellis of climbing plants. He sits at a table to the left of the opening, his face just visible in profile through the foliage. A WAITER comes out to serve him.

WAITER: *Good evening . . . What would you like?*

MURDERER: *Coffee.*

WAITER bending nearer: *Sorry?*

MURDERER controlling himself: *No . . . a vermouth . . . No, a brandy.*

The WAITER bows and withdraws.

MURDERER exhausted: *Brandy . . . brandy . . .*

The camera tracks in towards the foliage. The MURDERER starts to whistle and then takes out a cigarette as the WAITER's hand pours a brandy.

WAITER: *There you are.*

The MURDERER drinks the brandy in a gulp. The glass rings against the table, as he puts it down.

MURDERER in a broken voice: *Another one.*

The WAITER's hand pours another glass.

WAITER: *There.*

The MURDERER swallows the second glass, leans forward and stares fixedly in front of him. With a mechanical gesture he puts a cigarette in his mouth and immediately takes it out again. He presses his two bunched fists into his eyes and starts to whistle again. Then he covers his ears. In the background the lights of the café come on and faintly light up the table. He immediately stops whistling and gets up. We track away from him rapidly.

MURDERER: *The bill.*

WAITER coming up: *Two brandies. One sixty-five please.* Coins fall on the saucer. *Thanks very much.*

The MURDERER departs whistling, his hands in his pockets. Cut to LOHMANN, in his office, an enormous cigar in his hand. He sits at his desk thinking. Beside him, his ASSISTANT makes his report.

ASSISTANT: *Number 24: Beckert. He does not take the* Stadtischer Courier. *A walnut table with a cloth. No red pencil, nor any traces of such a pencil. No writing paper. In the wastepaper basket, a printed advertisement and a coloured postcard . . .* Medium close-up of LOHMANN thinking; behind him we see a map of the town . . . *of a bunch of flowers. Written on it: 'Regards, Paul.' No address of sender. An empty cigarette packet, Ariston brand. A bag of sweets with the name of a sweet shop . . .*

LOHMANN interrupting him: *Wait . . . wait a moment.* He screws up his eyes and thinks. *Ariston, did you say?* Track in. *A . . . ris . . . ton.*

Track in. Deep in thought he writes the name in the air. Camera tracks in closer.

LOHMANN: *That rings a bell . . . Ariston.* Camera tracks in even closer. Suddenly, LOHMANN seems to have got it. He grabs the telephone. *Hello. I want the file on the Marga Perl murder. Straight away.*

He hangs up. Camera cuts to the blind balloon seller's kiosk, where the BLIND MAN has just sold two balloons to a woman who pays and goes off.

BLIND MAN: *Thank you very much.*

From far off, we hear the MURDERER's whistling approach. His shadow passes. The BLIND MAN lifts his head.

BLIND MAN: *That's funny . . . I've heard that somewhere before.* Camera draws in closer. *It was . . . it was . . .*

The BLIND MAN walks forward tapping with his stick. Camera tracks back in front of him. Astonished passers-by watch him wave. Pan across a very busy street. In the foreground, some planks half cover a hole in the road. The Blind Man, still holding some balloons, comes up to it.

Blind Man: *Hey, hey, Henry.*

A young man in a cap pops up immediately. Medium close-up of them both.

Henry: *What is it?*

He takes the Blind Man's hand.

Blind Man: *Listen a moment. There's someone whistling. Can't you hear him?*

Henry cocks his head and cups his ear. Their two faces turn in the direction of the whistling.

Blind Man: *There.*

Henry listens. But the whistling suddenly stops.

Blind Man: *He's just stopped . . . Did you see him, the guy who was whistling?*

Henry: *Yes, yes, I can still see him.*

Blind Man: *Yes?*

Henry: *Sure.* Excited. *He's talking to a little girl as he walks down the street with her.*

Blind Man: *After him, and don't let him go.*

Henry: *But why?*

Blind Man: *The day Elsie Beckmann was killed someone bought a balloon off me. He was with a little girl . . .* Henry rushes off . . . *and the fellow whistled just like that!*

Henry runs to the end of the roadworks and looks round. Camera follows him, as he enters a quiet street running at right angles to the previous one. In a basement a greengrocer's shop is lit up. He approaches and looks through the window. Camera cuts to a view through the window from above. The Murderer and the Little Girl are being served by an old woman. She hands them a big paper bag and some sweets for the girl, who thanks her as the Murderer pays. Camera cuts back to Henry in the street, in front of the window; he stands up and hesitates for a moment. Taking one last look through the window, he runs off to the right out of shot. Camera now cuts to show him hiding in a corner of the roadworks between the tar boiler and a great roll of cable. He watches the street.

The Murderer and the Little Girl come out of the shop. She offers him the bag of fruit and he takes an orange. Anxiously, he looks right and left, but there is no one in sight. Then he sweeps back his coat and puts his hand into his trouser pocket. Huge close-up as he takes out a flick knife. The blade glints and flashes in the gloom.

Quick cut to show HENRY ready to jump out.

Return in close-up to the blade peeling an orange. Camera cuts back again to show HENRY, who is searching his pockets; he takes out a piece of chalk. Large close-up of the palm of HENRY's left hand on which he draws a large letter M.

Cut back to the MURDERER, facing the girl, his back to camera. He finishes peeling his orange and throws the peel onto the ground. HENRY comes up, hurriedly. As though by mistake, he knocks against the MURDERER and so gets a chance to place his left hand against the MURDERER's shoulder. Terrified, the MURDERER backs away, dropping the knife.

HENRY feigning annoyance: *Damn it, are you crazy, throwing your peel on the ground?* He shrugs his shoulders and goes out of frame.

Off: *I might have broken my neck. Unbelievable.*

Close-up of the knife on the ground, then back to show the whole scene.

HENRY: *I should report you to the police . . . You're a danger to the public.*

The LITTLE GIRL picks up the knife, gets up and hands it to the MURDERER. Camera rises with her and frames them both in profile. The LITTLE GIRL gives the still shaken MURDERER a little nudge.

LITTLE GIRL: *Uncle.*

The MURDERER takes the knife as the camera circles round behind him, to show, high on his back, an M outlined in chalk.

Cut to INSPECTOR LOHMANN's office where LOHMANN sits at his desk, his ASSISTANT standing beside him. LOHMANN studies a dossier, following the lines with his finger. Suddenly he raises his head.

LOHMANN: *There . . . that's it. They found three cigarette stubs where the crime took place — Aristons.*

ASSISTANT: *Yes, the cigarettes are the same, but there is no old wooden table.*

Nervously, LOHMANN waves away the objection and plunges back into the dossier, while his ASSISTANT faces the window.

ASSISTANT thoughtfully: *Of course . . . he could have written the letter somewhere else, but . . .* Suddenly he leans towards LOHMANN . . . *Heavens, the windowsill!*

Large close-up of the windowsill in the MURDERER's room. A hand holding a magnifying glass comes into shot. Through the magnifying glass in huge close-up, we see the grain of the wood. LOHMANN and his ASSISTANT closely examine the windowsill. LOHMANN holds the magnifying glass and we see them in profile.

LOHMANN: *You're right!*

ASSISTANT opening one of the windows: *Just a minute!*

He bends over the gap between the double windows and pushes a wet finger into it. Then he examines the bits of dust. Large close-up of his dirty finger.

ASSISTANT: *A red pencil!*

LOHMANN and his ASSISTANT stand in front of the window.

LOHMANN: *Good God . . . At last, we are getting somewhere!*

Cut to SCHRANKER sitting with his back to the camera, in the room where the underworld meeting was held. He is wearing his bowler. The SAFE-BREAKER is on the telephone opposite him. The BURGLAR and the PICKPOCKET are standing beside him. They all wear overcoats.

SAFE-BREAKER into the telephone: *Yes . . . yes . . . What?* To the others: *They're on his trail.*

CON-MAN off: *They've found him?*

PICK-POCKET: *The beggars found him.*

BURGLAR: *He was talking to a little girl.*

CON-MAN: *Tell me more.*

PICK-POCKET: *They put a mark on him.*

SAFE-BREAKER: *Can't you be quiet?* Into the telephone. *What's that?*

Medium close-up of HENRY in a telephone kiosk.

HENRY into the telephone: *They are following the sign. They are not letting him out of their sight for a second.*

The MURDERER walks slowly down a street with the LITTLE GIRL. They go out of shot. A passer-by throws down a cigarette end. A tramp comes up, picks up the stub and follows the MURDERER; he is accompanied by a colleague with one leg.

New shot of the MURDERER and the LITTLE GIRL, as they reach a column covered with posters. The two BEGGARS follow close behind. The ONE-LEGGED MAN disappears behind the column and a man in a cap takes his place. The BEGGAR jerks up one thumb.

Dissolve to a view of the street, shot through a half-open door. Behind the door is the outline of a man on watch. The MURDERER and the LITTLE GIRL cross the road. Followed warily by the man in the cap, he joins another beggar who takes over from him. Dissolve to the MURDERER and the LITTLE GIRL passing in front of a cheap café. The two beggars are still following. One of them taps on the window of the café. Immediately a man comes out and takes over trailing the MURDERER. Dissolve to the window display of a toy shop seen from the inside; it is showing dolls, teddy bears and all kinds of toys. There is a lot of traffic in the street. The MURDERER and the LITTLE GIRL stop in front of the window. He talks to her enthusiastically and she eagerly points out a toy to him. (*Still*). The MURDERER nods his head. Shot of the entrance of the shop from the street. The MURDERER is just about to go in, when the LITTLE GIRL sees the chalk mark and grabs his sleeve.

LITTLE GIRL: *Uncle.*

MURDERER: *What is it?*

LITTLE GIRL: *You're all dirty.*

MURDERER: *Where?*

He looks at himself in a mirror beside the doorway.

LITTLE GIRL: *There, on your shoulder.*

Close-up of the MURDERER's reflection in the mirror. He turns and sees the M reflected. His eyes bulge. Close-up of the letter M. Camera cuts to show the LITTLE GIRL and the MURDERER together.

LITTLE GIRL: *Here, I'll clean it off*

She tries to rub off the letter with her handkerchief. The MURDERER is still looking at it in the mirror. Suddenly he is frightened and turns nervously towards the street. Quick shot of a BEGGAR, who hides behind a beer-lorry. Camera cuts back to the MURDERER and the LITTLE GIRL.

LITTLE GIRL astonished: *Whatever's the matter?*

MURDERER: *Come on . . . let's go.*

He takes her hand and is about to leave when a whistle blows. He lets go of the LITTLE GIRL and runs away.

Resume on the BEGGAR, looking around, distraught. Then he

whistles through his fingers. Shot of a street corner with a street lamp, there is a pawnbroker's shop in the background. The MURDERER runs to the corner, where he hears more shrill whistles.

Desperate, he runs one way and then the other, before finally escaping down a side street. Pan after him. A man is waiting on a corner. Nervously, the MURDERER passes him, hesitates a moment, is about to go up to him, but then rushes off again. This man, too, follows him.

High shot from above of the MURDERER in an empty street, he is trying to shake off his pursuers. He turns sharp left and crosses the road, but at the far end two beggars appear. The MURDERER retraces his steps and stops undecided in front of a covered entrance gate. In the foreground, a pursuer blocks the middle of the street.

The gateway, a geometrical structure, leads to the inner courtyard of an office block. The MURDERER goes in and hides behind a buttress. Camera follows and tracks in on his shoulder; the letter M, although smudged, is still visible. Anxiously, he watches the gateway. Shot of a gate on the other side of the courtyard leading to another street. A policeman passes across it. Cut back to the MURDERER in his hiding-place; he is pressing back against the wall as the policeman passes in the background.

Two of the BEGGARS appear in the gateway which the MURDERER came through.

Cut to the MURDERER, poking his head out to look at the street. Shot of the three BEGGARS, who take stock of the situation. One of them gives a signal and the two others go out of shot to right and left to circle the building. The siren of a fire engine is heard in the distance. From the street we see the gateway where the MURDERER, a tiny figure, hides behind a pillar. Two fire engines roar past, sirens blaring and lights flashing. When they have gone by, the FIRST BEGGAR quickly crosses the road and goes through the arch. The MURDERER has disappeared. The two other BEGGARS return. Shot of the three BEGGARS.

2ND BEGGAR: *Anyway, he hasn't come out. We would have seen him.*

3RD BEGGAR: *Impossible.*

1ST BEGGAR: *He must be in the courtyard, then. He didn't come out this way either.*

2ND BEGGAR: *He must be somewhere.*

1ST BEGGAR off: *Perhaps he's gone to hide inside the building.*

Pan along the face of the building. A clock strikes six o'clock.

2ND BEGGAR: *Hell. The offices will be closing.*

1ST BEGGAR: *As long as he doesn't get out with all the people coming out.*

The 2ND BEGGAR rushes off to the other gateway.

2ND BEGGAR coming back: *Hell! Here come the first ones already.*

1ST BEGGAR: *Let's go out into the street.*

He disappears. A woman comes out of the building.

1ST BEGGAR: *Keep a sharp look out.*

The other two run towards the other entrance as the office workers start streaming out, some pushing bicycles. The 2ND BEGGAR, pretending to sell matches, watches them carefully.

VARIOUS VOICES: *Excuse me, I just want to light my cigarette . . . My holidays start tomorrow . . . First I'm going to Königsberg . . . With my ulcer, I can't eat things like that . . . The boss came and saw me today.*

In the foreground, a car passes, hooting.

Cut to LOHMANN'S ASSISTANT, who is sitting on the window-sill of the MURDERER'S room. Two other plain-clothes men are in the foreground.

ASSISTANT: *Put out the light, otherwise he'll suspect something when he gets back.*

With the light off, the ASSISTANT looks out of the window.

PLAIN-CLOTHES MAN: *What's the time?*

ASSISTANT: *Nearly six-thirty.*

A uniformed watchman finishes closing the imposing grille that goes right across the entrance to the office. He greets a passing policeman and goes back into the building.

Medium close-up of the 1ST BEGGAR in a telephone kiosk; he is talking to the underworld bosses.

1ST BEGGAR: *He must still be in the building. Anyway, he didn't come out with the others.*

The SAFE-BREAKER, a cigarette-holder in his mouth, is on the telephone in the crooks' headquarters. Standing beside him, SCHRANKER, still wearing overcoat and bowler, plays with his stick.

SAFE-BREAKER: *Okay . . . yes . . . yes . . . no, just a moment.* He covers the mouthpiece with his hand and talks to SCHRANKER. *The beggars have gone for reinforcements to search the whole area. They say the murderer must still be in the building.*

SCHRANKER: *Hmm . . . What sort of place is it?*

SAFE-BREAKER into the telephone: *What sort of building is it?*

BEGGAR in the kiosk: *Nothing but offices. I don't know what's in the cellar. There's a branch of the Savings Bank on the ground floor, and from the first to the fifth, nothing but offices, and above that lofts.*

Over bannisters, the camera frames the half-open door of the loft on the top floor of the office building. On the right of the door is the NIGHT WATCHMAN'S time clock. The WATCHMAN comes up and stops astonished in front of the door.

WATCHMAN to himself: *Look at that. It's not possible.*

He pushes open the door and looks into the loft, camera tracking in on him.

WATCHMAN shouting: *Anyone there?* He turns on the light. *Hello! Hello! Hello!*

Shot of the inside of one of the compartments in the loft. In the foreground, there is a jumble of old furniture and bric-a-brac. The loft area is cut off from the passage by fence-like partitions. The WATCHMAN passes behind them, camera tracking with him past several compartments.

WATCHMAN: *Anyone there?*

He checks one of the doors by shaking it to see whether it is firmly closed. He goes to the next one, where he does the same. Pan across to one of the compartments. In the gloom of the attic we can just make out the MURDERER, hiding in a corner. We hear the disappearing footsteps of the WATCHMAN and the rattle of doors.

WATCHMAN off: *Whatever next!* Shouting again. *Anyone there?*

Camera cuts to the WATCHMAN seen through the fence-like partitions. He shakes a door, looks once more along the corridor, then turns away.

WATCHMAN: *Bah! Damn carelessness . . . All that trouble for one door.*

He goes out, and camera goes with him. The light goes out.

Resume on the MURDERER, who stands up, tremendously relieved.

We hear the door out onto the landing close and a key turn in the lock. The MURDERER stands alert, breathing heavily.

Long shot of the crooks' room: SCHRANKER, the PICK-POCKET, the CON-MAN, the BURGLAR and the SAFE-BREAKER are grouped around the table. SCHRANKER, standing, looks down superciliously, holding his cane handle down on the table. The SAFE-BREAKER is on the telephone.

SAFE-BREAKER into the telephone: *Yes . . . ah. Good.* He puts down the receiver and turns to the others. *It looks as if the guy is really cornered now. I think we'd better tell the police straight away.*

CON-MAN: *I agree.*

The BURGLAR and the PICK-POCKET also agree.

SAFE-BREAKER picking up the telephone again: *Now then, listen carefully . . .*

SCHRANKER violently grabs the receiver from him.

SCHRANKER into telephone: *Hello. Just a moment . . . What . . . Okay . . . and ring straight back.* He hangs up.

Medium close-up of SCHRANKER between the BURGLAR and the SAFE-BREAKER.

SAFE-BREAKER: *What is it? What's got into you?*

SCHRANKER grimly: *Are you mad or something?*

SAFE-BREAKER: *Why?*

SCHRANKER: *The police? No . . . we're going to get the guy ourselves . . . Listen . . . now, the time is . . .*

There is a slight pause as each man is waiting for someone else to make the first move. Clumsily the CON-MAN fumbles for his watch. Group shot of them all round the table.

CON-MAN: *Eight o'clock.*

SCHRANKER in medium close-up: *Good . . . Then, at . . . nine . . . ten . . . eleven o'clock!*

Camera cuts to the gateway of the office block. From the street outside we can see through the sliding gates across the courtyard to the WATCHMEN'S office which is lit up. Somewhere a clock strikes eleven, as a uniformed policeman walks up to the gates and stops. He rings the bell. One of the watchmen comes out into the courtyard. Camera cuts to his point-of-view and shows the empty street through the gates and the policeman saluting behind them.

POLICEMAN, voice of SCHRANKER: *Good evening. Did you know your gates . . .* Big close-up of the lock . . . *weren't closed?*

WATCHMAN off: *What? But that's impossible!*

He comes forward, but only his hands holding a lamp are visible.

WATCHMAN off: *I've only just . . .* Close-up of his hand shaking the grille . . . *But it is . . .*

He stops suddenly. The camera pans to his shocked face. A sudden cut shows the POLICEMAN's gloved hand pointing a revolver through the ironwork.

POLICEMAN off: *Open up and no noise!*

Close-up of the WATCHMAN behind the grille. Reverse shot of the POLICEMAN who turns out to be SCHRANKER in disguise. He is pointing two revolvers. (*Still*).

SCHRANKER: *Are you going to open up, then?*

Camera cuts to a medium shot from the street. SCHRANKER is on the right, his body partly obscuring the WATCHMAN from view.

SCHRANKER brutally: *Come on . . . get on with it!*

The WATCHMAN slides back the grille. SCHRANKER goes through and with the barrel of one of his guns pushes the WATCHMAN towards his office. The grille stays open.

SCHRANKER: *Get a move on!*

Medium close-up of a key ring swaying from the key in the lock of the grille. SCHRANKER whistles a few bars of the song, '*Be faithful and honest.*'

Shot of the grille which has been pushed open just wide enough to let one person through at a time. Someone else echoes his whistling. The SAFE-BREAKER appears in the street and signals to a group of colleagues to follow him. They pass, loaded with bags and suitcases. They all gather in front of the WATCHMEN's office. Camera tilts down slightly over the heads of the whole group. Through the glass partition and half-open door, we see the WATCHMAN sitting terrified on a chair with SCHRANKER and the CON-MAN standing over him.

SCHRANKER: *How many watchmen are there in the building?* The WATCHMAN does not move. *Okay then, so you don't want to answer, eh?*

The WATCHMAN shakes his head. The CON-MAN grabs him by

the waistcoat.

SCHRANKER ironically: *Okay, then, Okay.*

He shuts the door from the inside. Through the glass panes of the door he can be seen saying something to the WATCHMAN who still refuses to reply. At a sign from SCHRANKER, the CON-MAN pulls back the WATCHMAN's arms and ties them behind the back of the chair. After a second's silence, there is a sharp scream. SCHRANKER opens the door and speaks to the crooks standing outside.

SCHRANKER: *There are two other watchmen on their rounds.*

Camera cuts to a corridor inside the building. One of the other watchmen comes through and resets a time switch on the wall, and then carries on out of sight.

Cut to the attic where the MURDERER can be seen through the slatted partitions trying to force the lock of the main attic door with his knife. He swears in a low voice.

MURDERER: *Bloody hell!*

Close-up of the lock over the MURDERER's shoulder. He has removed one of the screws round the lock, but it does not make any difference.

MURDERER rattling the lock furiously: *Damn it!*

He examines the lock from underneath. On his back the letter M is still visible. In huge close-up, he slips the blade of his knife between the lock and the door, trying to prize open the catch, but the blade snaps and the point falls to the ground. Camera cuts to show the MURDERER half-standing, half leaning on the door.

MURDERER: *Damn it!*

He raises his arm to throw the knife away.

MURDERER muttering: *Hell!*

He freezes abruptly, arm up and eyes rolling wildly. On the other side of the door, we see a WATCHMAN passing. He resets a time-switch and prepares to leave. Slight tilt up over the bannisters of the main staircase, the camera frames a door on the fourth floor. Two crooks are working on the lock; one makes an impression, the other passes him the appropriate skeleton key. A third man comes up the stairs. Slight tilt down on the stairs towards the entrance hall. SCHRANKER is standing on the bottom steps. Two crooks pass him carrying suitcases.

SCHRANKER: *Careful with the lights. And don't walk like elephants.*

The PICK-POCKET arrives wearing a raincoat and cap.

SCHRANKER: *What's up?*

PICK-POCKET: *He isn't in the basement. We've been through it with a fine comb and found nothing.*

SCHRANKER: *Hmm!*

PICK-POCKET: *Fried and Auguste are still going through the boiler rooms.*

The PICK-POCKET is going on up the stairs when SCHRANKER calls him back.

SCHRANKER: *Wait.*

Two crooks carrying an unconscious watchman pass them on the stairs.

CROOK TO SCHRANKER: *That's the last one.*

SCHRANKER to PICK-POCKET: *Go up and join Emile. He needs help.*

PICK-POCKET: *Okay.*

SCHRANKER: *Go on, get a move on!*

The PICK-POCKET hurries up the stairs.

In the WATCHMEN'S office, the SAFE-BREAKER is poring over a plan on the table. He is dressed rather incongruously in a smart overcoat, silk scarf, and bowler. There is another time-switch on the wall behind him. Propped up against the desk, the second watchman is lying bound and unconscious. The two men carry the third watchman in, followed by the PICK-POCKET.

PICK-POCKET: *Schränker sent me.*

SAFE-BREAKER: *Good. Listen carefully.*

He points to a time-switch, which is then shown in close-up. Cut to SAFE-BREAKER'S gloved hand as it comes into frame pointing at the alarm with his cigarette holder.

SAFE-BREAKER off: *It's a new type of time-switch.*

The gloved hand points to a plan of the building.

SAFE-BREAKER off: *Here is a general plan of the lay-out. If the time-switches are not reset at exactly the right time, they automatically set off an alarm at the nearest police station. Get it?*

Cut to a shot of the time clock.

PICK-POCKET off: *Sure.*

The SAFE-BREAKER'S hand puts a key into the lock and turns it.

SAFE-BREAKER off: *Like that.*

The two of them stand in front of the switch. The PICK-POCKET looks at the plan.

SAFE-BREAKER: *Have you got it?*

PICK-POCKET: *What do you think I am, some kind of idiot?*

SAFE-BREAKER: *Could be!*

He hands him the key. The PICK-POCKET sets off at a run to make his rounds.

Camera cuts to SCHRANKER, who is standing on the staircase, listening to the report of two more of his men.

1ST CROOK: *He isn't in the boiler room either.*

SCHRANKER: *Fine.*

Two men pass with cylinders of gas and an oxy-acetylene cutter.

2ND CROOK: *We moved all the coal.*

SCHRANKER shouting up to an upper storey: *Hey!*

Slight tilt up onto the upper landing, the BURGLAR is setting up the acetylene cutter in front of a door.

SCHRANKER: *Are you mad?*

The BURGLAR stops his work and straightens up. Camera tilts down from the top of the stairs to show SCHRANKER and the other two men looking up.

SCHRANKER: *What if that door's wired up already? Do you want to get the police round here right away?*

BURGLAR: *Okay. But we've got to get in if we're going to search the whole building.*

SCHRANKER exasperated: *But not by the door, you fool!* He taps his temple. *The office on the floor above . . . go through the ceiling.*

Shot from above of three crooks coming out of a corridor onto the fourth floor landing. Pan with them as they move towards the bannisters. One of them wearing a beret pulled down over his ears leans over and shouts.

CROOK: *Nothing!*

Camera cuts to the BURGLAR again, now in an office on the second floor. He is drilling with some difficulty through the floor with a power-drill. The SAFE-BREAKER's legs can be seen next to him where he is standing holding a torch. The BURGLAR's tool bag lies open on the floor beside him.

Cut to the MURDERER in medium close-up, who is now seen trying to lever a nail out of one of the wooden uprights on the partition. The broken blade is seen in close-up and then camera tracks back as he struggles to remove the nail by hand. In close-up again, the blade levers the nail out.

Cut back to the BURGLAR and the SAFE-BREAKER. They have now managed to make a decent-sized hole in the floor. Slight tilt down it. The BURGLAR throws down a rope ladder.

BURGLAR: *Right . . . let's go.*

He lowers himself through the hole. The SAFE-BREAKER leans over and watches him climb down.

The PICK-POCKET, still studying the plan of the building, has now reached the time-switch outside the main door to the attics. He is just about to put the key in the lock when there is a faint sound of knocking. After glancing round furtively he stops to listen.

Medium close-up of the MURDERER squatting behind the door, hammering a long nail. In very big close-up, we see that he is flattening one end of the nail with the handle of his knife.

On the other side, the PICK-POCKET creeps nearer to the door, listening carefully. The knocking continues. Wildly excited, he makes for the stairs; but he suddenly remembers the time-switch and turns back on his heels and quickly resets it. He pauses for a second to listen again, and then rushes downstairs.

From a long way below the PICK-POCKET is seen, plan in hand, leaping down the stairs four at a time from the sixth floor landing. Still tracing his descent from below, camera shows some men still forcing a door on the fifth floor landing. As the PICK-POCKET races past, one of them turns round.

CROOK: *Hey, what's up?*

The PICK-POCKET, who has not stopped, is now seen from the fourth floor landing.

CROOK from the fifth floor off: *Hey, can't you answer me? What's happening? Oy Paul, you might tell us.*

A man in a beret runs out of a passage, torch in one hand, revolver in the other. He leans over the bannisters to get a better view of the PICK-POCKET.

CROOK in beret: *What's going on?*

PICK-POCKET breathless, off: *I heard someone banging!*

Another crook emerges from the passage. Camera tilts down to the third floor landing. The PICK-POCKET races past.

SECOND CROOK off: *What did you say?*

CROOK in beret, off: *What's the hurry?*

Camera cuts to the SAFE-BREAKER, who is leaning over the hole through the floor, shining his torch, to light up the room below. Hearing the shouting, he jumps up.

From a new angle above the third floor landing, he is seen coming out and grabbing at the PICK-POCKET as he passes.

PICK-POCKET shaking free: *I must see Schränker!*

From below the second floor landing, camera pans with the PICK-POCKET as he hurls himself towards SCHRANKER, pointing frantically upwards.

PICK-POCKET out of breath: *In the attic . . . he's in the attic. I heard him knocking.* The SAFE-BREAKER joins them. *In the attic . . . he's in the attic!*

Camera cuts back to show the MURDERER has succeeded in bending the nail to make a skeleton key. He puts it into the key-hole and feels around with it.

Back outside the attic door, the metallic sound of the nail inside the keyhole can still be heard, as SCHRANKER and the others creep up on tip-toe. They stop to listen and the men nudge one another expectantly.

SCHRANKER: *Shhhhhh . . . keep quiet!*

The noise of the hammering can be heard clearly.

Close-up of the MURDERER, crouched behind the door, hammering at the nail. On the floor, he studies his skeleton key.

MURDERER, proud of his workmanship: *There!*

He turns back to the door and is about to push the key into the keyhole when the handle moves very slightly. The MURDERER backs away and presses himself against the wall, eyes bulging with terror and staring fixedly at the doorhandle.

Close-up of the lock from the outside. Two hands are testing a skeleton key selected from an assorted bunch on a large key ring.

Camera cuts back to the attic passageway, facing the door. The MURDERER presses his ear against the door to listen and then slips off down the passage towards camera. Halfway down, he turns back to switch off the light, plunging the place into darkness except for the light filtering in round the edges of the door. His shadow passes in front of the camera and disappears into the recesses of the attic. A moment later, the door is flung open and SCHRANKER appears in silhouette against the light.

Behind him three torches flash on.

SCHRANKER: *Get on with it, then.*

Torch beams pass across the wooden partitions.

SCHRANKER off: *He must be there.*

OTHER VOICES off: *There's the switch.*

Camera cuts to the passage seen from the door. The lights come on. The passage is now seen as it goes through the partition of a compartment, piled up with old furniture.

SCHRANKER off: *Force the locks.*

Some men pass down the passage.

VOICES: *Come on. Hurry up! Get a move on!*

Camera tracks back slightly and pans onto the door of the compartment. Then it tracks in again.

VOICES: *Come on. Off with it.*

Two crooks force the door.

Back in the WATCHMEN'S office, the CON-MAN is seated by the window. The PICK-POCKET comes in.

PICK-POCKET: *We've got him.*

CON-MAN getting up: *What?*

PICK-POCKET: *He's in the attic.*

CON-MAN: *Is that so?*

In medium close-up, the FIRST WATCHMAN moves. He is still lying tied up on the floor. While the two crooks are talking, he makes an effort to haul himself onto his knees and reach the alarm.

PICK-POCKET off: *Yes, I heard someone hammering . . .*

CON-MAN off: *Who?*

PICK-POCKET off: *. . . and immediately told Schränker . . .*

CON-MAN off: *What did he say?*

PICK-POCKET off: *He's already up there with eight men.*

CON-MAN off: *Oh, great!*

PICK-POCKET off: *They'll get him any moment.*

CON-MAN off: *You think so?*

Camera cuts back to the two crooks face to face.

PICK-POCKET: *I just came down to tell you.*

CON-MAN: *Great.*

PICK-POCKET importantly: *If I hadn't been on the alert we might have been looking for him for hours.*

The CON-MAN rises quickly and grabs the PICK-POCKET by the

shoulder. We see the WATCHMAN on his knees, his handcuffed hands lifted towards the alarm bell.

CON-MAN off: *Look out . . . the watchman!*

Large close-up of the WATCHMAN's hands as they snatch awkwardly at the alarm which is connected directly to the local police station. A bell rings as the camera cuts to a ticker-tape machine in the station which starts to operate by unrolling a punched tape. A POLICEMAN comes into shot and leans over to read the tape.

POLICEMAN: *Three . . . one . . . four.*

Close-up of the machine with the punched tape emerging.

POLICEMAN off: *Three, one, four.*

Close-up of a filing cabinet. A hand flicks through some cards and takes one out.

ANOTHER POLICEMAN: *Three, one, four.*

Cut back to the attic passageway; the PICK-POCKET bursts through to warn the men searching there. He shouts something incomprehensible.

A CROOK: *Are you crazy?* General hubbub.

PICK-POCKET: *Yes, the cops'll be here any minute. The watchman gave the alarm.*

CROOK: *Let's get out of here!* They make for the door.

SCHRANKER off: *Stop! Quiet!* He comes into shot. *We've five minutes more and six more compartments to search. Carry on. Get on with it. Only hurry! Come on, now!*

The CROOKS start work again. One of them fiddles with the lock on a door. SCHRANKER pushes him aside.

SCHRANKER: *Out of the way. You can't do it like that.*

He crashes against the door with all his weight to break it open. Camera cuts to the MURDERER hidden in one of the compartments, weak with fear. Light feebly penetrates a skylight. The sound of doors being forced open comes gradually closer.

VOICE: *He's not in here.*

SCHRANKER off: *Next door!*

Noise of splintering wood and tearing hinges.

SCHRANKER off: *Come on. Quicker.*

The noise draws nearer and the MURDERER ducks down further and further into his corner.

VOICE: *Not here either.*

SCHRANKER off: *Come on. Keep it up! Next door.*

As we hear the noise of another breaking door, the MURDERER disappears completely behind the bric-a-brac. Only his hat is visible.

SCHRANKER off: *Quick. We've only three minutes left.*

VOICE: *Hurry up. Quickly!*

SEVERAL VOICES: *This one hasn't got a padlock . . . he must be here . . . go on, open it . . . it's locked from the inside . . . let* me *do it!*

SCHRANKER off: *Hurry up. Only one minute left!*

The noise is deafening as the door is forced down and furniture crashes to the floor. Panic-stricken, the MURDERER leaps to his feet, spot-lit by a powerful torch beam. His face is grotesquely twisted with fear. Backing away, he stumbles against a grandfather clock. (*Still*).

VOICE: *Here he is . . . here he is . . . the bastard!*

Back in the courtyard, we see a parked car in the street behind the gates which are still pulled back. The SAFE-BREAKER is on guard by the opening and he checks on the men as they stream silently through, loaded with equipment, which they throw into the car before slipping out of sight down the street.

SAFE-BREAKER: *Get going. Hurry up!* He whistles through his fingers. *Everybody out!*

The CON-MAN runs past, pulling his overcoat on over a WATCHMAN's jacket. The SAFE-BREAKER pushes him outside.

SAFE-BREAKER: *Go on. Move!* Other crooks pass through. *Come on, hurry up. Quick!*

The CON-MAN goes back inside.

CON-MAN: *Christ! Get out while you can, you fool!*

The CON-MAN makes for the door as the SAFE-BREAKER runs past the WATCHMEN's office. Camera follows a few stragglers coming out of the building.

SAFE-BREAKER: *Anybody left?*

CROOK: *A few up top . . . they're on their way.*

SAFE-BREAKER: *No reason for you to wait for them. With or without the guy, it doesn't matter, get away.* He throws up his arms in despair. *What are they up to, for Christ's sake . . . Bloody hell.* He goes back into the building. *At last. Thank God!*

A final group leaves the building and the SAFE-BREAKER follows them. Camera tilts up slightly as two men carry the MURDERER down the steps, tied up and struggling inside a carpet. (*Still*). SCHRANKER, still in his policeman's uniform, dominates the scene as he stands behind them supervising the operation. He and the SAFE-BREAKER are the last to leave. The courtyard and the street beyond are left quiet and deserted. There is an ominous silence. Slight tilt from above of the WATCHMEN's office where the FIRST WATCHMAN lies unconscious, wrists handcuffed together, and then pan across to the two other watchmen who are slumped together in a corner, tied up and unconscious. (*Still*).

Shot from high above down the hole cut through the ceiling from the second floor. A torch beam sweeps across the floor of the room below and rises towards the opening.

BURGLAR off: *Hey! He's not down here.* No reply. *Oh! Who's pulled up the ladder?* The BURGLAR's face comes into view looking up from below, and repeats: *Who's pulled up the ladder?* Someone throws the ladder down into the hole. Irritably: *Bunch of morons.*

As his head and shoulders emerge from the opening, a torch clicks on and shines straight into his face.

BURGLAR: *Hello.*

A second torch lights him up.

A VOICE: *Hands up.*

BURGLAR curtly: *How can I put my hands up when I'm trying to hang onto the ladder, eh?*

THE VOICE: *Out of there.*

Camera tracks up and back. The BURGLAR climbs out of the hole, sits on the edge and raises his hands. Camera tracks further back. He is surrounded by policemen.

BURGLAR jokingly: *For once I'm innocent . . .*

The voice continues over as camera cuts to INSPECTOR GROEBER's office.

BURGLAR: *. . . as a new born babe.*

The BURGLAR is sitting by GROEBER's desk. A lamp shines into his face. Camera frames them both in profile. GROEBER is a distinguished, well-groomed man of about fifty. Behind them sits a secretary, a little old man who looks from one to the other over the top of his spectacles. GROEBER cuts a cigar and from behind the lamp leans towards the BURGLAR.

GROEBER: *This will surprise you, Franz, but I believe you.*

BURGLAR in reverse angle, not altogether reassured: *Hmmm. Ha, ha.* He laughs nervously. *Then everything is in order, Inspector.* He gets up. *I can leave then . . .*

GROEBER's hand comes into shot and gestures to him to sit down.

GROEBER off: *One minute!*

GROEBER is now seen facing the camera. He picks up a packet of cigarettes. Resume on the BURGLAR who is now standing. GROEBER's hand comes into shot holding the cigarettes.

GROEBER off: *Cigarette?*

BURGLAR: *Oh, boy.*

Crestfallen, he slumps back into his chair and takes a cigarette.

GROEBER: *I'll take your word for it.* He leans back, rocking his chair. *On condition you tell me . . .*

He pauses. The BURGLAR waits, holding an unlit cigarette in one hand and a burning match in the other. Camera intercuts between the two men.

GROEBER: *. . . who the man was you were looking for . . . and found in the building.*

On these last words, he lets himself fall forward, while the BURGLAR puts out the match and lays the cigarette on the table. He feigns surprise.

BURGLAR: *I don't understand, Inspector. A man, you said. No, I don't know anything about that, Inspector. There must be some mistake. I don't know anything.*

GROEBER and the BURGLAR are shown in profile, with the SECRETARY behind them at the end of the table, facing the camera.

BURGLAR: *Nothing at all.*

GROEBER: *Of course.* Slyly. *Only I don't understand why you are covering up for the gang who left you in the lurch.* He relights his cigar. *Funny friends! Leaving you right in it and running off. Bah!*

BURGLAR smiling maliciously: *That won't wash with me, Inspector.*

GROEBER takes some notes. The SECRETARY takes the opportunity to sharpen some pencils. The BURGLAR looks round him worriedly. He tries to read what GROEBER is writing, but cannot make it out.

BURGLAR: *After all* . . . Not very sure of himself, he pauses; then, after a moment, he begins again . . . *After all I'm not risking very much.*

Close-up of the hole in the floor.

BURGLAR off: *Maybe a little bit of damage. But nothing was stolen.*

Camera cuts back to GROEBER in medium close-up.

GROEBER: *Of course, something was stolen. In fact a good deal . . .*

The BURGLAR leans forward, surprised.

BURGLAR: *What?* He is rising to the bait. *Stolen? How much?*

GROEBER: *If you talk I'll tell you.*

BURGLAR: *I've already told you. I don't know anything.*

GROEBER: *All right.* He gets up. *Well think about it. It's amazing what one remembers* . . . turning on the ceiling light . . . *when one's left alone for an hour or two.* We hear the door opening. *Take him away!*

A hand is placed on the BURGLAR's shoulder and he rises and leaves the room. Camera tracks in on GROEBER, who watches him go thoughtfully.

GROEBER to the SECRETARY: *Get the night watchman sent in.*

He sits down and opens a dossier.

SECRETARY off: *Get the night watchman, Damowitz.*

GROEBER raises his eyes and looks towards the door. Camera follows his look. The SECRETARY shows the WATCHMAN in.

GROEBER off: *Sit down.*

The WATCHMAN sits in the armchair in front of the desk.

Pan to GROEBER, who continues to study the dossier.

GROEBER: *Now then, you said in your statement* . . . He raises his eyes to the WATCHMAN. *Listen carefully.*

The SECRETARY's hand turns off the light on the desk and picks up a pencil.

GROEBER: *You may have to repeat it under oath.* He reads from the dossier. *That you clearly heard . . .*

The WATCHMAN is seen in medium close-up, his right cheek swollen.

GROEBER off. . . . *that one of the burglars said to another, 'We've found him . . .'*

The WATCHMAN nods his head, winces with pain and holds his cheek.

GROEBER off: '. . . *I've discovered the bloke. He is in the attic.' Is that correct?*

WATCHMAN: *Yes, Inspector . . . ooooh.* He grimaces with pain. *Yes, Inspector . . . I'll swear to that whenever you wish.*

Reverse shot of GROEBER, who closes the dossier.

GROEBER: *Right. You may go home and rest now. But please keep yourself at the disposal of the police.*

The WATCHMAN gets up.

WATCHMAN: *Of course, Inspector . . . oooh.* Painfully. *Good day, Inspector.*

He goes out, holding his jaw askew.

GROEBER: *Good day.*

He remains for a moment, deep in thought. Then camera tracks in as he picks up the telephone.

GROEBER on the telephone: *Tell me, is Inspector Lohmann in the building? . . . Oh, good . . . He's talking to somebody? No, it doesn't matter. I'll come up.*

Camera cuts to show LOHMANN sitting at his desk smoking a cigar; he is framed against the large map of the city on the wall behind him. Now he is in shirt-sleeves, his collar open and tie loosened, and he looks tired and harassed. He is on the telephone, and with one hand pours out coffee from an enamel coffee pot.

LOHMANN on the telephone: *What? Good. Hasn't come in yet . . . You're watching the old girl, that Mrs. Winkler, eh?*

There is a knock on the door.

LOHMANN: *Come in.*

Shot from below under the desk at floor level, we see that LOHMANN is stretched out in his chair, lying rather than sitting. From this angle, the size of his stomach is enormously exaggerated and we can see that his trousers are unbuttoned at the waist; chewing at his cigar, he hangs up.

LOHMANN: *Hell!*

Camera cuts back to show LOHMANN behind his desk, and it pans slightly to pick up GROEBER who has just come in, a dossier under his arm. He sits on the edge of the desk. LOHMANN adds some milk to his coffee from a carton.

LOHMANN: *What do you want?*

GROEBER: *I wanted to ask you . . .*

Camera tracks in to isolate LOHMANN *who drinks his coffee.*

GROEBER off: *. . . a favour.*

LOHMANN in close-up, drinking: *Ugh . . . what muck.*

GROEBER off: *I wanted to ask you . . .*

Camera tracks back as GROEBER's hand places the dossier on the table.

GROEBER off: Anyway, read a bit of that.

LOHMANN takes a bit from a biscuit and picks up the dossier.

Close-up of LOHMANN's hand holding the dossier marked 'REPORTS.'

LOHMANN off: *Reports?*

GROEBER off: *Yes.*

The hand opens the dossier. The first typewritten sheet carries the date 25th November, 1930.

GROEBER off: *Burglary in an office block.*

The page is turned.

Dissolve to a shot of the ticker-tape machine and the punched tape.

Dissolve to a general view of the office building at Bennastrasse 29-33 and Ostend-allee 114-117.

LOHMANN off: *Bennastrasse?*

Dissolve to the main entrance of the building with gates half-open and the WATCHMEN's office illuminated.

LOHMANN off: *That's a very quiet neighbourhood.*

Dissolve to the WATCHMAN unconscious on the floor of his office.

LOHMANN off: *. . . Perhaps it's not as quiet as all that . . .*

Dissolve to the office again where the other bound watchmen are seen in the corner.

LOHMANN off: *Hell, this is becoming serious.*

Dissolve to an open door on the landing with the lock cut.

Dissolve to another door, also forced.

Dissolve back to a close-up of another page of the dossier. It is turned.

Dissolve to another door. A drill is still sticking in a hole and all round the lock there is a circle of holes.

LOHMANN off: *Did they intend to empty the whole place, then?*

Dissolve to the basement of the building where the door to the coal-hole has been forced.

LOHMANN amazed off: *What can they have been looking for in the coal?*

Dissolve to the boiler room, seen through a shattered door.

LOHMANN off: *Look at that. It's incredible.*

Dissolve to another page of the dossier as it is turned.

Dissolve to the corridor of the attic. The door of every compartment has been forced.

LOHMANN off: *Good Lord.*

Dissolve to the rear of the attic. The last few doors are completely smashed to pieces.

LOHMANN off, clicking his tongue: *This is madness!*

Dissolve to the last compartment showing all the furniture turned upside down.

Dissolve to a close-up of the hole in the ceiling on the second floor, with the rope ladder and the abandoned drill.

LOHMANN off: *Ah, now it makes sense. They were after the safe.*

Dissolve to a close-up of an old safe. It has not been touched.

LOHMANN off: *Good God. What's that all about?*

Dissolve to a close-up of another safe, also unharmed.

LOHMANN off: *I don't understand it at all.*

Close-up of another safe, also intact.

LOHMANN off: *They haven't even attacked that one. Were they all crazy or something?*

Dissolve to a quick shot of a page of the dossier turning.

Then camera cuts to show the two of them in the office.

LOHMANN lifting his head: *Well, I'll be damned!*

GROEBER: *Well, what have you got to say? Nothing stolen, but a man was taken away. God knows where.*

LOHMANN: *Fantastic!*

He puts his cigar-holder down on a plate and prepares another cigar.

GROEBER: *And Franz — the burglar we arrested — isn't talking. Frightened evidently. Actually I know him well . . . he is one of those burglars who would rather jump from the fifth floor than get mixed up in a murder.*

LOHMANN finishes cutting his cigar and starts to suck it.

GROEBER: *If we could . . . set a trap for him?* A huge smile spreads across LOHMANN's face. *Could you help me out, Lohmann?*

LOHMANN raising his cigar: *I see what you are getting at . . . well then, let's take a look at this Franz.*

Camera cuts to a prison cell where the BURGLAR is stretched out on a bed, his legs in the foreground. A DETECTIVE comes in.

DETECTIVE: *For questioning.*

The scene fades to black.

Back in LOHMANN's office, the BURGLAR is seen examining a plaque on the wall. The DETECTIVE who brought him in stands in the background.

Close-up of the plaque. It is a list of the members of the Murder Squad, with names, addresses and telephone numbers. Under 'Head of Department' we can read: 'Karl Lohmann,' followed by an address and telephone number. Camera cuts back to show the BURGLAR's back view as he stares at the list.

BURGLAR unhappily: *Inspector Karl Lohmann . . .*

A door opens. The BURGLAR turns. LOHMANN has come in, hands in pockets, sucking a cigar. The BURGLAR moves towards him.

BURGLAR frightened: *What do you want with me?* Shouting. *What does the Murder Squad want with me?*

After a moment, LOHMANN comes into shot. He stops in front of the BURGLAR.

LOHMANN: *Yes, old boy . . . Your case has been passed over to me now.*

The BURGLAR, very worried, wrings his hands. LOHMANN stands in front of him, in profile.

BURGLAR: *But . . . but why? Whatever for?*

LOHMANN: *You did your work a little too well.*

The BURGLAR nervously unbuttons his collar.

BURGLAR in a choked voice: *Yes?*

LOHMANN meaningfully: *One of the watchmen . . .*

Camera cuts to DAMOWITZ, the WATCHMAN, sitting at a table, in his home, an enormous plate of sausage and cabbage in front of him. He drinks some beer, wipes his moustache and digs into another sausage.

Camera cuts back to LOHMANN and the BURGLAR.

BURGLAR in a choked voice: *Dead?*

LOHMANN paces round his office; camera pans with him.

LOHMANN: *Planning and assisting with a murder . . . It's a bad show, Franz.*

BURGLAR off, still choking over his words: *I can't go on with it. I don't want to have anything to do with that.*

We see both of them as LOHMANN picks up a dossier and flicks through it.

BURGLAR breaking down: *I'll tell you everything . . . everything I know.*

LOHMANN off-hand: *Very wise, but unfortunately too late.*

The BURGLAR moves nearer and can be seen pleading with LOHMANN who turns his back on him.

BURGLAR: *Inspector, it* can't *be too late . . . please, Inspector . . . But, it isn't possible. Listen, I'm going to tell you everything . . . everything. Even who we were looking for in that damn building.*

LOHMANN straightens up, triumphant and interested, but does not turn round.

LOHMANN: *Well, then.*

BURGLAR: *The murderer . . . the child murderer.*

Medium close-up of LOHMANN as his mouth drops open in amazement, and his cigar falls out onto the table. There is a pause. LOHMANN is dumbfounded and without thinking he raises a shaky hand to remove the cigar from his lips. He looks confused for a moment, but quickly recovering his composure, he picks it up from the dossier where it had fallen.

LOHMANN with dawning realisation: *What? What? . . . Who?*

BURGLAR distraught: *The child murderer, Inspector.*

LOHMANN puffs out a great cloud of cigar smoke which completely obscures his face. He strides across the room flapping a hand to disperse the smoke-screen around him.

LOHMANN: *Wait.*

Very quick pan with him towards a door which he closes behind him.

In the toilet LOHMANN, seen from above, leans against the basin and puts his head under the cold tap.

Camera cuts back to the office in medium shot, where the BURGLAR waits in total despair.

BURGLAR sighing: *This had to happen to me! Of all people.*

A door opens behind him. He turns. LOHMANN comes back in, looking happy and satisfied. He has his jacket on and, rubbing his hands, sits down behind his desk.

Camera pans with him and then tracks back to frame him and the BURGLAR. After a while, LOHMANN takes out a cigar and cuts it, with a pair of scissors.

LOHMANN: *Right . . . Now, we're going to have a little talk.*

BURGLAR hopelessly: *If you want to, Inspector.* (*Still*).

LOHMANN: *And mind you don't lie.* He pauses. *Okay, let's start. What have you got to do with the murderer and where have you taken him?*

BURGLAR: *Well now, Inspector, you know the old . . . .*

Cut to the battered façade of an empty factory, almost a ruin.

BURGLAR off: *. . . distillery of Kuntz and Levy . . .*

Cut to a corner of the building.

LOHMANN off: *The one that went bankrupt?*

In the gloom of an abandoned workshop inside the factory, a staircase can just be made out to the right. Inarticulate cries are heard in the distance, gradually drawing nearer. Two men come down the steps and disappear into the gloom.

MURDERER off: *What do you want with me? Let me go . . . let me go!*

A VOICE roughly: *Go on . . . keep moving . . . go on.*

Shot of the two men reappearing, they are pushing the MURDERER up a short stairway. He is struggling furiously although his jacket has been pulled over his head. At the top of the steps a third man comes to help them. Group shot of them all.

MURDERER struggling: *I've done nothing to you . . . Let me go, you swine.*

From the bottom of another flight of steps, the camera tilts up to an iron door, which is flung open. A foot appears on the top step, but no one appears for a minute as there is obviously a scuffle going on at the top of the stairs. The third man comes down the steps.

MURDERER off: *Let me go.*

The two others push the MURDERER down the steps. He slips on the steps.

MURDERER: *Bastards!*

The MURDERER has fallen to the bottom of the steps and the two men stand on the platform at the top.

MURDERER: *Bunch of bastards!*

One of the men closes the door. The MURDERER drags his coat off his head.

MURDERER: *What do you want with me? Bastards! What do you want?*

He turns and stops dead in his tracks. (*Still*). Camera cuts back to show the huge factory cellar from his point-of-view, where assorted members of the underworld can be seen watching him. Camera pans along the entire length of the cellar to reveal that a vast crowd has assembled — crooks and their wives, tarts, pimps and beggars — most of them standing, with the older members seated on boxes and crates. There is absolute silence and no one moves. Pan continues until it reaches a trestle table set up in front of them. Behind it sit the PICK-POCKET, the CON-MAN and the SAFE-BREAKER on either side of SCHRANKER. It is obviously a crude form of tribunal and, as usual, SCHRANKER is in charge.

MURDERER: *Help!*

Camera cuts back to the MURDERER and the two men on the stairs.

MURDERER: *Help! Let me go. I want to get out* . . . He tries to climb up a few steps. *I want to get out. Get out.*

A general view of the tribunal, lit only by a single bulb hanging from the ceiling.

MURDERER off: *Let me out!*

SCHRANKER firmly: *You will not get out of here.*

The two men on the staircase block the MURDERER's way. He turns back to face the crowd.

MURDERER: *But gentlemen* . . . His hair falling over his face he comes down the stairs. Camera tracks in on him as he appeals to them. *Please, I don't even know what you want me for.* He takes a few hesitant paces forward. *I beg you. Set me free. There must be some mistake* . . . A hand comes into frame above his head, feeling around in the air. *A mist* . . .

The hand falls on the MURDERER's shoulder. His voice breaks off with a cry of terror.

BLIND BEGGAR off: *No . . . No . . . No mistake . . . Impossible. There's no mistake.*

Camera tracks back to show the MURDERER and the BLIND BEGGAR. The MURDERER turns towards him.

THE BLIND BEGGAR withdrawing his hand: *No, no mistake.*

MURDERER: *But . . . what do you mean?*

Camera tracks further back so that the BLIND BEGGAR's other arm comes into view. He is holding a doll-shaped balloon. He shows it to the MURDERER.

BLIND BEGGAR: *Do you recognise it? It is a balloon like the one you gave to little Elsie Beckmann.*

The MURDERER stiffens with fear at the mention of that name. The BLIND BEGGAR holds the string of the doll-shaped balloon and lets it rise up as far as the string will go. Seen from above, the MURDERER follows the balloon's ascent with horrified eyes. It sways gently very close to the camera. The faces of the crowd are a confused blur in the background.

BLIND BEGGAR off: *A balloon like that . . .*

MURDERER gibbering: *El . . . El . . . Elsie . . . El . . . Elsie.*

He backs away, terrified by the balloon, until he stumbles against the table. The camera follows him.

MURDERER, his voice becoming more and more high-pitched: *No, no, no . . .*

Camera cuts quickly onto the MURDERER's back. Behind him, we see the BLIND BEGGAR and the staircase guarded by the two men.

SCHRANKER off: *Where did you . . .*

On SCHRANKER's first words, the MURDERER turns to face the camera.

An immediate cut to SCHRANKER who has a photograph in front of him on the table of a little girl.

SCHRANKER leaning forward: *. . . bury little Martha?* (*Still*).

Cut back to the MURDERER who walks forwards towards the camera as the BLIND BEGGAR is led away by one of the crooks.

MURDERER: *But . . . but I never . . . I never even knew her.*

SCHRANKER sarcastically: *Oh yes, very good. You didn't even know her.* He waves another photograph. *And what about this one?*

Cut back to the MURDERER who backs away, now helpless with fright. A cutting from a newspaper is shown in medium close-up, lying on the table.

SCHRANKER off: *And this one?*

Camera cuts to the MURDERER, who chews at his fingers. Cut back to SCHRANKER's gloved hand showing a third photograph. We recognise ELSIE's face.

SCHRANKER off: *. . . and this one, you didn't know this one either eh?*

The MURDERER is seen now crazy with fright. Panic-stricken, he spins round in a mad dash for the exit. One of the men who brought him in is sitting at the foot of the stairs; he jumps up to bar the way as the crowd begin to jump up and shout hysterically. (*Still*).

VOICES: *Stop him . . . Stop him . . . don't let him escape!*

From one end of the cellar we see the crowd surging forward. Only SCHRANKER remains calmly seated.

VOICES: *Stop him . . . he mustn't get away!*

Camera cuts back to the MURDERER who barges past the crook on the stairs, pushing him violently out of the way, and manages to climb towards the door.

VOICES: *Quick, stop him . . . Hold him . . . Look out . . . the door!*

We now see the top of the stairs and the door which the MURDERER tries to open, but a crook grabs him by the collar.

A VOICE: *Hold him . . . hang onto him.*

From the same angle but closer, the MURDERER hangs onto the door handle with both hands. The crook holds him from behind. Two others come to his aid.

A VOICE: *Go on . . . Go on . . . Hit him . . . Belt him!*

Close-up of the MURDERER's convulsed face. A hand seizes him by the throat.

MURDERER in a strangled voice: *Let me go . . . Let me go!*

Medium shot of the three men trying to make the MURDERER loosen his grip. A fourth crook comes up the stairs to help them. One of them kicks him on the shins. The general shouting gets louder. Close-up of the crook kicking the MURDERER, then cut to a close-up of the MURDERER's hand still grasping the handle.

A VOICE: *Go on . . . on his shins.*

Camera cuts quickly to the fighter's legs. The MURDERER receives another violent kick in the shins. Cut back to a medium shot of the struggle at the door. A crook tries to hit the MURDERER's hands.

VOICES: *Heave . . . ho. Heave . . . ho.*

Close-up of the crook's fist violently striking the MURDERER's fingers. The shock makes him let go. Camera cuts back to a medium shot of the group as they draw back from the MURDERER and throw him down the stairs. The camera pans quickly as he falls. He lands heavily on the ground, banging his head sharply against some old timbers lying against the wall. He lies twisting with pain while the crowd cheers and hoots triumphantly.

MURDERER almost in tears: *You have no right to treat me like this!*

VOICES: *We'll show you what right we have!*

MURDERER groaning: *You have no right to hold me here.*

Camera cuts to part of the crowd, A prostitute gets up furiously.

PROSTITUTE screaming fanatically: *Right? Someone like you doesn't have any rights.* Roaring. *Kill him!*

A MAN next to her, rising: *Yes, kill him!*

PROSTITUTE: *We must put him down like a mad dog!*

There is a general view of the crowd, now very animated.

A VOICE: *Crush him.*

SCHRANKER turning impatiently to the crowd: *Quiet!*

A VOICE: *Kill him! . . . Kill him!*

SCHRANKER shouting: *Shut up!*

The crowd is calmed by an imperious gesture from SCHRANKER. When the noise dies down completely, he turns towards the MURDERER.

SCHRANKER: *You talk of rights . . . You will get your rights.* Camera tracks, in close-up, across the attentive faces of the crowd, as SCHRANKER continues off: *We are all law experts here, from six weeks in Tegel, to fifteen years in Brandenburg,** Close-up of SCHRANKER. *You will get your rights . . . you will even have a lawyer.* Ironically. *Everything will be done according to the rule of law.*

Camera cuts to the MURDERER crouching in a corner like a toad.

MURDERER screaming: *A lawyer? . . . A lawyer? . . . I don't need a lawyer . . . Who is accusing me? You, maybe?* You?

A hand taps him on the shoulder. The MURDERER turns round. Camera pans up, following his glance to frame a fairly old, ill-shaven man, who leans towards him across a wooden barrier. He is a LAWYER. In front of him, on a chest, a pile of Criminal and Civil law books.

LAWYER: *Eh . . . just a moment . . . If I were you sir, I'd keep quiet. Your life's at stake . . . in case you didn't know.*

The MURDERER rises and leans towards the LAWYER seated

* Tegel and Brandenburg are two of Berlin's prisons.

behind his chest. He stares at him in amazement.

MURDERER: *Who are you?*

LAWYER greeting him: *I have the dubious honour of being your defence counsel. But I am afraid it won't be much use to you.*

The LAWYER superciliously blows some dust from his notebook.

MURDERER: *But . . . but . . . Do you want to kill me then?* Horrified. *Murder me, just like that?*

SCHRANKER in close-up: *We just want to render you harmless. That's what we want . . . but you'll only be harmless when you're dead.*

Camera cuts back to a medium shot of the LAWYER and the MURDERER.

MURDERER begging: *But if you kill me it'll be cold-blooded murder!* Derisive laughter echoes round the cellar. The LAWYER sighs and shrugs his shoulders. *I demand that you hand me over to the police.* The laughter increases. He raises his voice. *I demand to be handed over to the jurisdiction of the common law.*

This is greeted by loud laughter from the crowd. Camera cuts to SCHRANKER and the CON-MAN unconcerned; behind them, the crowd rocks with laughter.

A VOICE: *Quite a performance . . . That's not bad, that, ha, ha, ha!*

SCHRANKER to the MURDERER: *That would suit you, wouldn't it?*

CON-MAN expostulating: *Anything else you'd like?*

SCHRANKER: *So that you can invoke paragraph fifty-one.*

A VOICE: *That's it.*

SCHRANKER: *. . . And spend the rest of your life in an institution at the state's expense . . . And then you'd escape . . . or else there'd be a pardon and there you are, free as air, with a pass, protected by the law because of mental illness.* Laughter. *Off again chasing little girls.* A pause. *No, no.* Very dry. *We're not going to let that happen.*

A VOICE echoing: *No, no, no.*

SCHRANKER: *We must make you powerless. You must disappear.*

A VOICE: *Bravo . . . he must disappear.*

Medium close-up of the MURDERER sobbing with fear.

MURDERER: *But I can't help what I do.* He falls to his knees and miserably hides his face in his hands. *I can't help it . . . I can't . . . I can't . . . I can't help it.*

Camera cuts quickly back to show the crowd from one side. In the front row, a crook rises to his feet.

CROOK with an evil laugh: *The old story.*

Camera tilts down slightly over the MURDERER, who has fallen to his knees. Helplessly, he lowers his hands.

MURDERER in complete despair: *What do you know about it? What are you saying? If it comes to that, who are you? What right have you to speak?* He turns his head to look at them all. *Who are you . . . All of you? . . . Criminals! Perhaps you're even proud of yourselves? Proud of being able to break safes, to climb into buildings or cheat at cards . . . Things you could just as well keep your fingers off . . . You wouldn't need to do all that if you had learnt a proper trade . . . or if you worked. If you weren't a bunch of lazy bastards . . . But I . . .* His hands clutch at his chest. *I can't help myself! I haven't any control over this evil thing that's inside me — the fire, the voices, the torment.*

Cut to a slight tilt on SCHRANKER sitting at the table; behind him part of the crowd.

Resume on the MURDERER.

MURDERER agonised: *Always . . . always, there's this evil force inside me . . . It's there all the time, driving me out to wander through the streets . . . following me . . . silently, but I can feel it there . . .It's me, pursuing myself, because . . .*

SCHRANKER: *You mean to say you* have *to murder?*

Medium close-up of an old man in the crowd, nodding thoughtfully, moved by the MURDERER's genuine anguish.

MURDERER off: *I want to escape . . . to escape from myself!* Camera cuts to two other crooks. One of them seems very moved . . . *but it's impossible. I can't. I can't escape.* Return to the panting MURDERER. *I have to obey it. I have to run . . . run . . . streets . . . endless streets. I want to escape. I want to get away.* Cut to two prostitutes, one of them nervously twisting a handkerchief. *And I am pursued by ghosts. Ghosts of mothers. And of those children . . . They never leave me.* Shouting desperately. *They are there, there, always, always.* In close-up. *Always . . . except . . .* He lowers his voice . . . *except when I do it . . . when I . . .* He raises his hands towards his neck, as though he were about to strangle a victim, then he lets them fall limp at his sides. *Then I can't remember anything . . . And afterwards I see those posters and I read what I've done . . . I read . . . and . . . and read . . . Did I do that? But I can't remember anything about it . . . But who will believe me? Who knows what it feels like to be me? How I'm forced to act . . .* His eyes close in ecstasy. *How I must . . .*

Don't want to, but must . . . He screams. *Must . . . Don't want to . . . must. And then . . . a voice screams . . . I can't bear to hear it.*

He throws himself against the wooden barrier in a paroxysm covering his ears with his hands.

MURDERER at the height of his fit: *I can't . . . I can't go on. Can't go on . . . Can't go on . . . Can't go on . . .*

Camera cuts back to SCHRANKER and the SAFE-BREAKER; the crowd behind them. SCHRANKER rises to his feet.

MURDERER off, his voice dying away: *I can't go on . . .*

SCHRANKER: *The accused has said that he cannot help himself. That is to say: he has to murder. As this is the case, he has pronounced his own death sentence.*

VOICES off: *Hurrah . . . that's true . . . Hurrah.*

SCHRANKER: *Someone who admits to being a compulsive murderer should be snuffed out, like a candle.*

A VOICE: *Hurrah.*

SCHRANKER louder: *This man must be wiped out, eliminated.*

Applause and shouts. Medium close-up of the MURDERER on his knees, he rubs his head against the barrier, his hands still over his ears. The noise continues.

Cut back to a quick view of SCHRANKER and the SAFE-BREAKER, the crowd in a frenzy behind them.

VARIOUS VOICES: *Hurrah . . . Perfect, just what I think . . . Hurrah!*

Medium shot of the LAWYER who gets up. On his right, the MURDERER crouches.

LAWYER: *I wish to speak.*

SCHRANKER off: The defence lawyer will speak.

LAWYER ironically: *Our very honourable President . . .*

He rubs his hands together. There is a quick shot of SCHRANKER who has just sat down.

LAWYER off: *. . . who is, I believe, wanted by the police for three murders . . .*

SCHRANKER very angry: *That's got nothing to do with it!*

LAWYER continuing: *. . . claims that because my client acts under an irresistible impulse, he is condemned to death.*

A VOICE: *That's exactly it . . . Yes . . . He's right.*

LAWYER louder: *He is mistaken . . . because it is that very fact that clears my client.*

Several close-ups of members of the crowd: a one-eyed crook, a prostitute, an older man who looks like a wrestler. They all look puzzled.

THE ONE-EYED CROOK: *Hey, just a moment, that's enough.*

We see other faces in the crowd. In the foreground a crook with a moustache, a hat and a bow-tie.

CROOK: *Are you mad, you drunken old sot?*

LAWYER: *It is this very fact of obsession which makes my client not responsible . . . And nobody can be punished for something which he is not responsible for.*

Whistles and cat-calls. Quick shot of a part of the crowd.

VOICE: *That's ridiculous.*

PROSTITUTE furious, jumps to her feet: *Do you want to suggest by any chance that this* brute *should get off?*

A CROOK bitterly: *That he should stay alive?*

Camera cuts back to the LAWYER and the MURDERER.

LAWYER: *I mean that this man is sick. And a sick man should be handed over, not to the executioner, but to the doctor.*

Cut to the SAFE-BREAKER in three-quarters profile, the angry crowd behind him.

SAFE-BREAKER: *Could you guarantee he'd be cured?*

LAWYER resume on him: *What use are asylums, then?*

Medium shot of SCHRANKER, the CON-MAN and the PICK-POCKET, seated at the table.

CON-MAN: *And what would happen if he escaped?*

SCHRANKER: *Yes . . . or if they released him as harmless? And what if the compulsion to kill returns? Yet another man-hunt for several months. Paragraph fifty-one again. Into the asylum again and then another escape or release. And then the compulsion all over again. And so on and so on till doomsday!*

LAWYER, shot of him: *No one has the right to kill a man who is not responsible for his actions. Not the state, and certainly not you. The state must take care that this man becomes harmless and ceases to be a danger to his fellow citizens.*

During this plea, the crowd becomes excited and they begin to shout and bawl at the top of their voices. His last words are almost lost in the general laughter. Camera cuts in to a group of onlookers gathered below an enormous heating pipe. They are laughing. A PROSTITUTE gets up.

PROSTITUTE: *You've never had children, eh? So you haven't lost any either. But if you want to know what it's like to lose one of your kids . . .* Another woman tries to calm her *. . . then go and ask the parents of those children he got at.*

We see different groups of onlookers. In their midst an enormous thug listens close to tears.

PROSTITUTE off: *Ask them what those days and nights were like when they didn't know for sure what was up . . . and about the ones when they finally knew what happened.* Camera cuts back to her, screaming: *Ask the mothers!*

Cut to the MURDERER still crouched against the barrier, his hands over his ears.

A WOMAN off: *She's right!*

Cut to a medium close-up of the MURDERER who crouches ever lower, then cut back to the PROSTITUTE who repeats her cry.

PROSTITUTE: *Ask the mothers!*

VOICES: *Yes, the mothers . . . the mothers . . . ask them . . . Do you think they'll have mercy on a child-murderer?*

Another group of onlookers is seen. The fever rises.

A CROOK: *She's right.*

ANOTHER: *And how.*

PROSTITUTE off: *No mercy . . . No pardon . . .*

A CROOK: *Give him to us, the murderer.*

2ND CROOK: *Kill him, the beast.*

We are shown several different faces in the crowd. A PROSTITUTE in the front row screams her rage. Behind her, a crook in a cap is also worked up.

YOUNG PROSTITUTE: *Crush him, the brute.*

MAN at the same time: *Kill him.*

Camera cuts to other faces already seen.

WRESTLER: *Bleed the beast.*

ONE-EYE: *Hang him.*

A VOICE: *Beat him down.*

A LITTLE MAN: *Kill him.*

ANOTHER: *Kill him.*

We see the whole furious mob.

CRIES: *To the gallows . . . Finish him . . . Kill him . . . Kill him . . . Kill him.*

Camera cuts quickly to the LAWYER.

LAWYER: *All that shouting won't silence me.*

The noise dies down. Another general shot of the crowd shows them waiting, but not appeased.

LAWYER: *I will not allow a crime to be committed in my presence. I demand that this man . . .*

A VOICE interrupting: *He isn't one!*

LAWYER carrying on: *. . . that this man be granted the protection of the law, which is everybody's right.*

A VOICE: *To hell with that . . . to hell with it.*

Whistles and shouts from the crowd.

LAWYER very loud: *I demand that this man be handed over to the police.*

Cut to a high shot of the crowd and the leaders of the tribunal, in uproar.

A WOMAN hysterically: *To the police!*

CON-MAN furious: *Filthy stooge!*

The excitement is at its height. Everyone shouts, whistles and screams at the same time. From every side, crooks and prostitutes throw themselves towards the MURDERER . . . then, suddenly, everyone freezes, and eyes fix on the door of the cellar.

VOICES and shrill whistles off: *Police . . . Hands up!*

Taken by surprise the crooks and women all stand with raised hands. Only SCHRANKER remains seated. He tips back his chair arrogantly. Having cast a long look round the assembled crowd and seen that there is no hope, he also gets up and raises his hands.

The MURDERER still crouches against the barrier. He rises even more slowly and looks round in absolute terror. Camera comes in closer and a hand is placed firmly on his shoulder.

A VOICE: *In the name of the law . . .*

The music of Peer Gynt is heard. Fade to black.

After a short pause the voice of MRS. BECKMANN can be heard: *We too, should keep a closer watch on our children.*

THE END

CREDITS:

Script by	Leo Lania, Bela Balasz, Ladislaus Vajda
from the play by	Berthold Brecht
Music by	Kurt Weill
Directed by	G. W. Pabst
Producer	Seymour Nebenzahl
Production company	Warner Bros.-Tobis
Photography	Fritz Arno Wagner
Sets	Andrei Andreiev
Musical director	Theo Mackeben
Sound	Adolf Jansen
Editor	Hans Oser
First shown	Berlin, 19th February, 1931
Length	3,097 metres

CAST:

Mackie Messer	Rudolf Forster
Polly	Carola Neher
Tiger Brown	Reinhold Schünzel
Peachum	Fritz Rasp
Mrs Peachum	Valeska Gert
Jenny	Lotte Lenya
The vicar	Hermann Thimig
The street-singer	Ernst Busch
Smith	Vladimir Sokolov
Mackie Messer's gang	Paul Kemp
	Gustav Püttjer
	Oscar Höcker
	Kraft Raschig
Filch	Herbert Grünbaum

(The French version, which was shot concurrently with the German version, using the same sets, had the following leading actors: Albert Préjean (Mackie Messer), Florelle (Polly), Jack Henley (Tiger Brown), Gaston Modot (Peachum), Jane Marken (Mrs Peachum), Margo Lion (Jenny), Antonin Artaud, Vladimir Sokolov, Marcel Merminod.)

THE THREEPENNY OPERA*

Scene 1. A street in London.

It is afternoon and the atmosphere is gloomy. A brick façade . . . one side of the street is taken up with solid-looking houses, warehouses, storage depots and old office buildings; we are to assume that the way down to the docks and the river is on the other side. The district is frequented by pallid-looking people — typical members of the lower middle classes and dock-workers on their way home. Some are lounging in doorways, children are playing in the street, housewives are going home laden with shopping-bags. The last notes of the overture are heard as the sequence opens on a long shot of the street. Among the passers-by are POLLY and MRS PEACHUM, shot unobtrusively from behind.

They are on their way home and the camera tracks behind them as they walk past a house with its entrance right on the street corner. An ornate signboard hanging over the doorway proclaims the name 'Highgate Marsh' and above that, on an iron bracket, is the red lamp that glows day and night to light people to brothels. At that moment the door opens and MACKIE MESSER, whom we can see only from behind, appears in the doorway with JENNY. The notes of the 'Tango Ballad' can be heard from inside the house. The camera comes to a standstill. POLLY and MRS PEACHUM walk out of the picture without noticing MACKIE, who happens to catch sight of them and hesitates, looking after them with interest.

We now see MACKIE from the side. In the twinkling of an eye his expression changes: this bleary-eyed fellow, who's obviously feeling rather morning-afterish, has visibly perked up; he straightens his hat and takes a step to the side to get a better look at the women. He pushes back JENNY as she tries

* The version presented here is taken from the original shooting script for the film, a copy of which was kindly provided by the Munich Film Archive. Major divergences from the final version of the film are indicated in the notes at the end of the script, which also contain stills references.

to follow him and sets off in pursuit, accompanied by the camera. As he passes a ground-floor window of the house, a woman rapidly hands him out his cane;[1] he takes it mechanically, without looking at the woman, and continues on his way. The music gets softer. The scene is repeated at the next window, except that this time another woman holds out his gloves. MACKIE is still looking straight ahead and again takes the gloves with a mechanical movement; he sets off after POLLY, who has now disappeared, swinging his cane. The music stops. Close-up of MACKIE from in front. The camera keeps pace with him as he goes faster and faster, his cane tapping feverishly along. Behind him in the distance, JENNY and the other women watch him as he walks away.

Now we follow POLLY as seen by MACKIE, with part of her mother's arm hanging onto her. The camera tilts up from POLLY's feet to her bottom and stays there, tracking with her. MACKIE is seen in back view, with MRS PEACHUM and POLLY now further ahead. The two women turn into a side alley; behind them, only a few steps away, MACKIE quickly follows and turns the same corner.

Scene 2. A small square.

We follow MACKIE as he enters the square, in the middle of which a crowd of people can be seen grouped around a STREET-SINGER, who is hidden from view. A barrel-organ is playing the beginning of 'The Ballad of Mackie Messer'. MACKIE walks up to the bystanders and joins the crowd, looking for POLLY.[2]

Seen from behind, MACKIE stands on tiptoe, looking for POLLY over the heads of the people in front of him. A tall man with a shabby top hat is blocking his view, and MACKIE quietly flicks the hat to one side with his cane so that it slides down over the man's ear.

A closer shot from MACKIE's point of view. In the middle of his field of vision is the STREET-SINGER, who is singing and illustrating his words with a series of pictures. Beyond him, in the front row of the audience, is POLLY's face, which we, and MACKIE, now see indistinctly for the first time.

Close-up of the STREET-SINGER as he sings, turning from side to side with comic gestures and pointing to the different pictures with his stick; each of the crudely painted designs illustrates one of the verses. Next to him is a bare-footed girl playing the barrel organ. The ballad continues.

Shooting from where the SINGER is standing, the camera pans across the spectators. The man with the top hat listens open-mouthed and mechanically straightens his hat, so that MACKIE's face disappears behind it. The pan continues as MACKIE moves in a wide semi-circle round the edge of the crowd so that he can stand beside POLLY. Among the audience we see a stout couple, a moustachioed petit-bourgeois with his plump wife, a servant girl with a soldier, who stands dumbly as if posing for a photograph, and two teenage girls sucking liquorice sticks. MACKIE has now come up behind POLLY; he pushes his way through to her and comes to a halt behind her and MRS PEACHUM as the first verse of the ballad ends.

Close-up of POLLY, seen from inside the circle of spectators. MACKIE's face appears just behind hers as the second verse of the ballad is sung. Unnoticed by POLLY, MACKIE looks at her, fascinated, and pushes closer. We get the impression that he wants to touch her. POLLY starts and turns her head towards MACKIE. He looks up simultaneously and, laughing, sings the last line of the third verse with the STREET-SINGER: '. . . But evidence is rather thin . . .'

We cut to the STREET-SINGER with his pictures as he sings the fourth verse.[3]

MRS PEACHUM is seen from behind. She is bored and leaves her place, dragging POLLY with her. POLLY can't take her eyes off MACKIE, and draws him after her with a look. All three of them go out of shot as the fourth verse comes to an end.

Resume on the STREET-SINGER with his pictures; he begins the last verse.[4]

We now see the ring of spectators from where the STREET-SINGER is standing. The camera pans round, showing the reactions of the audience, then holds on the faces of the girls, who as the SINGER comes to the word 'raped' leave their liquorice sticks in their mouths in a thrill of voluptuous horror.[5]

Scene 3. Outside the Cuttlefish Hotel.

We are at the entrance to a tavern with a signboard depicting a huge cuttlefish hanging up over the door. MACKIE is seen coming up the street behind the two women, who are laughing.

MACKIE: *May I invite you ladies to step into the Cuttlefish Hotel with me?*

He gestures invitingly towards the tavern. POLLY is still gazing at him with an ecstatic expression on her face, but MRS PEACHUM gives him a knowing wink and leads the way down the steps, looking a bit prim but clearly flattered by the invitation. POLLY follows her and MACKIE brings up the rear. As the women go in through the door we hear music coming from inside. MACKIE pauses at the bottom of the stairs, turns and whistles.[6] A man rushes down the first few steps and MACKIE goes back up towards him.

Seen from above, MACKIE gives an order to WAT DREARY.

MACKIE: *Tonight at two o'clock. In the Duke of Devonshire's stables. Bring a vicar with you. Furniture and fittings, the lot. I'm getting married at ten past two.*

WAT is flabbergasted, but MACKIE has already gone back down the steps and into the inn.[7]

WAT climbs the steps. He pauses a moment, peering furtively round in all directions. Then JIMMY, who has been unobtrusively patrolling the area round the tavern entrance, walks up to him. They have a whispered conversation. JIMMY nods and goes down the steps into the inn, while WAT quickly makes himself scarce. Loud music can still be heard from inside.

Scene 4. The Cuttlefish Hotel.

It is a typical London pub, clearly frequented by sailors, judging by the model ships hanging from the ceiling and the stuffed fish in cases round the walls. The decor is plushy, vulgar and Victorian — elaborate upholstered furniture, lots of copper knock-knacks, a portrait of Queen Victoria very much in evidence. In the middle is a small dance floor. The bar takes up the whole of one side of the room; the music is supplied by a band. The camera pans right round the room to show the clientele dancing, drinking or just sitting. They are all members of the lower middle classes — barge-owners, captains of small boats, plus a few tarts and shady-looking characters. WAT DREARY brushes past, giving whispered instructions. The drinks on sale are beer and whisky, and the dancing is highly decorous. The camera finally comes to rest on MACKIE and POLLY, who are dancing in the throng.[8] They gaze into each other's eyes, oblivious of what is going on around them. They continue dancing for a few seconds after all the other dancers have gone back to their seats, unaware that the music has stopped. MACKIE suddenly snaps out of it and they smile at each other as he leads the happy but dazed POLLY to the corner table where MRS PEACHUM is sitting. A waiter pours them out glasses of beer.[9]

In a close shot, POLLY settles herself slowly in her chair, her eyes still riveted on MACKIE, while MRS PEACHUM raises her glass to him. As MACKIE puts his glass to his lips, he notices someone at the bar. He slowly puts the glass down again and stares intently in that direction.

At the bar, CROOKFINGERED JACK is just raising his glass of whisky.[10] Feeling MACKIE's glance on him he instantly turns round and goes hesitantly over to MACKIE's table, his glass untouched. He is clearly embarrassed.

At MACKIE's table: JACK has come up and MACKIE whispers to him as he looks from MACKIE to the ladies. POLLY and MRS PEACHUM are sitting back in the corner out of earshot, busy with their beer.

MACKIE: *Two o'clock.*

JACK: *All right. We know all about it.*

MACKIE: *Make yourselves look spruce. Don't any of you come looking like that. After all, it's not just anybody who's getting married.*

The music begins again, gliding softly in a tango rhythm. MACKIE introduces JACK, who is trying to start on his drink, to the ladies.

MACKIE to MRS PEACHUM: *He's the best dancer in Soho.*

MRS PEACHUM is already getting to her feet; she takes JACK's arm as he looks first at MACKIE then at her, and reluctantly puts his glass down again. MACKIE has already danced off with POLLY. JACK throws one last glance at his beloved whisky as MRS PEACHUM nestles blissfully in his arms. They begin dancing near the table.[11]

The dancing couples are seen from the edge of the dance-floor, JACK and MRS PEACHUM and POLLY and MACKIE among them. MACKIE and POLLY move towards the camera and another couple, NED and his girl-friend, dance up to them. MACKIE speaks over POLLY's shoulder in a stage whisper as NED dances beside him.

MACKIE: *Tiger Brown must be invited to my wedding.*

NED still dancing: *The Chief of Police? He'll never come!*

MACKIE snapping at him imperiously: *Oh yes he will.* To POLLY, as they continue dancing: *I've arranged our wedding for two o'clock.*

POLLY: *Yes.*

The music continues as they dance off and the camera tracks in towards JACK and MRS PEACHUM. MRS PEACHUM has firmly taken possession of JACK, who is looking rather bashful.

POLLY and MACKIE dance past the bar, the camera panning with them from over the bar counter. MACKIE addresses MAT OF THE MINT.

MACKIE: *Don't forget the rugs. And a grandfather clock.*

He goes on dancing, looking at POLLY but speaking in such a way that MAT can't avoid hearing as well.

MACKIE: *A four-poster bed with a blue canopy.*

POLLY breathes her reply huskily, unable to tear her eyes from MACKIE's face.

POLLY: *Yes.*

The camera follows MACKIE as he goes on dancing.

MACKIE a shade more practical: *You've still got to have a wedding dress.*

POLLY whispering absent-mindedly: *Yes.*

MACKIE looks round; a lone dancer sidles up to him and he addresses him over his shoulder.

MACKIE: *Full bridal rig-out. Brocade.*[12]

He stops dancing and, with POLLY on his arm, disappears among the dancers.

MRS PEACHUM and JACK are seen dancing up to the table; JACK is clearly worn out. MRS PEACHUM sits down and pulls JACK down onto the bench beside her, in the corner. The camera tracks in on them. JACK is flushed, laughing unsteadily as he seizes his glass of whisky and makes to take a sip.

JACK: *I've always fancied the maturer type, ever since I was a kid.*

MRS PEACHUM moves very close to him, clutches his right hand so that he can't put the glass to his lips and gives an excited laugh.

MRS PEACHUM: *Yes.*

JACK has cooled down a bit now and doesn't really know what else to say; he struggles frantically to get at his whisky.

JACK: *You certainly know how to ginger a fellow up.*

MRS PEACHUM pushes JACK right into the corner, clutching his arm so violently that the whisky glass is in danger of falling.

MRS PEACHUM in great excitement: *Yes.*

JACK is virtually helpless. He's not really equal to the situation but he's doing his best to carry out MACKIE's orders, hesitating all the while between his thirst and his duty as a reluctant seducer.

JACK: *Wouldn't you like to . . .?*

MRS PEACHUM interrupts him, seizes hold of him and laughs immoderately.

MRS PEACHUM: *Yes.*

The glass of whisky finally drops from JACK's trembling hand and falls to the floor. There is the sound of breaking glass which continues into the next sequence. Fade out.

Scene 5. The window of a ladies' dress shop.

Fade in on the sound of breaking glass: the shop window has been shattered. In it there are various wax models arrayed in fashionable outfits; in the centre is a dummy wearing a wedding dress. Two men drag the dummy into the street, strip it and run off. The model is left standing in the street, stark naked. Fade out.

Scene 6. A furniture warehouse on the first floor of a department store.

Fade in; it is night. The large store room is crammed with beds, sofas, cupboards, tables etc. In the foreground are two elaborate double beds with canopies, one beside the other. In the darkness the STREET-SINGER's ballad is heard, being whistled from several different directions at once. Then we see the light of a strong torch as its owner gropes his way through the store room, leaping over various bits of furniture and finally coming to a halt by the first of the four-posters. The whistling continues. Into the beam of the torch comes the figure of a man — MAT OF THE MINT. He sits on the bed to test the springs — the bed bounces violently. A voice comes out of the darkness:

VOICE: *No good, Too much bounce.*

The torchbeam and the camera move onto the next bed. MAT lies down on it and it holds firm. The voice comes out of the darkness again.

VOICE: *All right.*

The beam and the camera tilt up from the bed to the canopy and the voice speaks again in a matter-of-fact tone.

VOICE: *Blue. O.K. Go on.*

Now the other burglars come into the beam of light from all directions at once and before you can say Jack Robinson the canopy's being taken down and the bed's being dismantled while the burglars softly but nonchalantly sing the words of the ballad.

(*Scene 7 cut.*)

Scene 8. Night scene by a small river.

There is a full moon shining down on a gloomy-looking refuse dump, with assorted pieces of junk interspersed with stunted trees. A patch of grass is covered with bits of waste paper. The first notes of the 'Love Duet' are heard as the camera shows POLLY putting the finishing touches to her *toilette* behind a twisted and broken bit of fencing. MACKIE meanwhile walks up and down in front of the fence, humming to himself. POLLY pushes aside several planks in the fence and comes through wearing the stolen wedding dress. The couple wander off over the rubbish, oblivious to everything, clinging closely to each other. They halt by a broken cart and lean against it, gazing up at the moon; their figures throw long shadows on the ground. They sing the 'Love Duet' while the camera tilts up to the sky and back down to the rubbish on the ground. The shadows fade as the song comes to an end.

Finally, the camera tilts up to the moon again just as it disappears behind a cloud. Fade out.

Scene 9. A narrow, crooked street in the City of London.

It is still night and the full moon emerges from behind the clouds and shines down over the rooftops. The camera tilts down from the moon onto the street. In the distance, a BEGGAR sits curled up beneath a lamp at the entrance to a drinking club, apparently asleep. Directly above him, on the other side of the street but nearer to the camera, JIMMY and WAT are climbing down a rope which is suspended from a window on the second floor. They are carrying a huge grandfather clock. JIMMY has now reached the bottom; WAT is still on the rope and hands JIMMY the clock, which he humps onto his back. At this very moment the clock begins to strike, emitting rumbling chimes accompanied by a carillon that shatters the silence of the night. The two burglars are appalled and very nearly drop the clock.

The BEGGAR is seen in close-up. He has a placard hanging on his chest announcing in capital letters that he is 'A DEAF MUTE FROM BIRTH'. But now he leaps up, startled out of his reverie by the clock's chiming.

BEGGAR bellowing: *Stop thief!*

The burglars, frightened out of their wits, glance towards the BEGGAR.

BEGGAR yelling, off: *Burglars!*

They drop the clock with a terrible crash and run for it.

We see them running away, pursued by the 'deaf-mute' BEGGAR, who is still shouting. People come rushing out from their homes. The thieves have now turned the corner and a POLICEMAN appears, coming in the other direction. He intercepts the BEGGAR as he rushes in pursuit.

The POLICEMAN seizes the BEGGAR, who is beside himself and shouting his head off. The local inhabitants gather round.

POLICEMAN haughtily, to the BEGGAR: *What are you yelling like that for? Who are you?*

BEGGAR pointing to his label in great indignation: *I'm the deaf-mute! Don't you know me, Officer? I saw it all. They'll have to give me the reward.*

POLICEMAN: *You'll get your reward, don't you worry! Come down to the station with me.*

Dissolve.

Scene 10. TIGER BROWN's *office.*

The POLICEMAN's last words mix into the roaring voice of TIGER BROWN, who is seen standing behind his desk.

TIGER BROWN: *The London Commissioner of Police will be hearing about you!*

He drums his fingers on the desk top in agitation. Before him stand the deaf-mute, who is under arrest and escorted by two policemen; behind them are a few more burly policemen, who stand like rocks as their chief's thundering washes over them. The camera tracks with BROWN as he comes out from behind his desk and walks along the ranks of policemen, spitting out his words at each of them in turn. Meanwhile the BEGGAR follows the roaring BROWN with his eyes, revolving on his own axis as the police chief passes behind him.

TIGER BROWN: *It's not for nothing I'm called Tiger Brown. Ten break-ins a day and yet you lot still doze away while the bandits snatch the sheets from under your backsides!*[18]

During this lecture BROWN has returned to his place behind the desk; he sinks down in utter exhaustion as he utters the last words. Then he catches sight of the deaf-mute, who is standing facing him.

Close-up of BROWN's face past the BEGGAR's head. It darkens and he starts shouting again.

TIGER BROWN: *What do you want now?*

The BEGGAR has resumed his 'deaf-mute' role. He pulls a little slate out of his pocket with a trembling hand and passes it across the desk to BROWN, plus a slate pencil, so that he can write his question down. At the same time he points at the label hanging round his neck.

BROWN, in close-up, looks momentarily perplexed; he glances from the label to the BEGGAR, then flies into a rage again, while the BEGGAR continues to point at his invalid's card as if to appease him. As BROWN is looking helplessly from the BEGGAR to the policemen, the POLICEMAN who arrested the BEGGAR bends down and tries to explain things to his chief.

POLICEMAN: *. . . but the man definitely isn't . . .*

BROWN pulls himself together and roars at the POLICEMAN.

BROWN: *You just shut up!*

He leans over the table and silently, but with particularly clear lip-movements, tries to get his question across to the deaf-mute. The BEGGAR doesn't look happy at this and begins to gesticulate right under BROWN's nose, using sign-language. BROWN retreats in alarm and the BEGGAR snatches up his slate, scrawls his message on it at top speed and hands it to him. BROWN reads it.

From above, we see BROWN's hands holding the slate. The text reads: 'I saw it all. It was Mackie Messer's gang. Please give me the reward.' BROWN's hands fling the slate aside. He takes a writing pad, tears a sheet out of it and writes: 'Reward for giving information. One pound.' Just as he is signing it, another hand is thrust into the picture. It pushes a printed visiting card onto BROWN's desk, which carries the pencilled message 'From the Captain' in ill-formed capital letters. For a second BROWN's hands hold both bits of paper. Then the fist clutching the visiting card crashes down onto the desk and BROWN begins to roar again.

BROWN: *What sort of a filthy joke is this?*

The trembling BEGGAR, who is staring as if hypnotized at the voucher for his reward, surreptitiously tries to fish the bit of paper off the desk. The policemen standing near look tense and harassed. Next to BROWN stands the OFFICIAL who handed him the visiting card.

BROWN bellowing: *Do you expect me to sit here all night? Get out!*

OFFICIAL trying to pacify BROWN: *Very good, sir. I'll chuck the fellow out right away.*

He turns to go, but before he gets to the door BROWN yells after him.

BROWN: *Show him in!* To the policemen: *Get out the lot of you!*

Meanwhile the BEGGAR has finally managed to slide the voucher for his reward off the desk. He and the policemen all make for the door and try to crowd through, but become tangled with MAT OF THE MINT, who is on his way in. Eventually one of the policemen grabs MAT by the collar and shoves him into the room. The door bangs shut. MAT remains by the door, looking round with a nonchalance he does not entirely feel.

Close-up of MAT at the door; BROWN walks over to him, gives him a severe look and moves his head in an inquiring gesture.

MAT, wavering between confidence and fear, delivers his message.

MAT OF THE MINT: *The Captain requests . . . He's getting married at 2 a.m. . . . at the Duke of Devonshire's . . . Two o'clock sharp in the stables, the Captain said — right on the dot.* He adds in a confidential tone: *If not, there'll be a real to-do.*

BROWN is clearly struggling with a welter of conflicting emotions; he tries to say something but can't get a sufficient grip on himself; he grinds his teeth, then looks as if he's about to burst into tears. The camera tracks with him as he wanders round the room in a state of great agitation, kicking at the furniture; he pounces on a bundle of documents and flings it into a corner.

At the door, MAT is getting more and more alarmed as he watches BROWN's towering rage. Behind him the door is opened by the OFFICIAL, who has come to see what the noise is all about. He sticks his head round.

OFFICIAL: *Shall I chuck him out?*

BROWN comes rushing into shot, kicks the door shut in the OFFICIAL's face and turns towards MAT; he goes so close to him that he blocks our view of him completely, almost squashing him against the door. Breathing heavily, he seems about to launch into a violent outburst — but in the end takes a deep breath and speaks in a resigned tone.

TIGER BROWN: *I'll come.*

MAT backs hastily away through the door without taking his eyes off BROWN. BROWN stares after him, then lets his head drop. Fade out.

Scene 11. On the rooftops of London.

The full moon is shining down on the roofs of a large block of houses. In the distance we can hear the STREET-SINGER's ballad being whistled softly. Over the ridge of a roof appears first the back of a large armchair, then a larger part of it.

A pair of hands push the chair over the ridge onto the roof. The camera tracks with them and then we see NED swinging himself along the roof. The whistling gets louder. NED prances perilously along the roof-ridge like a tightrope-walker, balancing the armchair. Suddenly a shot is heard from the street.

NED ducks, using the chair as a shield.
Cut to the street as seen from the rooftop. Policemen are firing their revolvers, people are rushing up from all directions and in no time the street is swarming.
Beyond the figures of the shooting policemen, the tiny figure of NED wriggles his way across the rooftops in a series of leaps, brandishing the chair like a trophy. Shots and screams can be heard.
Close on NED as he makes his way acrobatically over the rooftops, looking as if he is about to fall headlong at any moment. As the shots ring out he ducks behind the chair, using it as a shield. He is still whistling the ballad and stops only when a shot rings out, taking the tune up again immediately.
Close-up: a bullet rips a hole in the back of the chair.
NED takes a huge leap and disappears from sight. The notes of the ballad can be heard from somewhere far away.

Scene 12. The main hall in the Duke of Somerset's castle.
It is still night and there isn't much light, though the full moon is shining on the elaborate furnishings. A voice humming the ballad is carried over from the previous scene as the camera pans across the bound and gagged figures of the Duke's servants, who are spaced out around the room — propped against the walls or slumped on the ground in a variety of painful-looking postures. They are all in their night attire. The camera moves to a huge piano in the far corner. Several of the burglars are struggling to cart it away. Two of the legs have already been unscrewed, and the third is removed as we watch. The burglars hum the ballad as they work. Then the four of them hoist the piano onto their shoulders; a fifth steps up to it and, just as they are about to set off with their load, plays on it the last two notes of the song.

Scene 13. The outer wall of a large warehouse.
It is still night. A large open window on the third floor is seen from below. An enormous bundle of rags is pushed out from inside the room onto the windowsill and plunges down to the ground. It is immediately followed by a second bundle, then a third; this last bundle falls open and a large runner winds

down like a serpent from the third floor to the street. Two men run up and grab the end of the rug, stretching it taut.
The wall opposite, again shot from the street. Windows are flung open and figures in night attire gaze across at the warehouse.
We see the third floor of the warehouse again, from the first floor of the house opposite. The camera pans with the burglars as they swing themselves one at a time over the windowsill onto the carpet and then zoom down as if on a chute, bawling out the ballad as they do so.

Scene 14. A telegraph cable, stretched high above the street.
In the darkness a man works his way hand over hand along the cable, gripping a Venetian chandelier in his teeth. The glass tinkles in the rhythm of the ballad, taking up the song from the previous scene.

Scene 15. A street with the window of a large delicatessen.
It's midnight in Piccadilly; the traffic has stopped and the passers-by have gone home; a few night-birds are hurrying to their clubs and we can see prostitutes and men in evening dress. The shop-window is brightly-lit and full of enticing-looking delicacies. A van draws up unobtrusively, and the window is seen over its roof. Some men leap from the van and a stone is flung at the shop-window; there is an almighty crash and the sound of splintering glass.
Now seen from the van, the men start stripping the shop-window. Food and bottles fly in all directions; hams and tins of food are flung towards the van (i.e. towards the camera). Various passers-by rush up and a scuffle breaks out with the burglars using bottles, legs of ham etc, to beat their adversaries to the ground. Among the sounds of splintering, crashing, shrieking and the moans of the wounded can be heard the ballad which the burglars are bawling out at the tops of their voices like the ' Marseillaise '.
The burglars leap back into the van, which tears off, leaving behind it the empty window and, scattered on the pavement among the broken glass and debris, the victims of the Battle of Piccadilly. The camera moves rapidly in on the victims. The

face of one of them is smeared with jam, another is hidden behind a layer of caviar; a third is choking on a chicken leg that's been rammed down his throat to act as a gag. And all over the victims flows a miniature river of champagne from the broken bottles. Rapid fade out.

Scene 16. TIGER BROWN's *office.*
Fade in. All we can see is a file of papers on the desk, a hand holding it and a second hand leafing through the documents. The label on the front of the file reads ' Mackie Messer '. Sheet after sheet is flicked through and we scarcely have time to survey the long catalogue of crimes: two shopkeepers killed; breaking and entering; street hold-ups; murders; seduction; rape — and all these crimes were committed in a single month. Then come warrants for arrest, police orders, official minutes, and then suddenly in the middle of all these documents a large, yellowing photograph. The camera moves in and we see a picture of two solders riding on a gun-carriage; it moves in closer still and we recognize one of the faces as that of MACKIE, but the other one has been scratched out and cannot be identified. After a few moments one of the hands takes up a penknife and scrapes away at the face of the unrecognizable soldier, so energetically that it leaves a hole in the picture. Then the right hand snatches up the picture and thrusts it into a breast-pocket, as the camera tracks rapidly backwards to reveal TIGER BROWN. He pushes the photo down out of sight then rises from his chair, snatches up the bundle of documents and weighs it thoughtfully in his hand for a moment. He looks reflectively into the corner of the room, whence the camera now pans to show a large grate with a huge fire crackling away in it. BROWN reappears and the bundle of documents describes a broad arc as it flies through the air and into the fire.
BROWN's face is lit by the flickering flames as he watches the documents blazing away with a dreamy and contented look. It is the face of a man revelling in pleasant memories, happy in the knowledge that he has done his duty as a man and as an official. Slow fade-out.

Scene 17. A large disused stable at the Duke of Devonshire's.

Fade in. The door is flung open from the outside and in the moonlight we see the silhouettes of two of the burglars standing on the threshold; with revolvers and torches at the ready they jump down into the room.

First Burglar yelling: *Hello, anyone there? Hands up if you are!*

Second Burglar after a short pause: *Is anyone there?*

First Burglar: *Not a soul! We can celebrate our wedding here without any trouble.*

His companion turns towards the door and looks out into the street. A whistle signal is heard.

Scene 18. Open country in front of the stables.

They are long, barn-like buildings in the country on the outskirts of London and are surrounded by meadows and fields divided up by fences. Waggons laden with furniture are seen driving up to the gateway to the stables. The sound of wheels and the cracking of a whip echo through the silence of the night. The men jump out of the van and start unloading. Dissolve.

Scene 19. A London street.

Three waggons are driving rapidly past, one behind the other. Another two waggons emerge from a side street and join the procession. Dissolve.

Scene 20. A main road.

A long column of waggons is bowling along in the moonlight, joined at various intervals by other waggons pouring into the main road from various side roads. Soon the procession is heading rapidly towards its destination, the waggons travelling three abreast. Dissolve.

Scene 21. Inside the Duke of Devonshire's stables.

We look right through the stable to the open doors. There is a confused jumble of furniture, rugs, furnishings of one sort or another, and food. The stable is teeming with people feverishly arranging the furnishings, hanging curtains, fixing chandeliers to the ceiling or putting pieces of furniture in position, while more and more furniture is continually being carried through the gateway. There seems to be very little hope of ever bringing any order to this scene of chaos. The stable echoes with the sound of hammering, shouts, etc. Rapid dissolve . . . The stable is now fully furnished and has been transformed into an ultra-posh reception room. The door is closed and there is not a sound to be heard . . . All by himself in the centre of the room stands the helpless figure of the VICAR, a worthy fellow in a black frock-coat, a sort of missionary. He looks fearfully round the room, his hands clutching convulsively at his prayer-book.

The camera pans right round the room, following his gaze. As we catch glimpses of the splendid furnishings the burglars emerge from all corners of the stable, from alcoves and from behind folding screens and curtains. They are all in evening dress but unfortunately their subsequent behaviour hardly matches the elegance of their attire. They all gravitate towards a large cheval-mirror in one corner of the room to put the finishing touches to their *toilette.* On the way they give the VICAR a few words of encouragement; he looks nervously from one to the other, uncertain how to take their advances. One of them is stuffing the odds and ends from the pocket of his old suit into his dinner-jacket and in the process brandishes his revolver in the VICAR's face.

FIRST BURGLAR amiably: *Won't be long now, Reverend, and it'll all go off with a bang.*

A second BURGLAR claps the VICAR on the back in a friendly fashion.

SECOND BURGLAR: *The Captain'll be right pleased, Reverend, it's the happiest day of his life . . .*

Another, beaming, points to the furnishings.

THIRD BURGLAR: *A really first-class job, eh Reverend? Take a look at the stuff. It's all top quality . . .*

The camera tracks with the last speaker as he goes up to the mirror, which takes up a whole corner of the stable. It's a cheval-mirror with side-pieces, stolen from a tailor's workshop. As the burglars throng around it, helping each other to tie their bow-ties, we can see them reflected over and over again, their reflections grotesquely distorted.

Scene 22. Outside the stable.

The furniture-vans have disappeared, the gateway is shut and everything looks peaceful, as if nothing had happened. An open landau drives up and comes to a halt. MACKIE helps POLLY out and presses a note into the COACHMAN'S hand; the COACHMAN humbly thanks him and chases off lest the noble lord should repent of his generous tip. MACKIE offers his arm to POLLY and moves towards the door.

Scene 23. Inside the stable.

We see a table groaning under the weight of a wedding feast. Sofas, easy chairs, armchairs and even deckchairs are grouped round it, so that all the many guests can have somewhere to sit. Several of them are inspecting the table with a critical eye and tasting the different dishes. CROOKFINGERED JACK shoos them away from the table and pulls out his watch.

JACK solemnly: *Ten past two!*

As they all turn to look towards the door, JACK takes up a bottle of champagne and undoes the seal.

Scene 24. Outside the stables.

MACKIE, with POLLY on his arm, is about to ring the bell on the door. At that moment the champagne cork goes off with a loud report inside. MACKIE takes fright and draws his revolver. The door opens and we see into the stable, where the burglars are grouped in a semi-circle. They break into a resounding cheer as the orchestra plays a fanfare.

Scene 25. Inside the stable.

As the last two cheers ring out we move inside again. Seen past the assembled guests, the bride and bridegroom enter through the door. MACKIE takes no notice of the cheering and turns his attention exclusively to the furnishings. He walks towards a wall-cupboard next to the doorway.

MACKIE examines the cupboard critically, while POLLY stands at his side looking round her in fascination, but with apparent incomprehension.

MACKIE: *Trash!*

JACK comes into the picture and bows low.

JACK: *Congratulations! There were people on the first floor at 14*

Ginger Street so we had to smoke them out first.

The camera tracks with MACKIE and POLLY, leaving JACK behind. MACKIE stops in front of a sofa and examines it critically; just then ROBIN OF BAGSHOT comes up to him.

ROBIN: *Congratulations! A constable kicked the bucket down in the Strand.*

MACKIE continues his tour of inspection. When he gets to the piano WAT DREARY approaches.

WAT: *Congratulations! Only half an hour ago, ma'am, the piano belonged to the Duchess of Somerset.*

MACKIE: *A rosewood piano and a Renaissance sofa! It's inexcusable.*

He opens the piano, plays two notes with one finger, then lets out a yell of rage.

MACKIE: *It's out of tune!*

He slams the lid shut, and the camera tracks with him as he sets off rapidly towards the table. He is pulled up short by the splendid armchair, looks startled, bends over to get a better look, then glances up reproachfully. NED appears in the frame, an anxious expression on his face.

NED: *Congratulations.*

MACKIE motions scornfully to the chair with his cane.

Close-up: the tip of the cane digs into the bullet-torn fabric of the chair.

NED sounding distressed, off: *I did what I could but the whole of Scotland Yard had turned out. Congratulations.*

MACKIE shrugs his shoulders, speechless. He goes over to the banquet, notices something on the food and bends over to look more closely.

Close-up of a dish of egg-mayonnaise. There are splinters of glass in it; MACKIE picks one up between two fingers and raises it in the air.

We see MACKIE holding up the tiny splinter of glass; his expression is withering but he maintains a scornful silence. The burglars look very upset. JIMMY steps forward, removes the bit of glass from between MACKIE's fingers and tries to smooth things over.

JIMMY: *The eggs are from Selfridge's. There should have been a vat full of pâté foie gras as well, but . . .*

MACKIE cutting in scornfully: *From Selfridge's eh? And what about the splinters?*

JIMMY: *They're from Selfridge's too. Fourteen people rather fell by the wayside, but I don't think it's anything serious. Congratulations.*

MACKIE looks past him, at a loss for words; his expression is one of real consternation. (Throughout this scene POLLY has been hanging onto his arm, uttering not a word but merely looking at him rapturously whenever he says something.)

MACKIE: *And the clock? There's no grandfather clock!*

JIMMY pacifying him: *It's sure to arrive sooner or later.*

MACKIE: *My wife is very upset. You've really let us down!*

The burglars, who are still standing round in a semi-circle, turn and point proudly to the back of the stable.

BURGLARS shouting: *Reverend!*

The VICAR is standing bewildered in a far corner of the room. He looks lost and helpless, but comes hesitantly forward in answer to their shouts. The bride and groom come into shot.

MACKIE: *This, Reverend, is Miss Peachum, who loves me so much that she has followed me and wishes to share the rest of my life.*

As he introduces POLLY, we cut to a close shot of the three of them. The VICAR bows low to POLLY, then leafs through his prayer-book and begins to read the marriage service. We hear MACKIE's and POLLY's responses.

The camera now pans over the faces of the listening burglars as they follow the ceremony; they look very moved and solemn. The ceremony ends and the VICAR quickly joins the couple's hands. The burglars hurry forward from all sides, thronging round MACKIE and POLLY, almost knocking over the VICAR in their haste. Finally, JACK thrusts the others aside and takes up his position before MACKIE.

JACK: *Please allow us, Captain, on this happiest day of your life, in the spring-time of your career, I mean to say at this turning point . . .*

MACKIE interrupts him because he has just noticed that the VICAR is taking advantage of the general excitement to slip past the guests and out through the door.

MACKIE: *Come, Reverend, won't you honour us with your presence on this special day?*

Close-up of the VICAR, who is already at the door.

VICAR: *Thank you, thank you, but I must hurry away to a christen-*

ing.

NED off: *We'll soon be needing you for one of those too!*

While he is speaking the VICAR makes good his escape. MACKIE reprimands NED.

MACKIE severely: *Shut your trap. We'll have none of your dirty jokes in the presence of a lady!*[14]

The orchestra sounds a fanfare and the guests rush towards the banquet. They begin to eat and drink greedily, while the orchestra plays.

A series of quick close-ups shows the guests eating greedily, stuffing caviar into their mouths with their knives, dipping their fingers into the bowls, with gravy running down their chins etc. There is a chorus of lip-smacking and munching over the music.

MACKIE is seated beside POLLY, eating nothing and surveying the whole banquet disapprovingly.

MACKIE: *I didn't want to start on the eating yet. We could have done with a bit of entertainment before you all rush to the trough. Other people always manage something of the sort on days like this.*[15]

JACK: *Such as what?*

MACKIE: *Well, why not sing a song to brighten the day up a bit? Do you want it to be just the same old wretched, gloomy day as ever?*

POLLY looks round in surprise, then glances anxiously at MACKIE as he continues to stare grimly at the company.

POLLY: *Well, gentlemen, if none of you wants to perform, I'll do my best to sing a little something myself.*

Everyone cheers and the orchestra strikes up.

The table is hastily pulled away from in front of POLLY; the rest of the furniture is also shoved aside.

Dissolve to a high shot over the guests seated around the walls to the large empty space in the middle of the room, where POLLY stands alone, looking small and lost. The orchestra plays 'Pirate Jenny' and POLLY sings.[16] There is applause and laughter as she comes to the end of the song.

Suddenly ROBIN rushes in through the door, shouting over the applause:

ROBIN: *Hey, Captain! The rozzers! It's the Chief of Police himself.*

There is a deathly silence.

Shot from the door, the burglars all scuttle out of sight behind the furniture and screens. MACKIE remains standing beside POLLY, who looks round in consternation.

BROWN enters the stable and looks round. He is not in uniform.

MACKIE goes over to him and shakes him by the hand.

MACKIE: *Hello Jack!*

BROWN: *Hello Mack! I haven't got much time so I'll have to be going shortly. I'm on night duty. Did it absolutely* have *to be someone else's stable? Yet another break-in!*

The camera tracks with MACKIE as he leads BROWN along by the arm.

MACKIE: *But Jack, it's so convenient. I'm so glad you've come to join in your old friend Mackie's wedding celebrations.*

They have now come up to where POLLY is standing.

MACKIE: *May I introduce my wife, née Peachum? Polly, this is Tiger Brown, London's Chief of Police, the pillar of the Old Bailey, isn't that right, old boy?*

Cut to a high spot of the men grouped round the walls. While MACKIE goes on speaking, the burglars come shyly and cautiously out from their hiding-places. MACKIE makes a sweeping gesture.

MACKIE: *My Polly, and my men!*

BROWN interrupting: *Don't forget I'm here in a private capacity, Mack!*

MACKIE: *So are we, so are we . . .*

As he goes on speaking, BROWN bows to POLLY, kisses her hand and talks to her in an undertone.

MACKIE: *Gentlemen, you see in your midst today a man who has been placed far above his fellow men by the king's inscrutable decree and yet has still remained my friend, through all life's trials and tribulations and so on.*

MACKIE puts an arm round BROWN.

MACKIE: *Do you remember, Jack, how we served side by side in the Army in India?*

While MACKIE is asking this question BROWN looks with interest at the rug on which he's standing. MACKIE has followed his gaze.

MACKIE aside: *Genuine Shiraz.*

BROWN: *From the Oriental Carpet Company.*

MACKIE: *Yes, that's where we always get them. You see, Jack, I had to have you here today; I hope it's not too awkward for you, in your position.*

BROWN: *You know very well I can't turn you down, Mack.*

He hands him the photograph from his pocket. MACKIE shows it to POLLY, looking happy and moved.

The photo, in close-up, is seen past MACKIE's and POLLY's heads.

CROOKFINGERED JACK now approaches the group with a huge camera, simulating an elegant walk.

JACK: *And now a nice big smile!*

He sets the camera up. BROWN rapidly shakes hands with MACKIE and POLLY and speaks in a horrified whisper.

BROWN: *I really must go . . .*

The camera tracks with him as he rushes over to the door. MACKIE hurries after him and asks:

MACKIE softly: *Have they got anything against me at Scotland Yard?*[17]

BROWN equally softly: *They haven't got the tiniest thing against you at Scotland Yard. I've seen to that. Good night.*

While this short dialogue is going on — BROWN is already moving out through the door as he says the last words — JACK's voice rings out.

JACK off: *And now for the big surprise!*

We see JACK as he pulls aside the curtain.

MACKIE off: *What's going on?*

Amid general oohs and aahs, JACK unveils the four-poster. MACKIE comes into shot with POLLY on his arm. MAT OF THE MINT steps up to the bed from the other side and points at the canopy.

MAT: *Sky blue.*

A VOICE off: *Now for the photograph.*

All the burglars converge on the bed, grouping themselves round POLLY and MACKIE for the photograph.

The group are seen past the photographer. Someone tries to push to the front.

TWO VOICES off: *Stop! We're here too!*

JIMMY and WAT DREARY rush breathlessly into shot, still wearing their ragged clothing; they pose right in the front, next to POLLY and MACKIE, thrusting the others aside.

MACKIE looks severe.

MACKIE: *What about the clock? Where's the grandfather clock?*

The two of them seem to shrink under his gaze, and slink away to the side; the camera pans with them as the other burglars push them further and further towards the end of the row.

VOICES off, from the other end of the row: *Are we still in the picture?*

The guests all stand in fixed poses, seen past the PHOTOGRAPHER again.

PHOTOGRAPHER: *Lights out!*

The lights go out; voices are heard in the darkness.

PHOTOGRAPHER: *Hold it!*

NED: *How marvellous! It's a shame the bride's parents aren't here.*

MACKIE severely: *And the grandfather clock.*

JIMMY replies soothingly from the end of the row.

JIMMY: *We'll get it here yet.*

PHOTOGRAPHER: *A nice smile, please.*

As the flash flares we see the middle part of the group, with MACKIE and POLLY posing formally in the centre. As the flash goes out, the picture fades.

During the fade we hear the voice of the STREET-SINGER, which seems almost unnaturally loud. He calls out like a town crier.

STREET-SINGER off: *You have been watching the love and marriage of Polly Peachum . . . And now I'm going to show you the strength of the Beggar King!*

As he finishes his speech, we fade into the next scene.

Scene 26. Outside a church.

The façade of the church is seen from below, with a flight of steps leading up to the doorway; the bells are ringing and the sound of an organ can be heard from inside the church on this grey morning. A pair of beggars are standing on the steps as the members of the congregation, mostly women, walk past them into the church. The church-goers are all coming from the same direction, and none of them gives the beggars anything. One of the beggars is blind, the other lame, and they are making a great show of their infirmities, in a particularly blatant way.

Seen closer now, they hold a whispered consultation. The BLIND BEGGAR gives his colleague a stealthy wink as if to enquire why it should be that not a single charitable donation is finding its way into their outstretched hands today. They turn to the edge of the steps and peer in the direction from which the members of the congregation are coming.

From the beggars' point of view, the camera pans over the steps and the parapet until it comes to the street along which the church-goers are approaching. It finally holds on a third beggar in the distance, who has his back to us and is being given some money by a passer-by. A second passer-by follows suit.

The other two beggars exchange comments in a rapid whisper. Then, as if nothing had happened and they had given up hope of receiving any alms, they get ready to set off for home. The camera tracks with them as they grope their way slowly and carefully down the steps, the lame one leading the blind one, a pair of pathetic-looking wrecks.

Resume on the street leading to the church, where the third beggar — FILCH — can be seen. The other beggars, SAM and HONEY, stumble haltingly past. When they come up to FILCH, the blind beggar, still hanging onto the lame one's arm, walks straight into him, making him step backwards a few paces. The two of them push relentlessly forward, the lame beggar barring FILCH's path with a threatening gesture. FILCH is visibly alarmed and shrinks back step by step until all three of them have progressed as far as the nearest street-corner.

At this moment the lame one — SAM — leaps forward, so that FILCH finds himself surrounded. SAM seizes his crutch and brandishes it at FILCH like a cudgel, while HONEY lands him such a blow that he staggers back against the wall.

HONEY in a rapid whisper: *How come you're pestering the passers-by, you swine? Have you got a licence?*

FILCH trembling: *Please, gentlemen, I'm broke. It's the wages of sin . . .*

SAM dealing him another blow: *So this small fry comes here and think's he's only got to stick out his paws and he'll land himself a nice steak.*

FILCH is doing his best to stammer out an excuse.

FILCH: *The thing is, gentlemen, I've been unlucky ever since I was a kid. My mother was an alcoholic so I sank deeper and deeper into the mire of the big city. And now you see me . . .*

HONEY interrupts him and gives him another bang on the head with his crutch, so hard that the crutch breaks.

HONEY: *We see all right. And if you let yourself be seen again you'll get it in the neck.*

As HONEY speaks, FILCH sinks to the ground beneath the blows, trying desperately to protect his head. The two beggars stop hitting him and HONEY presses a card into his hand. FILCH takes it nervously. But then the beggars transform themselves back into helpless cripples with lightning speed and disappear round the corner.

FILCH, in close-up, picks himself up awkwardly. He's been so badly beaten up that he can scarcely stand. He looks in amazement at the card the beggars have pressed into his hand, turns it over and over and then reads it.

We see the card in FILCH's hand, which reads: 'Jonathan Jeremiah Peachum & Co. — The Beggar's Friend — Beggar's outfits and licences — 83 Shaftesbury Avenue.' Dissolve. (The sounds of the church-bells and the organ music that have been audible at intervals throughout this scene mix into the 'Morning Anthem' which accompanies the following scenes.)

Scene 27. PEACHUM'S *shop.*

We see the large signboard outside the shop which reads: 'Give and thou shalt be given. Shut not your ears to misery.' Dissolve.

Scene 28. Inside PEACHUM'S *shop.*

There is a large office with cubicles for changing in, and in the centre stands a double desk at which PEACHUM is seated, totally absorbed in his huge ledgers. The place is full of crutches, invalid chairs and old clothes hanging up, as in a second-hand clothes shop. Placards inscribed with biblical sayings are very much in evidence. On one side of the desk there is a large chest with five wax dummies representing the basic types of human wretchedness and on the other side a modern strong-box or safe. In the background we can see a wrought-iron staircase leading up to PEACHUM's apartment on the first floor. PEACHUM sings the 'Morning Anthem.'[18]

Scene 29. POLLY's *room.*

It is a typical teenage girl's room, in the kitsch style of the turn of the century, with little lace mats all over the place, photographs arranged in a fan on the wall, pious texts, a guardian angel above the bed and above that a canopy with stuffed white doves. The last lines of PEACHUM's 'Morning Anthem' can still be heard wafting up from the shop below. The sequence opens with a shot of MRS PEACHUM opening the door and entering the room.

The camera pans slowly round the room from the door, eventually holding on the bed. It clearly hasn't been slept in, since POLLY's night things are all still laid out ready for the night. MRS PEACHUM stands in the doorway, too startled to say anything; she nervously wrings her hands and looks helplessly round.

PEACHUM off: *Mrs Peachum!*

MRS PEACHUM takes fright. She runs over to the bed and hurriedly rumples it to make it look as if it's been slept in.

Scene 30. PEACHUM's *shop.*

PEACHUM is seen with the crumpled-looking figure of FILCH beside him, looking at a map of London.

PEACHUM sounding businesslike: *Anyone intending to practise the trade of the beggar in London needs a licence from Jonathan Jeremiah Peachum & Co.*

FILCH: *A few shillings stand between me and ruin . . . But with two shillings in hand . . .*

PEACHUM: *Twenty!*

FILCH looks unhappily round the shop and then points to a placard.

Close-up of the placard; it bears the text: 'Shut not your ears to misery!'

FILCH off: *Ten!*

PEACHUM points to another placard behind him.

The text reads: 'Give and thou shalt be given.'

PEACHUM off: *Twenty!*

PEACHUM brings the deal to a close.

PEACHUM: *And fifty per cent of your weekly takings!*

FILCH sounding downcast: *All right.*

He fumbles about with his money and counts it out onto the desk while PEACHUM opens a ledger.

PEACHUM: *Name?*

FILCH: *Charles Filch.*

PEACHUM writes it down.

PEACHUM at the top of his voice: *Mrs Peachum!*

We see the staircase, past PEACHUM and FILCH at the desk. MRS PEACHUM appears on the stairs; as she comes down a whining voice is heard from the doorway.

BEGGAR off: *Greetings and peace be with you!*

A BEGGAR with a wooden leg comes into shot and walks up to the desk to stand beside FILCH.

BEGGAR: *I must complain most vehemently. This stump is just no good.* He lays his wooden leg down on the desk. *It's a really shoddy piece of work and I'm not going to throw my money away on it.*

PEACHUM is furious and shoves both the BEGGAR and his wooden leg away from the desk.

PEACHUM: *Wait there!*

MRS PEACHUM finishes coming down the stairs and walks over to stand beside her husband at the desk. As she does so the doorbell jangles several times and we hear a rapid succession of greetings from the people who come in, such as 'Good day to you' and 'Praise the Lord'.

We look past PEACHUM to FILCH and the BEGGAR with the wooden leg, who are still by the desk. HONEY and a fourth BEGGAR now join them. HONEY walks very warily over to the desk and hands his broken crutch over the top of it to PEACHUM. PEACHUM doesn't look up from his book.

PEACHUM snapping at HONEY: *Wait there!* To MRS PEACHUM, pointing towards FILCH: *Number 314, Baker Street District, outfit number C.*

MRS PEACHUM moves away, motioning FILCH to follow her. But FILCH has recognized HONEY and has been observing him in obvious fury for some time. HONEY has recognised him too, and as he makes to follow MRS PEACHUM, he grabs him by the sleeve.

HONEY to PEACHUM: *This witness here can confirm that it wasn't my fault that my crutch got broken.*

PEACHUM to HONEY growling: *Clause No. 12: The firm cannot be held responsible for damage to items of equipment.*

FILCH tries to tear himself away from HONEY's grasp, but HONEY won't let go and starts spluttering.

HONEY: *But . . . it wasn't my fault!*

PEACHUM: *Shut up!*

HONEY beside himself with fury: *He got his thrashing in accordance with the statutes . . . it was in the service of the Organisation . . . and now I've got to pay for a new crutch?!*

PEACHUM slams his fist down on the table-top.

PEACHUM to FILCH: *Go and get changed!* To HONEY: *Wait there!*

FILCH slips hurriedly out of shot. The fourth BEGGAR pushes his way forward to hand PEACHUM his membership card.[19]

FOURTH BEGGAR: *Here's my takings!*

He lays the card and the money down on the desk.

PEACHUM goes over to the safe, takes out a smaller cash-box and stows the money away in it. MRS PEACHUM is standing nearby, busy hunting among the clothes on hangers to find an outfit that will fit FILCH. FILCH watches her with interest, then takes a look round and walks over to the wax dummies to get a better look.

We see the dummies past FILCH. He stops in front of a dummy wearing a large label marked with the letter C and looks round enquiringly.

FILCH pointing to the dummy: *What's that?*

PEACHUM, who is now back at his desk, interrupts his work to look up.

PEACHUM to FILCH: *Those are the five basic types of misery most likely to touch the human heart. The sight of such wretchedness puts people in that unnatural frame of mind in which they are actually prepared to part with their money!*

MRS PEACHUM brings FILCH his ragged outfit on a coat-hanger.

MRS PEACHUM to FILCH: *Get undressed and put this on, but look after it.*

FILCH looks uncomprehendingly from the rags to the dummy labelled C and then to PEACHUM and MRS PEACHUM (the dummy does in fact look very like FILCH); he then looks down at himself.

FILCH: *And what happens to my own things?*

PEACHUM: *They become the firm's property! Outfit A: Young man who's seen better days or who never thought it would come to this.*

FILCH: *Ah, I see. You're going to use them again, are you? Why can't I do the 'better days' bit?*

PEACHUM: *Because nobody ever believes in real misery, my son!*

The camera now shows the queue of beggars (there are about five of them) who have been lining up in front of the desk during this scene. PEACHUM picks up the wooden leg, which is still lying there, and examines it with a critical eye.

PEACHUM: *What are you after? It's no worse than any other stump.*

BEGGAR: *In that case why don't I earn as much as all the others?*

THE BEGGARS grumbling: *It's rubbish!*

ANOTHER BEGGAR: *You might as well hack off your own leg!*

ANOTHER BEGGAR: *It's nothing but trash!*

PEACHUM trying to appease them: *Well, what do you expect? I can't help it if people have got hearts of stone! Here's another stump for you if that one's not good enough!*

FIRST BEGGAR: *All right, Mr Peachum, that'll do me better.*

He leaves the shop and the others move forward.

Meanwhile, MRS PEACHUM pushes FILCH into one of the changing cubicles in the background.

MRS PEACHUM: *Get a move on, young fellow, I'm not going to go on holding your trousers till Christmas!*

Resume on PEACHUM, busy with his counting and surrounded by a group of beggars. The door-bell jangles loudly.

VOICE off: *You can't do that to me!*

PEACHUM and the beggars look over towards the door. A BLIND BEGGAR walks rapidly into shot, pushes the other beggars aside and steps firmly up to PEACHUM. He raises his eye-shield in great indignation and brandishes his stick in PEACHUM's face. PEACHUM wards it off with both hands.

BLIND BEGGAR: *Is that what you call a rig-out? I paid for a brand new costume!*

PEACHUM finally losing patience: *Mrs Peachum! Tell Polly to come here! Polly!*

He looks up the stairs, expecting POLLY to appear.

PEACHUM: *Polly! How often have I told you that a gentleman doesn't wear filthy clothing next to his skin!*

As he says these last words he walks over to the staircase and starts to go up. The beggars watch him. When he is half way up the stairs he turns round.

PEACHUM to the beggars: *Just a second!*

MRS PEACHUM rushes after him and hurries up the stairs, puffing and panting.

PEACHUM: *Polly!*

The two of them disappear. We can half hear PEACHUM shouting in the room on the floor above.[20]

PEACHUM off: *. . . Hasn't been home all night?!*

The camera tilts down from the top to the bottom of the stairs, where the beggars are crowding round to listen, in great curiosity. They all have their backs to the doorway. Fragments of the quarrel come floating down.

MRS PEACHUM: *. . . in the Cuttlefish . . .*

There is muffled swearing, then PEACHUM's voice is heard again.

PEACHUM: *And you didn't even ask what the fellow's name was?*

MRS PEACHUM tearfully: *. . . white kid gloves . . .*

PEACHUM: *. . . and a cane with an ivory handle? Your Captain, as you call him . . .*

A muffled shout is heard from the doorway.

VOICE off: *Hands up!*

The beggars huddle together in terror, their hands above their heads; they all turn towards the door.

Shot of the sight that greets them in the doorway. Two of the burglars (the two that tried unsuccessfully to steal the clock) cover the beggars with their revolvers. The camera tracks with them as they walk over to the beggars; one continues to keep them covered while the other rushes over to the safe, flings it open (PEACHUM has left the key in the lock) and takes out the cash-box. Then the two of them retreat towards the door, walking backwards, revolvers at the ready. Meanwhile, bits of the quarrel continue to waft down from upstairs.

PEACHUM agitated: *And spats? And patent-leather shoes . . .? And a scar . . .?*

MRS PEACHUM tearfully: *Yes . . . on his neck.*

PEACHUM his voice cracking: *Mackie Messer!*

Just at this moment the bandits disappear through the door, which bangs shut so that the bell jangles.

We see the beggars' hands, which are still above their heads, and beyond them the top of the staircase. PEACHUM now appears on the stairs, in a state of great agitation; MRS PEACHUM follows him. He stops short and leans over the bannisters, dumbfounded, looking at the beggars.

MRS PEACHUM weeping: *Oh my Gawd! Mackie Messer! Lord Jesus save us!*

PEACHUM hurries down the stairs and the camera moves down with him; when he gets to the bottom he starts bellowing at the beggars, who are still facing the door, motionless, hands above their heads.

PEACHUM: *What's the matter with you?*

The beggars come to and begin to explain confusedly.

THE BEGGARS simultaneously: *Robbery! Mackie Messer! The safe!*

The camera tracks with PEACHUM as he forces his way through the crowd of beggars. He stands stock still in front of the now-empty safe, at a loss for words. The beggars stick close behind him, whispering in an undertone.

FILCH, in close-up, emerges from the cubicle in his new outfit. He looks at himself despairingly, shaking his head; then he walks past the beggars, who have their backs to him and are still gazing at the safe, past PEACHUM, who is rummaging about inside it, and up to the mirror. He looks at his reflection. He is close to tears as he takes off his cap and holds it out as if he were begging. He seems to be going through a dress rehearsal for his new career.

FILCH: *My mother was a drunkard, my father a . . .*

The doorbell jangles and we hear the cheerful humming of a happy man.

Cut to show the DEAF-MUTE as he comes cheerfully into the shop. FILCH looks at him in amazement; some of the beggars turn round as he marches over to the desk, holding himself exaggeratedly erect. He salutes, then makes his triumphant announcement.

DEAF-MUTE triumphantly: *Mr Peachum, one pound for denouncing Mackie Messer! Here's your fifty per cent!*

PEACHUM, apparently seized by an attack of hysteria, pounces on the DEAF-MUTE, who looks at him uncomprehendingly.

PEACHUM bawling: *Ten shillings! For a paltry ten shillings you've set the whole gang at my throat!* He turns to the other beggars. *Get out, the lot of you!*

FILCH and all the other beggars retreat nervously to the doorway in the face of PEACHUM's fury.

Scene 31. The street outside PEACHUM's *shop.*

In a shot towards the door of the shop, POLLY drives up in an open cab, wearing her wedding dress. She climbs out of the cab just as the beggars back hastily out of the shop, then walks up to the door.

As she goes to open the door, in a close shot, PEACHUM's face peers through the glass; he looks at his daughter with a mixture of bewilderment and fury. POLLY presses down the latch and then enters. The beggars gather curiously round the glass door and peer through into the room.

Scene 32. Inside PEACHUM's *shop.*

As the bell rings, we look in through the glass door from the beggars' point of view. POLLY is standing happily in the middle of the room, while MRS PEACHUM is tearing her hair and PEACHUM is waving both fists excitedly at POLLY. We get the impression of a heated scene, but we cannot hear what is being said until a shout comes from PEACHUM.

PEACHUM: *Thieves' slut!*

MRS PEACHUM sinks onto a chair in a dead faint. PEACHUM fetches a bottle of brandy to revive her and she eventually comes to. PEACHUM looks up, catches sight of the beggars the other side of the door and flies towards them in a fury.

Seen from inside, PEACHUM goes up to the door and angrily throws it open. The beggars take to their heels; he closes the door, turns and says heatedly:

PEACHUM: *If you were going to be so immoral as to get married at all, did it have to be a horse-thief and highwayman, of all people?*

MRS PEACHUM off: *First we deck her out with dresses and hats and gloves and parasols . . .*

Close-up of POLLY, who continues to smile happily as her parents shout at her. MRS PEACHUM continues:

MRS PEACHUM: *. . . and when she's cost as much as a ship in full rig, she throws herself onto the dungheap like a rotten cucumber.*

PEACHUM: *You'll get a divorce!*

POLLY: *But I love him!*

MRS PEACHUM: *I'll tan your backside.*

POLLY: *That won't do any good. My love's greater than any hiding!*

PEACHUM: *One more word and I'll box your ears for you!*

POLLY: *Love is the most important thing in the world!*

The opening bars of the song 'Barbara' are heard. POLLY skips up the stairs to her room while her parents gaze after her, speechless with fury.

Scene 33. POLLY'S *room.*

POLLY comes in, walks over to the mirror and starts to undress, singing the first verse of 'Barbara' as she does so.

When she is down to her petticoat the camera moves with her to the sofa; she kneels down on it and sings the second verse as she examines the photographs, which are arranged in a fan shape above.

We see the photos in close-up, over POLLY's head. Then she stretches herself out on the sofa, puts her arms behind her head and sings the third verse. She lies there pensively for a moment, then suddenly leaps up decisively and starts to pack various odds and ends (keepsakes, trinkets etc) into a bag; she then throws dresses and blouses into a suitcase. The final notes of the song are heard.

Scene 34. PEACHUM'S *shop.*

On the lowest landing of the staircase, we see the heads of POLLY'S parents as they discuss the situation, whispering heatedly. A barrel organ is playing off.

PEACHUM: *. . . notify the Chief of Police. If only they can catch him.*

MRS PEACHUM: *You leave that to me.*

POLLY appears on the top landing. She is still in her petticoat and is clutching a dressing gown, a comb, a brush and a powder-puff. She listens to what is being said downstairs.

MRS PEACHUM: *He's sure to be hiding with his gang. If he's got a date with one of his girls in a couple of hours he'll be well and truly sunk.*

The parents are seen from above, with POLLY listening to them in the foreground.

PEACHUM: *Before the week's out they'll be taking him to the gallows, just as he deserves. I'm going to the Chief of Police.*

MRS PEACHUM: *And I'm going to his whores in Turnbridge.*

The parents grab their hats and coats and dash off; the door slams.[21]

Close-up of POLLY's face from below; her expression is one of utter dismay and full of conflicting emotions. As if to herself, she begins to sing the first lines of the First Finale (' Is it a lot I'm asking?'), apparently trying to justify herself in her own eyes.

Scene 35. The STREET-SINGER *with little girl and woman.*

The location is indefinite. To the accompaniment of a barrel organ, the little girl takes up POLLY's words (' Is it a lot she's asking?' etc). This is followed by an abbreviated version of the First Finale. Fade out.

Scene 36. A store-room in the Duke of Devonshire's stables.

We are in a room partitioned off from the main stable, glimpses of which (the four-poster bed etc) can be seen behind a curtain. The room looks distinctly like an office, with bookshelves, a typewriter and a huge armchair, though the remainder of the furniture contrasts strangely with this office equipment. The shelves carry a card index and there are some fat ledgers lying on the table next to the typewriter. MACKIE is lolling back in the armchair, while CROOKFINGERED JACK is struggling painfully to master the typewriter, laboriously picking out the letters. We can hear the machine clattering away as MACKIE dictates.

MACKIE: *Item number 7: Only strong rooms are to be burgled, after Oak Street. Nothing but cash is to be taken. No securities.* In an aside to JACK: *We must stick to safe stuff. We won't have anything to do with stock-market fiddles.*

MACKIE is seen past JACK. He is leaning arrogantly back in his chair and issuing his orders like a general.

MACKIE: *Item number 8: Wat Dreary will merely be the lookout man.* To Jack: *He's an untrustworthy scoundrel, always putting money into his own pocket . . . No need to write that down.* He continues his dictation. *Jimmy No. 2 is in charge of the explosives squad.* To Jack: *If he gets done in it'll be no loss to us. He's not on a retainer any more.*

Jack is seen past Mackie. He is laughing so much that he has to clutch his sides.

Mackie barking at Jack: *Your retainer's no laughing matter, either.* He leafs through a notebook. *One, two, three, four, five gold watches — that's not much for a month's work, my friend!*

Jack chokes back his laughter, assumes a solemn and gloomy expression and looks submissively at Mackie as he waits for him to continue dictating.

Mackie dictates and Jack takes it down.

Mackie: *Item number 9: The break-in must be effected by 8.30.* Aside: *That's when the big fireworks will be held as part of the Coronation celebrations. All the doormen and caretakers will be watching the display.*

Jack: *And all the nobs'll be roaring drunk.*

Polly comes into the room looking very upset.

Polly: *Mack! Mack! Don't be afraid!*

Mackie: *What's up? What's the matter with you?*

Polly comes right up to him and puts her arm imploringly round his shoulders.

Polly: *You must disappear for a while, and fast! You must start packing straight away.*

Mackie draws her to him.

Mackie: *What nonsense! Come here, Polly . . .*

Jack discreetly withdraws, looking thoroughly put out.

Close shot of Polly seated on Mackie's lap.

Polly very agitated, to Mackie: *I'm so frightened, Mac. They kept talking about hanging.*

Mackie annoyed: *I don't believe a word of it. They've got absolutely nothing on me at Scotland Yard.*

Polly: *They may not have yesterday, but suddenly there's an awful lot against you today.*

Mackie: *I can rely on Brown. He's my best friend.*

Polly rapidly, the words tumbling out: *I went to see Brown. And so did my father. And they arranged it between them that they were going to have you arrested. Brown stuck up for you but my father made some terrible threats and he gave in.*

MACKIE losing his assurance, but still incredulous: *What sort of threats did Peachum make?*

POLLY: *I don't know. But Brown stopped me in the corridor and said he couldn't do any more for you now.*

She goes to embrace him, weeping as she does so.

POLLY: *Oh, Mack . . .*

MACKIE leaps up, suddenly transformed into a trembling heap of misery. The camera tracks back a little as he stares at POLLY wordlessly, like a ghost. POLLY is so alarmed by MACKIE's alarm that she too stands stock still and stares at him aghast. MACKIE is seen past POLLY as he suddenly bursts out:

MACKIE: *Your father . . .! That's all the thanks I get for marrying his daughter!*

POLLY looks at him wordlessly for a moment, then collapses sobbing into an armchair. MACKIE has suddenly got control of himself again. The camera tracks with him as he walks rapidly over to the curtain that separates the room from the stable and pulls it violently aside. JACK has been eavesdropping behind the curtain. He starts back.

MACKIE barking at JACK: *Come here, all of you!*

JACK turns and rushes off.

POLLY is seen in close-up with tears in her eyes. She looks up and her grief slowly gives way to total bewilderment. MACKIE comes back and walks thoughtfully past her, taking no notice of her. She gazes fixedly at him, her face a picture of conflicting emotions but chiefly full of admiration and devoted love.

The burglars step out from behind the curtain one at a time; despite their nonchalant air they are obviously feeling awkward. POLLY looks from them to MACKIE, amazed at first, then calmer. MACKIE stands in the middle of the room and announces.

MACKIE: *I am unfortunately compelled to embark on a little trip.*

The burglars exchange glances of amazement.

MAT grumbling: *What, just before the Coronation? The Coronation without you'll be like soup without a spoon.*

JIMMY 2: *And what about our big bank job? You don't get Corona-*

tion jamborees every year! It's such a good opportunity . . .
MACKIE snarling at JIMMY 2: *Shut your trap.*

In a closer shot, MACKIE walks over to POLLY, who looks at him with a mixture of amazement and love. He strikes a pose and announces:

MACKIE: *I'm handing over the running of the business to my wife while I'm away.*

POLLY involuntarily rises to her feet, still staring at MACKIE, clearly unable to grasp what he is saying but happy just to see him speak. The burglars give a suppressed titter. MACKIE flashes a look at them, then the camera tracks with him as he strides rapidly over to the burglars, who instinctively line up in a row. He paces along the row, looking at each one of them in turn; they each stand to attention.

Shot of the line-up of burglars. MACKIE has now got to the end of the row.

MACKIE addressing the burglars: *The national celebration . . . The Queen's Coronation . . . must be a matrix . . . I mean a turning point for our business.*

As he speaks the camera tracks in closer and closer to him.

MACKIE continuing his address: *Let's have no more of this petifogging rubbish! Highway robbery, pickpocketing and all that sort of stuff is a loathsome business . . . you still haven't brought the grandfather clock!*

He glances reprovingly at the other flank of the line-up.

The two burglars who attempted to steal the clock bow their heads in remorse, then camera pans across to POLLY, who is standing in front of the line-up but on the other flank from MACKIE. She still has eyes for him alone. Meanwhile MACKIE is still talking.

MACKIE: *With the money we have from the deposit bank — I mean the money that will be ours tomorrow, we must put our business on a new and broader footing.*

He is seen in close-up as he finishes his speech.

MACKIE: *Let's away from Soho! And into the City!*

The burglars cheer.

MACKIE: *You've got some very hard work ahead of you. From now on you take your orders from my wife.*

We see him walk quickly past the line-up to where POLLY is

standing; she moves forward to meet him. He gives her a quick pat, then, as she clings to him and makes as if to accompany him, he walks on, speaking to her over his shoulder.

MACKIE: *Farewell, my love. Keep your chin up and don't forget to wear make-up every day — that's very important, Polly!*

MACKIE and POLLY disappear behind the curtain. The line-up disperses. At first the burglars gaze blankly at each other for several seconds; then one of them gives a scornful laugh and the others join in, digging each other in the ribs as though to say 'A fine mess we're in now!'

Scene 37. The doorway of the stables.

POLLY and MACKIE stand in the open doorway outside, silhouetted against the street.

POLLY clinging on to MACKIE: *Oh, Mac! Don't tear my heart from my body! Stay with me!*

MACKIE: *I'm tearing my heart from my own body, since I must go away and nobody knows when I'll be back!*

POLLY: *Don't forget me, Mack, in those foreign cities!*

MACKIE: *Of course I shan't forget you, Polly. Give me a quick kiss.*

POLLY: *And Mack, promise me you won't ever look at other women? Don't go to Turnbridge, don't go with other women . . .!*

MACKIE: *But it's you I love, and you alone! At midnight I shall fetch my black horse from some stable or other and before you see the moon from your bedroom window I shall be riding over Highgate Marsh!*

POLLY weeping: *Farewell Mack!*

MACKIE: *Farewell Polly!*

He tears himself away from her and leaves.

MACKIE singing off: *Love endures or fades away, either here or elsewhere . . .*

The distant sound of bells can be heard.

POLLY helpless as a small child:

The Queen to London is wending her way
Where shall we be on Coronation Day . . .?

Scene 38. The room partitioned off from the stables.

The camera pans rapidly across the burglars who are lounging in groups around the room. Some are stretched out on the armchair, others on the table, CROOKFINGERED JACK is sitting on a pile of books; they are all puffing away at cigarettes, spitting on the floor, passing a bottle round. When the cat's away . . .

POLLY off: *I am taking over the command!*

The camera pans back across the groups of burglars as they react to POLLY's surprising command. One of them, possibly JACK, stares at her, his jaw dropping, and hesitantly hides the bottle of brandy, from which he was about to take a swig, in his pocket. Another BURGLAR in the second group, who has greeted POLLY's words with loud laughter, grows suddenly solemn and rises hesitantly to his feet, clearly called to order by the look on POLLY's face. A third BURGLAR, looking sullen and unwilling, but not daring to offer any resistance, straightens up and takes a last drag on his cigarette before stuffing it in his pocket.

The camera tracks with POLLY as she steps forcefully up to one of the burglars and looks him up and down with a critical eye; he stands almost timidly before her, holding himself stiffly. She reviews the whole line-up in the same way, and all the gang instinctively line up one behind the other, all of them looking stiff and awkward.

We look along the whole line-up from the opposite flank to where POLLY is standing. The burglars have dressed ranks as though they were on the parade-ground.

POLLY addressing the assembled ranks: *Now boys! I think our Captain can leave with an easy mind. We'll pull it off all right without him. Right boys?*

As she is speaking the camera tracks in towards her and holds when it comes to MAT. The others have been exchanging puzzled glances during POLLY's pep-talk, but MAT is still grumbling.

MAT OF THE MINT: *I haven't really got anything to say, but I don't know whether a woman, at a time like this . . .*

POLLY walks quickly up to him.

MAT weakening somewhat: *I didn't mean anything personal, ma'am.*

POLLY snapping at MAT: *You've certainly started off well, you swine! Of course you didn't mean anything personal, or these gentlemen would have shut your filthy trap for you. Right gentlemen?*[22]

The line-up is seen past POLLY. She looks up and down the row and they clap and cheer. JACK takes a pace forward.

JACK like a soldier: *You just give us your orders, ma'am, while your husband's away. Pay-day Thursdays, ma'am.*

POLLY: *Thursdays, boys. Dis-miss!*

The burglars slink quickly away behind the curtain.

POLLY calling after them: *Crookfingered Jack!*

JACK has got as far as the curtain but now turns and walks back. POLLY points silently to the typewriter.

Seen in close-up, he seats himself at the typewriter; POLLY comes into shot, reads through the last lines on the sheet that is still in the machine, then settles down in the armchair in exactly the same posture as MACKIE earlier on. She continues the dictation from where he left off.

POLLY: *Item number 10 . . .*

Just as she is about to begin she stops short and the camera tracks in towards her.

POLLY repeating dreamily: *Item number 10 . . .*

The camera closes in on her face. Dissolve.

Scene 39. A vision of an imaginary marsh.

Dramatic music. The vision opens with a long shot of an eerie marsh landscape, beneath a stormy night-time sky with tattered clouds. A lone horseman appears in the distance.

MACKIE is struggling against the rigours of the storm and the marsh, into which his horse is sinking. A peal of thunder is heard, and a dazzling flash of lightning lights up the sky, forming the words 'Highgate Marsh' in fiery letters. Dissolve.

Scene 40. The entrance of the 'Highgate Marsh'.

Close-up of the signboard of the brothel, with the words 'Highgate Marsh' inscribed in an ornate script. A thunderclap is heard. The camera tilts down to the street entrance as MACKIE marches blithely in through the door, whistling a little song and swinging his cane. He slams the door shut with a thunderous noise.

Scene 41. The salon of the 'Highgate Marsh'.

The room is furnished with tawdry elegance, full of plush

upholstery, mirrors, gilded furniture, little mats everywhere, little cupids, the whole atmosphere very bourgeois. The salon, which in the evening serves a large and bustling clientele with the aid of a piano and an upholstered sofa, is now, at five o'clock in the afternoon, being used as an ordinary living-room. An ironing board is laid across the backs of two armchairs; there is underwear lying on the piano; girls sloppily dressed in negligees are sewing and reading the papers at the same time. The sequence opens on a close-up of a pair of woman's hands laying out a pack of cards. At the same time a woman's voice is heard reading, stumbling over the words like a child.

WOMAN'S VOICE off: *Two shopkeepers killed, thirty burglaries, twenty-three hold-ups, eighteen cases of arson, seven premeditated murders . . .*

SECOND VOICE off, cutting in: *He's certainly managed to get together a tidy list, has Mackie Messer . . .*

As she utters MACKIE's name, the hands deal the last card — the knave of hearts.

FIRST VOICE off: *And in Winchester he seduced a pair of sisters, both minors.*

JENNY'S VOICE off: *I bet they weren't as minor as all that!*

In the middle of this sentence, the camera tracks back to reveal JENNY with her cards, then pulls back further to show us a GIRL READING THE PAPER perched on a stool nearby; beside her is a GIRL IRONING. A FOURTH GIRL is lying face downwards on a sofa reading an illustrated paper.

FOURTH GIRL interrupting the dialogue: *Look, girls, isn't this beautiful!*

The GIRL IRONING comes over to the sofa, the iron still in her hand, and so do two of the other tarts; they all peer over the recumbent girl at the magazine, while JENNY remains totally absorbed in her cards.

The cover of the magazine is seen over the heads of the girls. It depicts the Queen and the caption reads: 'The Queen's Coronation robe'.

JENNY pensively, off: *He's not coming back.*

The camera swings round to focus on JENNY, who is looking at her cards, lost in thought.

MACKIE off, from the door: *My coffee!*

JENNY jumps up, flabbergasted, and looks over to the door. The camera swings over from her to MACKIE, who has just come in, and tracks with him as he walks serenely across the salon, hangs his hat on the hat-stand and finally, crossing his legs, settles himself with great nonchalance into an armchair in the middle of the room.

MACKIE: *What's happened to my coffee?*

He looks round with a superior air.

The girls stare fixedly at MACKIE, looking as if they've seen a ghost. The GIRL READING THE PAPER is holding out the sheet from which she has been reading out the long list of MACKIE'S crimes.

GIRL READING THE PAPER stuttering: *Here's the warrant for your arrest . . .*

We see her hand holding out the page of the newspaper with MACKIE beyond. He pulls another paper out of his pocket, a bored expression on his face.

MACKIE: *I know. This is my usual Thursday visit. I really can't let such trifles upset my routine.*

He tosses the paper disdainfully onto the table.

Scene 42. Part of a corridor with doors, in the brothel.

Shot of a door in the corridor. BETTY (the tart who was reading the paper) flings it open. Inside the room a half-naked girl is standing in front of a mirror making herself up. As if announcing some unheard-of sensation, BETTY whispers:

BETTY: *Mack's here!*

Scene 43. The brothel kitchen.

The water for the coffee is boiling over on the stove, while a dirty little MAID of about fifteen sits huddled on a bench crying her eyes out; she has a well-thumbed novel on her lap. The door is flung open.

BROTHEL MADAME off, from the doorway: *Coffee for Mackie!*

The MADAME comes into the shot, rushes over to the stove and grabs the kettle.

MADAME snarling at the MAID: *What are you howling for? Nothing'll happen to him!*

The MAID is absorbed in her reverie and her voice is choked

with tears, while more tears fall onto her book.

MAID: *'. . . It looked as if Count Botho would never see the golden-haired Else again . . .'*

A VOICE off, from the corridor: *Jenny . . .!* Then more softly: *Jenny!*

Scene 44. The door of the salon from the corridor.

The door is opened from inside and JENNY comes out into the corridor. Piano music issues from the salon.

JENNY annoyed: *Coming . . .!*

We see part of the salon through the door, past JENNY's head. She shuts the door and walks out of the shot.

Scene 45. The salon.

The camera tracks with the MADAME as she carries a large tray bearing the coffee-pot, cups and a large cake over to the big oval table which is being rapidly laid by two of the girls. They unload the tray and the other girls come over and gather round the table. MACKIE is seated on the sofa in the centre. Everyone has been eagerly awaiting the coffee.

Scene 46. A dark corner in the corridor leading to the stairs.

MRS PEACHUM is on the stairs and JENNY is two steps above her, both of them seen from above. MRS PEACHUM is saying something eagerly and secretively and JENNY listens in fascination.

JENNY's face is seen past MRS PEACHUM, from below. Behind JENNY the first door in the corridor opens; a girl's head appears in the shaft of light coming from inside and she cocks her head to listen. MRS PEACHUM draws JENNY closer to her, whispers to her and then takes a banknote out of her handbag and presses it into JENNY's hand. JENNY stuffs it into the top of her stocking, with a swift but sure movement.

Scene 47. The salon.

Shot of the table with the coffee things, the door of the salon beyond. The scene is a real middle-class idyll with the table laid for coffee, the MADAME cutting slices of cake and everyone eating with great enjoyment. MACKIE is saying something as he raises his cup to his lips with his left hand and puts his right arm round the girl sitting next to him.

MACKIE: *That's a nice bit of underwear!*

The girl laughs.

THE MADAME judiciously: *From the cradle to the grave underwear comes first!*

While these last words are being spoken JENNY appears and walks slowly over to the table; she sits down on a chair beside MACKIE but he takes no notice of her and continues to concentrate on his neighbour on the other side. JENNY helps herself to coffee.

JENNY casually, as she starts to eat: *Congratulations on your wedding, Mack!*

MACKIE, struck by her tone, hesitates; he stops flirting with the other girl, though he leaves his arm round her, and turns slowly towards JENNY. The girls all watch JENNY and MACKIE, surprised and interested.

Close shot of the two of them.

MACKIE: *Jealous, are you?*

He tries to draw JENNY towards him, realizing that she is angry and trying to calm her down.

MACKIE: *I'm married to you too, you know!*

JENNY pushes his arm away and retreats into her chair.

JENNY: *Yes — and to all of them.*

She points to the other girls, who laugh loudly. MACKIE looks down at her, thinking that she's in a very hostile mood today. Then he suddenly grabs at her brutally as if to say 'Stop playing the fool' and with a sure touch pulls the money out of the top of her stocking.

MACKIE surprised and approving: *Ten pounds — good girl!*

He pockets the money as he says this, then lets go of the other girl and draws JENNY close to him; she is so stunned at having lost her money that for a moment she forgets her hostility, but when he gives her a kiss she tries to ward him off. He takes a last sip from his cup, stuffs the last few crumbs of cake into his mouth and stands up. The camera tracks back.

MACKIE: *Now I must be going.*

JENNY, who is holding his left hand, suddenly looks at it and says:

JENNY: *Mack, when the bells of Westminster ring out for the Coro-*

nation you'll have a bad time.

The other girls draw closer, looking interested. They bend low over MACKIE's hand, their heads close to JENNY's. MACKIE looks nonchalant at first, then suddenly becomes interested.[23]

MACKIE looking at JENNY: *Just tell me the good part, please, nothing unpleasant.*

A GIRL: *Yes, Jenny, read his hand, you're first rate at that!*

ANOTHER GIRL: *What can you see then?*

JENNY: *I see a confining darkness without much light. And then I can see a capital C, which stands for a woman's cunning . . . Then . . .*

MACKIE is fascinated; he sits down again slowly and pushes the women aside.

MACKIE: *Stop! I'd like to hear a bit more about the confining darkness and the cunning. What's the name of this cunning woman, for instance?*

JENNY: *All I can see is that it begins with a J.*

MACKIE: *Then it's wrong. It begins with a P.* He stands up. *Goodbye!*

One of the girls brings him his hat and his sword-stick. JENNY is still clinging onto his hand, so MACKIE caresses her and strokes her hair.

MACKIE: *No, it doesn't begin with a J, Jenny! You've always been true to me . . .*

He turns to face the other girls as he pulls JENNY to her feet and hugs her tightly; she looks up at him; her face is full of conflicting emotions but her love for MACKIE and his fascination for her gradually get the upper hand.

MACKIE to the assembled girls: *And even though I'm Mackie Messer today, and my luck has turned, I shall never forget the companion of my darker days: Jenny, who was my favourite of all the girls!*

He begins to sing the 'Tango Ballad', holding JENNY close to him. When he gets to the end of the first verse, JENNY seems to snap out of her reverie. She notices the banknote in MACKIE's waistcoat and shakes off this indulgent mood. The camera tracks with her as she goes slowly over to the window, leans against window sill and starts singing the second verse.

A high shot past JENNY's head framed in the window to the street below, where MRS PEACHUM and two policemen are standing. While Jenny continues the second verse she makes an unobtrusive signal to the group in the street.

Jenny walks over to Mackie as she sings the last words of the ballad; she puts her arms round him and they start dancing to the refrain. The camera tracks with them as Jenny gradually leads Mackie over to the door, which slowly opens a crack. Jenny looks over Mackie's shoulder and as the pair of them get close to the door we can see the figure of a man outside. Mackie has his back to the door and is dancing happily.

The dancing couple are seen from outside the room. Several policemen are lurking in the corridor and a detective is waiting in the half-open doorway. In the background we can see the girls congregated round the table; they are gazing anxiously at the door.

Shot of a group of the girls. One of them has her hands to her open mouth as though she is about to scream, while another tries to signal to Mackie.

Jenny and Mackie dancing. Mackie can't see either the door or the girl's warning signal because Jenny is dancing him right up to the door, keeping him with his back to it. At this moment Smith springs forward and lays his hand on Mackie's shoulder. He swivels round, startled. Smith grabs his hands and goes to put handcuffs on him. Mackie deals a blow at his chest, draws his knife out of his stick and escapes backwards to the window.

The policemen come tearing through the door. One of them raises his revolver but Smith knocks his arm down.

Mackie, having swung himself onto the window-sill, starts to slide down the drainpipe and disappears from view.

Jenny rushes over to the window and leans out.

Scene 48. The street outside the brothel.

The camera follows Mackie as he slides down the drainpipe to the street. As he reaches the bottom the policemen who have been lying in wait for him grab him from behind and clap handcuffs on him. Mackie is under arrest. Mrs Peachum, who is standing nearby, gives a scornful laugh. Mackie, having regained his composure, asks her politely:

Mackie: *How is your husband?*

The policemen drag him off. MRS PEACHUM follows at a distance, but turns round again to signal to JENNY. The camera tilts up to JENNY, who at that moment turns away from the window.

Scene 49. Inside the salon.

The girls are standing roughly in a circle, watching JENNY at the window. She has just turned back into the room and is clearly very disturbed, but has got herself well under control and looks serious, lost in thought. The tension is broken when one of the girls walks over to JENNY and spits contemptuously on the floor in front of her. JENNY does not react; with an angry and defiant expression she walks past the girl who has spat at her and through the circle formed by the other girls. They make way for her, staring in bewilderment as she continues over to the table where the playing cards are still laid out, and sits down.

Seen in close-up, she starts dealing the cards. The camera closes on the cards (as at the beginning of Scene 41).

JENNY murmuring to herself: *I wonder if they'll hang him?*

The grid pattern in which the cards are arranged dissolves into the prison bars in the next scene.

Scene 50. A prison in the Old Bailey.

The prison cells are more like cages on either side of a series of corridors; they are separated from each other by lateral corridors. The cells are in darkness but all the corridors are harshly lit from above. Most of the cells are occupied by prisoners. The sequence opens with a shot of MACKIE's cell. First of all we see nothing but the bars, then MACKIE emerges from the background and steps up to the bars. BROWN approaches the cage from the outside. He seems very agitated and addresses MACKIE in an anxious and imploring tone.

BROWN: *It wasn't me: I did everything I . . .*

BROWN is seen in back view, with MACKIE on the other side of the bars. MACKIE is gazing at BROWN with a scornful and crushing look on his face. BROWN is almost in tears.

BROWN: *Don't look at me like that, Mack . . . I can't stand it:*

We see his face from the other side of the bars, past MACKIE.

BROWN is thoroughly agitated. He presses his face, which is running with sweat, against the bars and is clearly on the verge of tears.

BROWN: *Your silence is awful: Say something, Mack! Say something to your poor old Jack!*

He virtually collapses and turns away from the bars, his hands to his face.

He staggers down the corridor between the cells, a broken man.

BROWN mumbling to himself: *He didn't even deign to speak to me!*

As he stumbles past the cells the prisoners inside gaze after him. SMITH comes past and looks him up and down, shaking his head, then walks on to visit MACKIE.

Inside MACKIE's cell: SMITH opens the door and walks in, handcuffs at the ready. MACKIE looks at him enquiringly.

SMITH: *What's bitten the Chief?*

MACKIE: *It's a good thing I didn't shout at him. I just gave him a look and he wept bitterly. A little trick I got out of the Bible.*

While he is speaking SMITH has been putting the handcuffs on him. MACKIE inspects them critically.

MACKIE: *These must be the very heaviest you've got, Mr Jailer! With your permission I should like to put in a request for a more comfortable pair.*

SMITH: *But we've got them at all prices here, Captain. It all depends on how much you want to fork out.*

MACKIE: *How much does it cost not to have any at all?*

SMITH: *Ten pounds.*

MACKIE rummages in his waistcoat pocket to find JENNY's ten-pound note and presses it into SMITH's hand. SMITH promptly removes the handcuffs and backs away to the door, bowing obsequiously. MACKIE stands at the bars to watch him leave and begins to sing a shortened version of the 'Ballad of Gracious Living'.

Scene 51. The entrance to the cells.

We see a massive iron door with bars, set in a wall; it has a judas window which opens as LUCY, muffled up and wearing a veil, comes up and knocks shyly on the door. A vague outline of a warder's head appears framed in the judas.

WARDER: *Who goes there?*
LUCY: *Is my father still here?*

The door opens and the WARDER appears.

WARDER: *The Chief of Police has already left.*
LUCY: *Let me through!*
WARDER saluting LUCY: *Certainly, Miss Brown!*

Scene 52. The prison in the Old Bailey.

Shot of the corridor past MACKIE as he stands at the bars of his cell. LUCY is coming along the corridor, looking timidly about her as she does so. MACKIE clasps his hands together.

MACKIE: *The slut! That's all I needed. Now I'll have a fine time up to the execution!*

MACKIE turns away, pulls his collar up and his hat down to hide his face, then stands there with his back turned. LUCY comes rapidly up to the bars, reaches through and pulls at MACKIE's coat-tails.

LUCY: *You dirty swine! How can you look me in the face after all there's been between us!*

MACKIE turns to LUCY with a look of great surprise.

MACKIE: *Lucy?!*

We see the two of them, separated by the bars.

MACKIE trying to calm LUCY down: *Have you no heart, seeing your husband like this?*

LUCY: *My husband! You monster! I suppose you think I didn't know anything about your goings-on with Miss Peachum!*

A loud altercation can be heard coming from the entrance to the cells and POLLY's voice wafts towards us, the words tumbling over each other.

POLLY off: . . . *my husband!* . . .

Close-up of LUCY, with MACKIE in front of her.

LUCY taking no notice of the uproar: *I could scratch your eyes out! You're married to her, aren't you, you beast?*

MACKIE, one ear on the shindig outside, tries nervously to calm her down.

MACKIE: *Married! That's a good one! I visit this house regularly, I chat to her, I give her a peck on the cheek now and then, and now the old bag's rushing around shouting from the rooftops that we're married!*

TOFFEE
LUXE

dem
Elend

POLLY off, but coming closer: *Where's my husband?*

She rushes into shot, not even noticing LUCY in her excitement, since she has eyes only for MACKIE.

POLLY clinging onto the bars: *Oh Mack, you told me you wouldn't go to those women ever again! Just think what your Polly's suffering to see you like this!*

LUCY scornfully: *The slut!*

POLLY noticing LUCY for the first time: *What's all this, Mack? Who on earth is this? Please tell her I'm your wife!* As MACKIE tries to pull her back her tone becomes more insistent. *Aren't I your wife?*

LUCY: *You dirty swine! Do you mean to say you've got two wives, you monster?*

POLLY speaking at the same time as LUCY: *Aren't I your wife?*

MACKIE trying to address them both at once: *If only you'd both shut your traps for two minutes I could explain everything.*

MACKIE is seen past the two women. POLLY and LUCY turn on each other and he tries unsuccessfully to separate them through the bars as they virtually tear each other's hair out. They begin to sing the 'Jealousy Duet'.

Shot of the corridor past the two women. As they sing the last lines of the duet we see MRS PEACHUM in the distance. She is arguing violently but inaudibly with SMITH, hurrying towards us as she does so. As the last words of the song die away we hear part of MRS PEACHUM's outburst.

MRS PEACHUM: *My son-in-law . . . I must see him!*

As she speaks she thrusts SMITH aside and storms towards the cell like an avenging fury, then lets fly at POLLY.

MRS PEACHUM: *You filthy little slut! Come home at once!*

POLLY: *Let me stay here mama, please, it's very important!*

MRS PEACHUM giving POLLY a box on the ears: *Oh yes? Well, that's important too! Quick march! When your fellow's hanged you can hang yourself with him!*

She drags POLLY away, while the girl yells and tries to resist her.

LUCY scornfully watches the pair of them leave, while MACKIE stands aloof. He gives LUCY a calculating look, then reaches through the bars and strokes her arm in a sort of caress, which makes her turn to him in surprise.

MACKIE: *You see how right I was? Is that how people treat their son-in-law? Do you believe me now when I say there's no truth in it?*

LUCY is convinced. She caresses him through the bars, an expression of utter devotion on her face.

LUCY: *How happy I am to hear you saying that from the bottom of your heart! I love you so much that I'd almost rather see you on the gallows than in someone's else's arms!*

MACKIE urgently: *Lucy, I'd love to owe my life to you!*

LUCY: *It's wonderful the way you say that. Say it again.*

Seen past MACKIE, SMITH approaches along the corridor carrying MACKIE's dinner. MACKIE notices SMITH and his voice becomes excited.

MACKIE whispering to LUCY: *Lucy, I'd love to owe my life to you!*

SMITH comes up to them and greets LUCY, beaming with pleasure.

SMITH: *Excuse me — may I serve the dinner?*

He walks along the cell towards the door; the lock clicks, while LUCY nods to MACKIE and then says something to him in a whisper.

Shot of the open door, past MACKIE. SMITH has come into the cell and is setting out the meal. Then we hear a cry from LUCY, as if she's about to faint. SMITH rushes out, leaving the door open.

LUCY is clinging to the bars as she swoons in a mock faint; SMITH comes into shot and catches her; He can't take his eyes off her, but she turns her head away and winks in the direction of the cell.

Seen from her point of view, MACKIE slinks over to the door and out of the cell.

LUCY, still pretending to be in a dead faint, is weighing SMITH down so heavily that he looks round despairingly for help, not knowing what to do; on the one hand he would like to summon help, but on the other hand he's thoroughly enjoying the situation.

In another cell, a prisoner sits gazing up in amazement at the wall above. The camera tilts up past him to show MACKIE decamping through a trap door high up in the wall. The prisoner follows his movements in great excitement.

Cut back to SMITH as he notices that the cell is empty. He

makes as if to abandon LUCY and goes to put his whistle to his lips so as to sound the alarm. But LUCY opens her arms wide and pulls him towards her, and he forgets MACKIE and the need to sound the alarm in the face of this outburst of passion.

Scene 53. The roof of the prison.
MACKIE saunters along the ridge of the roof and looks down.

Scene 54. The prison yard.
Seen from the roof, the prisoners are walking round the yard in a circle.

Scene 55. The prison roof.
It is now evening. MACKIE, having seen the prisoners, turns to the other side of the roof, and skips over towards the fire escape.
Seen in close-up, MACKIE prepares to climb down the fire-escape.

Scene 56. The prison yard.
In a corner of the yard, a couple of steps lead up to a side-entrance. The prisoners are still circling round the yard, and as the camera holds on the steps and the entrance it intersects a segment of the moving procession. MRS PEACHUM and POLLY are standing on the steps, framed in the doorway. POLLY is fighting tooth and nail to get away.

POLLY weeping and shouting at the same time: *Mackie! Mackie!*

MRS PEACHUM struggles to pull POLLY after her. As the prisoners come into the shot, they turn their heads to look at this scene, a mixture of boredom, sadness and indifference on their faces, but then calmly continue their circular walk.

Scene 57. The fire-escape on the outer wall of the prison.
MACKIE climbs down with effortless ease and the camera tilts with him until he reaches the bottom. As soon as his feet touch the ground he glances round in all directions, then stops short.
Wide shot past MACKIE of SUKY, who is just turning the

corner some distance away.

MACKIE, in close-up, dusts himself down feverishly, pulls his gloves out of his pocket, puts them on and then sets off behind SUKY.

Scene 58. The Old Bailey prison, MACKIE'S *cell.*

LUCY is still locked in SMITH'S arms. He is quite oblivious to everything else as he abandons himself to her kisses.

MACKIE'S cell is surrounded by corridors on three sides. The scene with SMITH and LUCY takes place in front of the cell, while the door through which MACKIE escaped is on the right hand side. It is along this right-hand corridor that BROWN now approaches, seen from behind.

Shot of BROWN past SMITH and LUCY as he comes along the corridor, then notices the open door and stops dead.

We see BROWN from inside the cell as he comes in through the door. His initial amazement gives way to joyous surprise and then to sheer delight as he satisfies himself that the cell is empty. Then his glance rests on the corridor in front of the cell and his face takes on an expression of bewilderment. The camera shoots past him on the embracing couple.

BROWN at the top of his voice: *Lucy!*

LUCY releasing SMITH: *Papa!*

SMITH has come to his senses and starts blowing his whistle like a man possessed. LUCY clutches onto the bars and speaks exultantly to her father, who is inside the cell, at the bars.

LUCY to BROWN: *I've freed him!*

Policemen rush along the corridors from every side.

Scene 59. In the street.

POLLY is being dragged along, weeping, by her mother; she has virtually given up trying to resist, but wails continually:

POLLY: *My husband! My poor husband!*

Scene 60. A narrow alleyway.

SUKY is seen from the front, with MACKIE in pursuit a few paces behind. The camera tracks ahead of them.

Now the camera tracks behind SUKY, from MACKIE'S point of view. It tilts up from her feet to her bottom, lingers there a

moment, then tilts on up to her head. She turns her head and smiles, then slows down.
Resume on SUKY from in front as MACKIE catches her up and takes her arm. They walk away like a pair of lovers.

Scene 61. The Old Bailey prison, MACKIE'S *cell.*
The policemen are standing round outside MACKIE'S cell, seen from inside past BROWN, who has sunk exhausted onto the plank-bed. Also in the shot are LUCY, who is leaning against the bars, smiling, and SMITH, who is totally bewildered. Two policemen appear with PEACHUM.

ONE OF THE POLICEMEN: *Here's the Chief of Police.*
We see PEACHUM in the doorway of the cell, with BROWN in the foreground.

PEACHUM quite taken aback: *Oh! I suppose the other gentleman's gone for a stroll?*
BROWN sits on the plank-bed, struggling to hide his embarrassment. PEACHUM, in the foreground, looks at him spitefully.

BROWN: *Mr Peachum, I am quite beside myself.*

PEACHUM: *I come in here to visit a criminal and who do I find? London's Chief of Police!*

BROWN springing indignantly to his feet: *Damn it! I can't help it if the fellow gets away. The police can't do a thing!*

PEACHUM in a threatening tone: *I see. The police can't do anything, do you say? Hmmm . . .*
Close-up of PEACHUM past BROWN as he continues, with an increasingly triumphant expression:

PEACHUM: *. . . I'm curious to know what the police will do when the brillance of tomorrow's Coronation celebrations is marred by a march-past of a thousand or so beggars!*

BROWN: *What's all this?*

PEACHUM triumphantly: *Do you really think it'll look good if a few hundred crippled and mutilated people have to be struck down during the Coronation festivities?*
The two of them in close-up.

PEACHUM: *It would look bad. It's a disgusting sight, enough to make you sick.*

BROWN in a voice like thunder: *That's a threat! It's sheer blackmail! Policemen!*

The policemen stand stiffly to attention.

POLICEMEN in chorus: *Yessir!*

BROWN to PEACHUM: *Now you'll find out all about the Chief of Police's iron hand! It's not for nothing they call me Tiger Brown!* To the policemen: *Lock him up!*

Two policemen walk over and clap handcuffs on the totally bewildered PEACHUM. BROWN leaves the cell with the policemen.

BROWN to LUCY: *Come here, my girl.*

The door of the cell clangs shut. PEACHUM stands at the bars watching BROWN and LUCY as they go out of sight, the policemen marching behind them.

PEACHUM in a threatening tone: *You'll be browned off good and proper tomorrow, Mr Brown!*

Fade out.

Scene 62. The STREET-SINGER *with a small girl and a woman.*
Fade in to the STREET-SINGER singing a shortened version of the 'Second Threepenny Finale' accompanied by the barrel-organ. There is no indication of where the scene is taking place. Fade out.

Scene 63. A corner of the stables (MACKIE'S '*office*').
POLLY is seated at the desk, while the burglars are lounging about in the foreground, some of them standing, some sitting down. A babble of voices can be heard. Then POLLY stands up and raps on the table with her pencil. Silence.

POLLY: *Let's away from the seedy streets of Soho and into the elegance of the City! My dear husband — I mean our illustrious chief — hit the nail right on the head when he said that! And now that he has once again escaped from prison and must lie hidden in unknown cities, he can rest assured that we'll pull off this bank business properly. Right, boys? We'll do a first-rate job, so that we can put our business on a broader basis at last!*

Cheers from the burglars. POLLY sits down.

Shot of the burglars past POLLY as she turns her attention to the accounts.

POLLY: *And now for the accounts.*

As the burglars don't stir, but just glance at each other eloquently, she looks up.

POLLY: *It's Thursday today, gentlemen.* She looks at the account book. *Crookfingered Jack!*

JACK steps reluctantly forward, assuming a troubled expression.

JACK: *Times are bad, ma'am! One silver watch.*

He lays it on the table and POLLY makes an entry in the book.

POLLY: *One silver watch.*

Some of the burglars titter. POLLY glances suspiciously round the circle and the titters die away.

POLLY reading from the book: *Mat of the Mint!*

MAT comes forward.

MAT: *It's been a very bad week, ma'am. One purse, contents five shillings and sevenpence.*

POLLY again writes it down, while the burglars burst out laughing.

POLLY: *Five shillings and sevenpence.*

She looks up very suspiciously and uncertainly; the laughter fades to a suppressed titter, which continues when she calls the next man forward.

POLLY: *Robin of Bagshot!*

He steps forward, looking very contrite.

We see ROBIN standing in front of the desk and POLLY behind it, with CROOKFINGERED JACK, clearly enjoying himself hugely, standing behind ROBIN.

ROBIN sounding troubled: *One coffee spoon. Real silver.*

A roar of laughter from the men. POLLY is furious and can scarcely contain herself.

POLLY trembling with anger: *Real silver?*

Close-up of ROBIN, looking crossly round while the merriment gets louder. As he does so, JACK pulls his fat wallet out of his pocket and waves it triumphantly in the air. This act of burglary is accompanied by a breathless hush.

The whole group of burglars is seen past POLLY. They are staring open-mouthed at ROBIN'S wallet, but ROBIN himself is still confused and doesn't yet understand why his mood has changed so suddenly. Then he sees the wallet in JACK'S hand and tries to snatch it from him, while the others push him aside, booing him. JACK counts out the contents of the wallet for POLLY to see.

POLLY'S hand draws the money across the table towards her;

on either side, the heads of ROBIN and JACK. JACK is smirking contemptuously, while ROBIN is furious.

ROBIN snapping at JACK: *And what about your silver watch? How about the diamonds you got from that shop in Regent Street the day before yesterday?*

The laughter fades from JACK's face.

JACK hissing with fury: *Shut your trap!*

ROBIN grins; JACK pulls himself together.

JACK gasping: *And what did you hand over these last three Thursdays? You've been cheating the chief for years!* He turns to the others. *Isn't that so?*

Shot of the burglars.

A BURGLAR with a scornful laugh: *That's right!*

ROBIN leaps on him.

ROBIN fuming: *And how much did you put in your own pocket during the Thompson burglary?*

The other burglar looks embarrassed. JIMMY boos.

JIMMY: *Give it to him!*

WAT DREARY spins furiously round, making a threatening gesture towards JIMMY.

Close-up of JIMMY laughing.

WAT DREARY off: *You've got nothing to laugh about! Come and show us what you've put aside!*

JIMMY furiously: *Why me? Ned made more out of it than I did.*

The camera moves quickly to NED.

NED yelling fiercely: *That's not true at all! Jack's stowed away more money than all of us put together!*

The camera moves rapidly over the other burglars, who all start shouting threats at one another with angry faces.

BURGLARS: *Scoundrel! . . . Scoundrel yourself! . . . Cheat! . . . Crook! . . . Traitor! . . .* etc.

It comes to rest on JACK, who is pale and silent as he tries to retain his composure. Holding his head high in the face of the storm, he buttons up his coat and sticks his hands in his pockets.

Cut to POLLY. Her arms folded over the money, she looks warily at JACK and then her gaze wanders from one to the other as the uproar continues. She suddenly raps on the table with her pencil.

Polly in a sharp voice, full of authority: *Silence!*

They fall silent. She continues in a vigorous tone that has a dangerous edge to it:

Polly: *Bring out the money you've been embezzling!*

The burglars are seen past Polly. They look grim and sullen and flash looks of hatred at each other.

Polly: *Come on now! Are you going to do it? Otherwise I shall go straight to the Chief of Police and tomorrow . . .* Pointing at each of them in turn . . . *the whole rotten lot of you will have disappeared into the cells at the Old Bailey!*

The burglars, annoyed but beaten, turn sullenly round; some of them pull out their wallets and slam them angrily down on the table under Polly's nose. A rapid series of close-ups shows:

A pair of hands lifting up one of the floorboards and pulling out a money-box.

A hand slitting open a straw mattress with a knife, whereupon a stream of banknotes gushes out.

From above, a hand turning the lining of a pocket inside out; a whole lot of pearl necklaces and other pieces of jewellery pour out onto the table-top. The camera moves higher and we see the top of the desk with an ever-growing heap of jewellery, coins, wallets and little iron money-boxes. Polly's voice can be heard above the clinking of the coins and the jewellery.

Polly off: *The burglary will not now take place. Why do we need to rob a bank when we've got enough capital here to open our own Bank?! Away from Soho and into the City!*

The mountain of coins and jewellery dissolves into the sign hanging outside a bank, which reads ' City Bank '. Dissolve.

Scene 64. The directors' office in the bank.

The room is furnished in a modern style and contains a desk, club-type fittings and a glass wall at the back giving onto the banking hall, where bank-clerks can be seen working feverishly. Beginning at the door, the camera tracks right through the room, past Polly and Jack — absorbed in paperwork at their respective desks — and past three of the other burglars, now smartly dressed and smoking fat cigars as they recline in club armchairs. It finally holds for a moment on the glass wall through which we can see the clerks slaving away. A bell has been ringing continuously during the fade-in. Now one of the clerks, a woman in her forties (the 'elderly spinster' type) stands up, walks up to the glass wall, knocks on the door, then opens it and comes into the directors' office.

FEMALE CLERK very humbly: *Did you want something, sir?*

JACK leans majestically back in his chair.

JACK: *Come and take dictation!*

The SECRETARY comes into shot and sits down at the typewriter near the desks. She has barely sat down when she suddenly leaps up again.

SECRETARY bowing to POLLY: *Good morning, Madam President!*

The camera tracks over to POLLY, who nods graciously and then becomes engrossed in her papers once again.

POLLY in a detached tone, to the SECRETARY: *Good morning, my dear.*

JACK has already begun to dictate and we hear the clattering of the typewriter.

JACK dictating: *First sales letter. In accordance with the honourable traditions of our institution etc, etc, we will endeavour to build up and increase the confidence of our customers . . .*

POLLY correcting him: *. . . clients . . .*

JACK: *. . . by the credit-worthiness of our bank in all transactions . . .*

The camera pans over to the three new members of the board, who are listening with broad grins on their faces, beaming contentedly. At that moment a voice bawls from the doorway:

VOICE off: *'Morning, boys!*

The men turn in horror and the camera pans to show WAT DREARY at the door. His clothes are not quite right somehow; he is not only unshaven and somewhat tipsy, but he is also wearing a long, brightly checked cravat with his tail-coat. The camera moves with him as he enters the room.

WAT DREARY waving to POLLY: *Pulled it off a treat, didn't we, ma'am!* He comes up to POLLY and holds out his hand. *Congratulations!*

Shot of POLLY, past WAT. She fails to notice his outstretched hand, stands up with great dignity and turns to the SECRETARY and dismisses her.

POLLY to the SECRETARY: *Thank you, my dear.*

She looks after the SECRETARY's retreating back, then turns her gaze on WAT, who has watched this little scene with a bewildered expression. He stares in amazament first at POLLY then at the disappearing figure of the SECRETARY, and finally at his colleagues in the background, hoping for a word of advice from them. POLLY's voice becomes very severe.

POLLY: *Do you really expect to fulfil the role of a director and member of the board in a suit like that, Mr Dreary? I really can't help laughing.*

The three 'members of the board' laugh, while WAT looks furiously round at them, utterly confused.

POLLY: *Silence! It's no laughing matter!*

The camera tracks back to show the members of the board standing stiffly to attention, while CROOKFINGERED JACK watches POLLY from his chair like a benevolent grandfather, nodding his approval.

POLLY: *In this new business of ours we can only use people of the highest calibre. Any fool can be a highwayman or a pickpocket. But what we're doing now is serious and you're incapable of rising to the situation, Mr Dreary! I'm going to pension you off!*

She sits down and writes something down on a piece of paper, shaking her head and muttering to herself as she does so.

POLLY: *A tail-coat with a green tie!*

She finishes writing and hands the piece of paper to JACK, who countersigns it. Then she hands it to WAT, addressing him in her former tone.

POLLY: *Go and report to the Chief of Police with this and get yourself locked up. You've earned the opportunity to retire!*

She claps him on the shoulder. He is totally bewildered and looks round to his colleagues for help, but they only shrug their shoulders. He staggers out of the room. The others watch him go.

POLLY breaking the silence: *It's eleven o'clock, Mr Mat of the Mint! Why aren't you over at the Stock Exchange?*

MAT snatches up a briefcase from where it is lying on a chair and darts through the door. POLLY sits down at her desk and gets back to work. Fade out.

Scene 65. A street in London (as Scene 1).

Fade in on part of a monument that was seen in the opening scene of the film. But whereas in the first scene it looked rather the worse for wear, and was dirty and inconspicuous, it is now being given a brilliant new coat of paint. There are people perched on various parts of the statue, washing down the great man's face and painting it over. The camera tracks back to show the whole of the statue and then more of the street. There are rugs hanging out of the windows, plus flags and garlands. Brushwood has been scattered on the roadway and workmen are feverishly working to get the decorations up, while the street is swarming with light-hearted throngs of people. A brass band can be heard in the distance. Policemen with white gloves and wearing dress uniforms are struggling vainly to control the traffic on this brilliantly sunny day. In a few hours the Coronation procession will be passing by. Our attention is immediately caught by a banner reading 'Long live our new Queen!' The camera tracks along the street and eventually holds on JENNY, who is caught up in the throng of passers-by, gaping at the preparations for the Coronation procession that are going on all round her. She looks up at the windows of the houses above her.

The camera tilts upwards from her point of view, over the rugs and garlands hanging down from the windows. As if by chance, it comes to rest on a window on the third floor of one of the houses. It is open and MACKIE and SUKY can be seen struggling to fix an enormous flag which is fluttering down almost as far as the first floor. MACKIE is in his shirtsleeves. Rapid dissolve to a shot of the two of them; they are totally engrossed in their work, like a pair of children absorbed in a game.

Then back to a close-up of JENNY's head, which is tilted back to look at them. Staring open-mouthed, she lets out an involuntary cry.

JENNY: *Mackie!*

The camera pulls rapidly back to show her pointing up at the window with one hand, the other hand to her mouth. She is staring at MACKIE oblivious of what is going on around her. People begin to collect round her, looking up also, and then a policeman pushes his way up to her. He too looks up at the window. Fade out.

Scene 66. PEACHUM'S *shop.*

The shop is full to bursting with beggars getting ready for the demonstration and painting placards and banners. There's a great deal of noise, what with the babble of voices from all sides, the distant sound of a brass band (which mixes in from the previous scene), the doorbell jangling repeatedly, the telephone ringing etc. The scene opens on a close-up of one of the banners with a hand painting it. It reads: 'I gave my eyes for the King!'

MRS PEACHUM off, at the top of her voice: *Come on! Come on!*

The camera tracks back slightly to show us the BLIND BEGGAR, who has pushed his glasses up onto the top of his head and is busy painting. MRS PEACHUM pushes her way through the assembled beggars, urging them on.

MRS PEACHUM: *If you're not willing to work you can't beg!* She walks over to the BLIND BEGGAR and examines his work with a critical eye. *You call yourself a blind man and you can't even form a 'K' properly?*

The camera pans over the various different types of beggars as they work away. A renewed roll of drums is heard from the street.

A BEGGAR to one of his colleagues: *The Coronation procession!*

A moment's silence — all the beggars listen to what's going on outside. The camera tracks on and over to FILCH, who is feverishly taking orders behind the desk, using the telephone continuously.

FILCH: *Drury Lane branch? 350 men ready to go? Right you are! . . .* He hangs up, but the telephone rings again straight away. He snatches the receiver off. *Turnbridge branch? . . . Come on now, come on! Everything must be under way in one hour's time! How many banners? All right . . .!* He leaps up onto the desk. The camera tracks rapidly backwards . . . *Ladies and gentlemen! At this very moment 1,432 of our colleagues in eleven branches are working feverishly so as to be able to play a fitting part in our Queen's coronation.*[24] *In one hour from now we will assemble in front of Buckingham Palace and line the street. Departure of the poorest of the poor half an hour later!*

The beggars let out a cheer, which mixes in with the cheering of the crowd in the next scene.

Scene 67. The street (as Scene 1).

The cheering of the crowd takes over from the cheering beggars in the previous scene. The police thrust the crowd to the side of the street, where they stand waving and shouting. Accompanied by the skirl of bagpipes, a platoon of Scots guards marches along the street, which is now clean and cleared of people. The sun is blazing down.

Scene 68. BROWN'S *office.*

Several telephones on the desk are all jangling loudly at once. BROWN is half in his dress uniform and is clearly in a state of terrific excitement. He tears over to the desk, snatches up three telephones and speaks into all of them at once.

BROWN into the first telephone: *Yes! . . . No! . . . What a filthy trick! What? In Piccadilly as well? . . . Over 400 beggars?* Into the second telephone: *What? In front of Westminster as well? How many? More than 700? Arrest them! All of them! . . . Disperse them! . . . No, no, you fool! I can't scatter more than 10,000 beggars, on Coronation Day of all days!* Into a third telephone: *What? In front of Buckingham Palace . . .?*

He sinks exhausted into a chair. A POLICEMAN appears, looking agitated, walks over to BROWN and announces:

POLICEMAN to BROWN: *The Coronation procession is assembling!*

A roll of drums and a flourish of trumpets can be heard. SMITH appears, in a state of utter hysteria.

SMITH: *The beggars are setting off!*

The telephone rings. BROWN, who has completely lost his grip on things and doesn't know where to turn, puts his head in his hands. The telephone rings again. The camera tracks out as BROWN rushes round the office, completely at a loss, his head in his hands. SMITH walks over to the telephone and lifts the receiver. After a few moments he begins to speak.

SMITH in a strangled voice: *They've got him back!* Shouting aloud: *Mackie Messer has just been committed to prison!*

Everyone is paralysed for a moment. BROWN'S eyes are popping out of his head as he stares at SMITH blankly. Then he grasps what is happening, comes to a decision and, still only half-dressed, runs out of the door, pulling his coat on as he goes. SMITH and the policemen follow him.

Scene 69. The prison, MACKIE's *cell.*

PEACHUM is seen from the side, lying on the plank-bed, his legs drawn up and gazing at the ceiling. The lock rattles and the door is opened. At this sound PEACHUM quickly closes his eyes and begins to snore. BROWN comes into the picture and walks over to him.

BROWN: *Look here, Mr Peachum, you must leave!*

He shakes him, whereupon PEACHUM turns his back on him. BROWN sits down beside him, as if he were an invalid, and gives him a gentle but nervous shake, trying to convince him.

BROWN: *Pull yourself together, man! I'm revoking your arrest!*

PEACHUM stretches, yawns, raises himself on one arm and looks at BROWN sleepily as though he's just woken up from a deep sleep. BROWN's hopes begin to revive.

BROWN very quickly, to PEACHUM: *You must stop your demonstration!*

As PEACHUM makes no sign of having understood him, BROWN tries a new tack.

BROWN: *As one man to another — as one friend to another . . . You can't make difficulties for me today! I've fulfilled your requirements — Mackie Messer is under arrest! Look — they're bringing him in now!*

From PEACHUM's point of view, we see MACKIE approaching along the corridor outside the cell. He is literally buried under a welter of chains and the police escort is so big that it fills up the whole corridor. The policemen are all heavily armed. They line the corridor, their revolvers levelled at MACKIE. He gradually gets nearer to the cell.

Shot of PEACHUM, past BROWN; PEACHUM sits up on the plank-bed, pushing BROWN aside so as to get a better view. He looks at MACKIE with interest, a triumphant expression on his face. We see MACKIE in the doorway, then cut back to BROWN and PEACHUM. PEACHUM makes a disparaging gesture and sinks back on the plank-bed.

PEACHUM: *You'll only release him again!*

He rolls over on his side again, turning his back on BROWN. MACKIE stands in the doorway, waiting to come in. He tries to catch BROWN's eye, but BROWN takes no notice of him and instead rages up and down the cell, in terrible agitation. Then he walks over to PEACHUM once again.

BROWN to PEACHUM: *We won't release him! I give you my word of honour! He'll be hanged!*

MACKIE realizes he has no hope of awakening BROWN's interest, loses his assurance and almost faints. He is virtually shaking with fear.

BROWN to PEACHUM: *Well, then, get out of here.*

PEACHUM does not move but replies in a honeyed and affable tone:

PEACHUM: *I'm fine here.*

BROWN loses his last vestige of self-control and roars:

BROWN: *Police! Take him out!*

The POLICEMEN rush in, push MACKIE into the cell so as to get him out of their way, drag PEACHUM off the plank-bed and throw him out through the door and into the corridor, tossing him from one to the other. In the process, MACKIE gets whirled round on his own axis in the cell. BROWN disappears behind PEACHUM, snorting with rage. All the policemen follow him. The cell door slams shut. MACKIE is left speechless, scarcely grasping what's been going on, since it's all happened at such a speed. He stands in the middle of the cell, looks all round and then as the camera tracks slightly backwards we see a pair of heavily armed policemen patrolling the corridor on either side of the cell.

The camera tracks ahead of PEACHUM as he walks slowly along the corridor with BROWN beside him.

BROWN: *Here's a concrete proposal for you! You stop the demonstration — I hang* Mackie *— and the authorities will extend your licence for another three years!*

PEACHUM throws BROWN a searching sideways glance, but then keeps to his pose of indifference and walks on without saying a word. His steps get slower and slower. BROWN whispers to PEACHUM in an even more urgent tone:

BROWN: *And a hundred pounds in cash — for your trouble!*

PEACHUM, realizing that he has won, shows no sign of being interested, whereupon BROWN increases his offer.

BROWN: *A hundred and fifty!* Then as PEACHUM doesn't stir: *Two hundred!*

PEACHUM has almost come to a standstill, but still shows no interest, BROWN loses patience.

BROWN: *All right, then — no deal! Go and have your demonstration! !* He walks off, snorting with rage.

PEACHUM is at first bewildered, but then he pulls himself together. The camera closes in on his mouth as he yells after BROWN.

PEACHUM: *Hey, stop! Give me a chance to get a word in!* After a moment's pause: *Right! Two hundred! Done!*

Fade out.

Scene 70. The directors' office at the bank.

Fade in to a close-up of POLLY at her desk, speaking into the telephone. The last words from the previous scene mix into her first words.

POLLY: . . . *Five thousand? . . . Convert another three thousand into cash at once . . . Yes! By hook or by crook . . .!*

The camera tracks back a bit. POLLY hangs up and turns to the directors, amongst whom is JACK. They have been following the conversation with bated breath as they stand in a circle round POLLY.

POLLY: *Right, so we've rustled up the bail for the release of our chief.*

We hear the sound of the glass door being opened. They all turn towards it. The camera pans to show us a bank-clerk coming in with bundles of banknotes on a wooden tray. The camera tracks with him as he walks over to the desk, and lays the tray down on it. POLLY turns to JACK as the clerk begins to count out the packets of notes.

POLLY to JACK: *The money must be in the Chief of Police's hands within the hour, Mr Jack!*

JACK rushes eagerly forward and goes to pick up the money; the other two directors instinctively do the same. But POLLY, looking at them suspiciously, pushes their hands away with an equally instinctive gesture and bends right over the desk so that she can both protect the money and ring the bell.

A member of the bank's staff appears in the doorway. He is a very venerable-looking elderly man with a majestic beard; he is in uniform and holds his cap in his hand; a huge bank bag is attached to his belt. The camera tracks with him as he walks in a dignified manner over to the desk, opens the bag with a key and puts the money into it. The directors watch it disappear with unconcealed envy. While this is going on, POLLY speaks to him.

POLLY: *This is the money for the bail. Have the policemen we asked for arrived?*

ELDERLY EMPLOYEE: *Yes they have, Madam President.*

He hands over the key to POLLY, who shuts the bags and gives the key to JACK. Then he walks majestically out of shot towards the door.

At the door, he lets in the two policemen who have been waiting outside.

POLLY very vehemently, off: *These gentlemen from the police are personally responsible to me for the safe transport of the money!*

The policemen salute. The ELDERLY EMPLOYEE walks out first and they follow him stiffly. Then JACK comes into shot, nods towards POLLY and follows the others out.

We see POLLY standing beside the huge green-baize conference table. The seven main members of the board are either seated in the armchairs or about to sit down.

POLLY: *We will postpone our board-meeting so that my husband — I mean, our chief, can take part in the discussions.*

Scene 71. The street outside the bank.

We see an enclosed car (an old-fashioned model, 1900 vintage) parked in front of the door. Some policemen ward off curious passers-by who are trying to form a crowd. The ELDERLY EMPLOYEE comes out of the bank, followed by the policemen and JACK, and gets into the car. JACK and the policemen get in after him, one of the policemen sitting beside the driver. The car drives off.

Scene 72. The Old Bailey, MACKIE'S *cell.*

In the cell, MACKIE is wandering round and round like a caged lion, half-crazy with fear.

MACKIE *murmuring to himself*: . . . *They're going to hang me . . . they're going to hang me . . . they're going to hang me!*

There is a distant sound of hammering on wood. MACKIE starts, walks over to the bars and listens anxiously. The banging gets more eerie and more hollow. He stares wildly into space and then a vision appears before his eyes . . .

Sinister-looking torturers are busy constructing a gallows . . .

MACKIE stuffs his fingers into his ears and rushes backwards into a distant corner of the cell, his eyes glued to the vision. The vision continues, accompanied by a distant roll of drums . . .

MACKIE is no longer chained but wearing a condemned person's shift, his neck bare. Two torturers lead him between a double rank of policemen, all heavily armed and drumming away. The drumming gets louder . . .

MACKIE covers his face with his hands and escapes to another corner of the cell, where he clings onto the bars. The drumming stops and instead we hear a bell tolling in the distance. It sounds like the sort of bell that is tolled when a condemned man is about to be executed. As he gazes through the bars, MACKIE sees a different vision . . .

A huge pair of gallows: MACKIE is being dragged up the steps. The vision disappears . . .

MACKIE collapses onto the floor of the cell and screams.

Scene 73. The street scene (as Scene 1).

The Coronation festivities have reached their climax; the crowds are roaring, enjoying themselves hugely. The police can scarcely keep them off the road. They are all laughing and looking in the same direction — the Coronation procession will soon be coming. A band is playing somewhere.

We see the car with MACKIE's bail inching its way through the throngs of people. As it is on the point of turning into the street a POLICEMAN stretches out his arm to prevent it going any further. JACK opens the door and perches on the running-board to peer ahead.

Scene 74. The Old Bailey, MACKIE'S *cell.*

Behind the bars, MACKIE picks himself up from the floor, struggling to his feet as though he has just come round from a dead faint. Still on his knees, he sings 'A Cry from the Grave' (a shortened version, possibly combined with 'The Epitaph'). He rises to his feet and continues singing with his face pressed against the bars. Fade out.

Scene 75. Outside PEACHUM'S *shop.*

A vast throng of beggars are gathering in preparation for their march. Signboards, placards and banners rear up above their heads. There is total silence as they form ranks.

Seen past the front rank of beggars, PEACHUM approaches along the street. At first a tiny figure, he gets larger and larger and while he is still some way away he starts signalling and calling out:

PEACHUM: *Call off the demonstration! . . . Call it off! Call it off!*

At first they can't make out what he's saying, but eventually he comes up to them, breathless, bedraggled and pouring with sweat. Since the beggars merely look at him, not reacting to his shouts at all, he furiously pushes back the first two, who are carrying a large banner.

PEACHUM screaming: *Take it all back. The demonstration is cancelled.*

He tries to tear the banner from their hands. A shrill whistle is heard from behind.

Shot of the assembling crowd of beggars from in front, with PEACHUM in the foreground. The ones at the back push their way forwards, all whistling and yelling, waving their hands and brandishing their crutches. FILCH rides to the front of the column on a high old-fashioned bike and shouts:

FILCH: *Forward march!*

The front ranks begin to move. PEACHUM is very nearly trampled underfoot. He leaps out of the way and rushes over to FILCH.

We see FILCH on the bike with the furious figure of PEACHUM beside him, while behind them the crowd of beggars begins to march.

PEACHUM clutching at FILCH: *Back, I say! I'm in charge here!*

He tries to pull FILCH off his bike. FILCH struggles with him, the beggars pull PEACHUM off as they march past; there's momentary confusion, during which PEACHUM gets thrashed and FILCH rides on, the main body of the beggars behind him.

Scene 76. Inside PEACHUM'S *shop.*
The open doorway is seen from inside the shop. There is a frightful noise coming from the street. MRS PEACHUM rushes towards the door and as the column marches past, PEACHUM retreats backwards into the shop and tries to shut the door, helped by MRS PEACHUM. But some of the beggars break in and give him a good thrashing, smashing the glass door in the process. More and more of them push their way in from the street. The camera tracks out to show the roaring throng of beggars tearing the shop apart.

Scene 77. A dark, narrow street.
Seen from a high angle, the procession of beggars march slowly and silently along. More and more people, the very images of poverty, come out of every nook and cranny, round every street corner. But these are figures of genuine wretchedness, among them haggard women holding small children by the hand. They join the beggars, so that the well organised procession soon breaks up into a jumbled mass of people shuffling slowly forwards.

Scene 78. Inside PEACHUM'S *shop.*
We look down from the staircase above MRS PEACHUM as she runs down with a jug of water and over to the battered and unconscious figure of her husband. She tries to revive him and he slowly comes round and looks about him.
The camera pans from his point of view, showing the devastation in the shop and then, through the shattered door in the street, the legs and artificial limbs of the beggars. Fade out.

Scene 79. BROWN'S *office in the Old Bailey.*
Close-up of some bundles of banknotes lying on BROWN'S desk. The camera tracks out to show us BROWN himself on one side of the table and in front of him the ELDERLY BANK

Employee, who is still taking bundles of notes out of his bag, with Jack standing beside him. The two policemen who escorted them stand stiffly behind them. Brown sits down, takes a printed form and begins to write something.
The form is seen in close-up as Brown puts his signature to it. We can make out only the bottom half of the form, the last words of which read '. . . is to be released at once'. After signing it, Brown's hand takes a large round rubber stamp and presses it down on the form, then puts the stamp back, allowing us to read the words 'London's Chief of Police'. The image fades, so that we can see nothing but the circular inscription on the stamp, then this too dissolves into the next shot.

Scene 80. The street outside the prison.
Close-up of the circular inscription 'London's Chief of Police' over the door of the prison. The camera tracks back to show us the door and a crowd of people besieging it. The police are holding the crowd back so that a passage is left clear from the door to the car from the bank, which is parked outside. Some photographers push their way to the front of the crowd, aiming their cameras at the door.

Scene 81. Brown's *office in the Old Bailey.*
Brown is seated at the desk on which he has stacked up the piles of notes. He walks over to the window and looks out into the street as distant cheers are heard from outside.

Scene 82. The street outside the prison.
The street is seen from Brown's window, with the waiting crowd being held back by police. In front are the car and the ring of photographers, still with their cameras pointing at the door, from which Mackie now emerges, triumphant and wreathed in smiles. He pauses on the top step and the ring of photographers closes in on him. He waves affably in all directions, while the crowd cheer in the background. He walks over to the car and climbs in. Jack climbs in and sits down behind him, while the Elderly Bank Employee, his bag now empty, gets in beside the chauffeur. The car drives off. Fade out.

Scene 83. A dark, narrow street.
Fade in to a high shot looking down onto the street. The throng of wretched humanity pours through, disappearing beneath the camera. The crowd entirely fills the street, in total disorder, the beggars disappearing in the welter of genuine poverty and misery. Distant cheers can be heard from the direction in which the crowd is marching.

Scene 84. The street scene (as Scene 1).
The cheers continue: the festivities are at their height in a blaze of sunshine and merriment. In the foreground, the crowds wait lining the street. Beyond them at the next intersection, the front of the Coronation procession is just turning the corner into the street and gradually getting nearer.
The procession is now seen in the foreground, beyond it the cheering crowds and a side street along which the throng of beggars, real and fake, are approaching. They turn into the main road. The cheering crowds and the policemen scatter, as the paupers surge forward and line the street in their place. More and more of them pour out of the sidestreet, swelling the waiting ranks.
Shot of the Coronation procession. In the foreground, the beggars stand waving their arms and artificial limbs threateningly and raising high their banners. A magnificent gilded Baroque calèche surrounded by heralds and pages breaks into a hurried trot; the slow and ceremonial pace observed hitherto is thrown to the winds and pages and maids of honour start to run like hunted animals. A chorus of threatening shouts begins to arise from the beggars, leading us into the next scene.

Scene 85. The directors' office in POLLY'S *bank.*
The beggars' chorus continues, faintly at first, but rapidly getting louder. MACKIE is addressing the members of the board, who are assembled round the green-baize table in the foreground. POLLY is seated beside him and looks up at him lovingly as he talks. MACKIE suddenly stops in mid-sentence, his mouth open, and turns nervously to the window. All the others gaze in the same direction, as the noise and singing rise to a threatening crescendo.

MACKIE in a commanding tone: *Let the shutters down!*

The rattle of the shutters being rolled down continues into the next scene.

Scene 86. The main banking hall.

The clerks have leapt onto their desks in panic. Beyond them we see the wide plate glass windows and large entrance doors. Various members of the bank's staff are feverishly letting down the shutters.

We see the shutter over the main entrance, now lowered to less than a man's height above the floor. The sweating and tattered figure of BROWN rushes into the hall beneath it, just before it finally crashes down to the ground.

Scene 87. The directors' office.

The directors and MACKIE are standing in a group as BROWN rushes in in the background, wild-eyed and out of breath. MACKIE hurries over to him and virtually catches him in his arms. JACK pushes up an easy chair and BROWN sinks exhausted into it. The noise and singing in the street are ebbing away.

Close on BROWN as he seizes MACKIE's hand and whispers to him in an agitated and stricken tone:

BROWN: *The Coronation procession is ruined! I'm done for! . . . I shall have to resign! Oh Mack, I have been sacrificed on the altar of our friendship!*

MACKIE calming him down: *Chin up, old chap!*

JACK brings a glass of whisky to revive him.

MACKIE: *Drown your sorrows in this whisky!* . . . BROWN drinks it down and pulls himself together . . . *It's mutual, after all.*

MACKIE turns to his colleagues and the camera tracks slightly back to show them standing round.

MACKIE: *There's a lesson for you!* To BROWN: *There's no reason why a retired Chief of Police shouldn't make an excellent bank director!*

BROWN shakes MACKIE by the hand, beaming and breathing a sigh of relief. POLLY walks over to BROWN and addresses him in a solemn and businesslike tone.

POLLY: *What sort of stake can you put in?*

BROWN looks perplexed, but then a thought strikes him.

BROWN triumphantly: *I managed to rescue the bail money!*

He pulls bundles of banknotes out of all his pockets and lays them on the table. MACKIE and BROWN embrace each other, exactly as they did in the wedding scene, and in the photograph of the two of them in uniform. They begin to sing 'The Song of the Heavy Cannon', with the burglars joining in the chorus.

Scene 88. The street in front of the bank.

The shutters are down. In the far distance we can see the tail end of the throng of beggars turning the corner as their singing fades softly away into the distance. PEACHUM, now scarcely recognizable, drags himself painfully along the street.

He walks past the bank, a broken man, leaning heavily on his stick, and the chorus of 'The Song of the Heavy Cannon' swells out from behind the lowered shutters.

We see him from behind as he stumbles on. The camera is stationary and he grows smaller and smaller until he finally disappears into the mist. Fade out.

NOTES

By comparison with the script published here, the final version of *The Threepenny Opera* is considerably condensed and reconstructed in a number of important ways. The dialogue, while following the sense of that given in the script, is often condensed almost to silent screen standards, while many scenes are cut or transposed. Significant divergences, both in structure and dialogue, are indicated in the following notes. It should be noted that the first half of the film follows the script fairly closely, and it may be assumed that scenes are included unless they are mentioned as being cut. From *Scene 48* onwards, the film diverges substantially from the script, and the only scenes included are those mentioned in the notes.

Scene 1

[1] In the film, as MACKIE grabs the cane by the handle, it comes apart and we see that it is a sword-stick with a long blade in it.

Scene 2

[2] In the film, our first view of MACKIE in this scene is as he comes round a corner between two spectators. The incident with the man with the top hat is omitted. During the initial action, the first three verses of 'The Ballad of Mackie Messer' are sung as follows:

Now the shark he has his teeth
And he wears them in his face.
Mackie Messer has a knife but
Wears it in a discreet place

On a lovely, sunny Sunday
A man lies dead upon the shore.
Another man strolls round the corner,
Mackie Messer strikes once more.

And Schul Mayer still is missing
And many other fine rich men.
Mackie Messer has their money
But evidence is rather thin.

[3] The next two verses of the song now follow:

When they found poor Jenny Towler
With a knife stuck in her breast,
On the quay walked Mackie Messer
As innocent as all the rest.

Seven children and an old man
Burned alive in our Soho —
In the crowd is Mackie Messer,
He's not asked and does not know.

4 At this point, instead of showing us the girls with their liquorice sticks, the camera tracks away from the scene, showing the two women with MACKIE in pursuit. The STREET-SINGER delivers the final verse off-screen:

And the widow, under age
The one whose name we know so well
Raped one night as she lay sleeping . . .

Camera tracks ahead of MACKIE, smiling.

. . . Mackie, how much could you tell?

We resume on the SINGER as he repeats the last two lines of the song.

5 Before *Scene 3*, the film shows the two women coming up the street and stopping in front of a shop with a sign saying MILLINERS. There is a wedding dress in the window and as POLLY gazes at it thoughtfully, she notices the reflection of MACKIE, who has come up behind her. She turns and MACKIE leans hungrily over POLLY, who is dragged unwillingly away by her mother.

Scene 3

6 The exchange with WAT DREARY does not take place at this point. Instead, MACKIE sees JENNY approaching, and tells the doorman not to let her in.

7 Once inside the inn, MACKIE tells one of his henchmen to go and deal with JENNY. The henchman goes outside and blocks JENNY's path as she tries to go in.

Scene 4

8 The film first shows them arriving at a table in a corner of the bar. MACKIE stands menacingly over two characters seated at the table, who nervously raise their hats and vacate their places. (*Still*).

9 Meanwhile, outside, JENNY is screaming at the doorman: *He's in there with a woman, isn't he?* The henchman restrains her bodily.

10 In the film, this scene has even more point, since it is JACK's girl, not his whisky, from which he is torn away to dance with MRS PEACHUM.

11 MACKIE stays at the table with POLLY and they gaze into one another's eyes. He silently asks her to marry him and she nods.

[12] Apart from the comment on JACK's abilities as a dancer to MRS PEACHUM, these are the first words which MACKIE is heard to utter in the bar scene. There then follows a condensed version of MACKIE's instructions for the wedding, which the man addressed passes on to the other burglars. MACKIE finally disappears upstairs with POLLY, leaving a written invitation to be delivered to TIGER BROWN, which the horrified burglars pass from hand to hand. The final dialogue between JACK and MRS PEACHUM is omitted.

Scenes 5 to 9

The scenes involving the burglars are much condensed in the film. The episode with the double bed is omitted, and the serenade is displaced to a later point. The deaf-mute BEGGAR is also omitted, both from the scene with the clock *(Scene 9)* and from the scene in BROWN's office which follows.

Scene 10

[13] In the film, MAT OF THE MINT is brought in as BROWN is berating his men: they have caught a thief 'red-handed'. BROWN turns on MAT and gives him dire warnings of the treatment he can expect, but is cut off in mid-flow by the sight of MACKIE's invitation, which is fastened inside the crown of MAT's hat so that only BROWN can see it. BROWN nervously orders the policemen out. (*Still*).

Scene 11

After the episode with NED and the armchair (*Still*), the film moves straight on to *Scene 17*.

Scene 17

In the film, the scene of the marriage, and MACKIE's headquarters, is a large warehouse beside the river, and not the stables of the Duke of Devonshire. All references to the place in the film are therefore to the 'warehouse' rather than the 'stable'. At the beginning of this scene, the two burglars first appear through a trapdoor in the floor, leading from a lower storey of the warehouse. (*Still*).

Scene 18

The following scenes of the waggons approaching the stable are omitted. Instead a ramp is let down from the upper floor of the warehouse and the burglars, who have been waiting outside, swarm in with their stolen goods. At this point the serenade *(Scene 8)* is inserted, but takes place on a boat moored to the quayside by the river. POLLY appears in her wedding dress, and the following dialogue takes place:

MACKIE: *Can you see the moon over Soho?*

POLLY: *I see it, dearest . . . Can you feel my heart beating, beloved?*

MACKIE: *I feel it, beloved.*

POLLY: *Where you are, there will I be too.*

MACKIE: *And where you are, I'll be at your side.* He begins to sing:

We have no licence from the registrar
And no nice flowers on the high altar.
Your wedding dress comes from somewhere afar
And no myrtle crown for your hair.
The platter from off which you now eat your bread,
Don't look at it, cast it down.
Love endures or fades away
Either here or elsewhere, my own.

He helps POLLY off the boat onto the quay and they walk away into the distance. (*Still*).

The scenes of the preparations in the warehouse then follow.

Scene 22

The coachman is, of course, omitted, since in the film, MACKIE and POLLY are coming from the boat moored at the quayside.

Scene 25

The comments from the various burglars are omitted in the film, and after a brief chorus of congratulations, MACKIE begins his tour of inspection; one of the burglars carries POLLY's train. At the end, POLLY comments:

POLLY: *How lovely! All stolen, Mackie?*

MACKIE: *Of course.*

POLLY: *A pity we've no home for these lovely things.*

[14] At this point, MACKIE instructs NED to escort the VICAR from the warehouse with the words: *The district is none too safe.* However, as soon as they get outside the terrified VICAR runs away.

[15] One of the burglars responds by standing on his hands on the table, juggling with some plates etc, but gets a very frosty reception.

[16] The song which POLLY sings is not ' Pirate Jenny ' but the following:

Once I believed, when innocent I was —
And I really was once, same as you —
Perhaps someone will soon be my suitor,
Then I must know what to do.
And if he's rich and if he's nice,
And if his collar's white as snow,

And if he knows how to treat a lady,
Then the answer's No.

Then you stick your nose up in the air
And let your righteous virtue glow.
Sure the moon is brighter than before,
Sure the boat goes gliding from the shore,
But that's as far as you should go.
Yes, but you don't simply lay yourself down,
Yes, be as cold and heartless as you know,
Yes, there's so much that can happen,
Yes, there's just one answer, No!

The first was a man who came from Kent,
He was all that a man should be.
The second had three ships in the harbour,
The third was mad about me.
And they had money, and they were nice,
And their collars were as white as snow,
And they knew how to treat a lady —
To them I answered No!

Then I stuck my nose up in the air
And I let my righteous virtue glow.
Sure the moon was brighter than before,
Sure the boat went gliding from the shore,
But that's as far as I would go.
Yes, but you don't simply lay yourself down,
Yes, be as cold and heartless as you know,
Yes, there's so much that can happen,
Yes, there's just one answer, No! . . . No?

Then came another who didn't try to beg
One day when the sky was blue.
He hung his hat on the peg in my room,
Then I didn't know what to do.
He had no money, he wasn't nice,
His collar was never white as snow.
He didn't know how to treat a lady,
Yet I couldn't say to him No.

I couldn't stick my nose up in the air,
And forgot my virtue's glow.

Oh the moon was brighter than before,
But the boat never glided from the shore,
Then I had no choice and so . . .
Yes, then you must simply lay yourself down,
Yes, then you can't be cold and heartless, you know.
Yes, there's so much that did happen.
Yes, I couldn't hope to answer No.

The song is accompanied by alternating shots of POLLY, MACKIE and the listening burglars. At the end of the song the burglars applaud enthusiastically and one of them says: *I like the words, very nice.* To which MACKIE replies scornfully: *Nice! It's not nice, it's art, you fool!* To POLLY: *Wonderful! Too good for this trash.*

[17] *Still.*

Scene 26

This scene is omitted from the film, and so is all reference to the fight between the three beggars in the later scenes in PEACHUM's shop.

Scene 28

[18] PEACHUM's song is omitted from the film.

Scene 29 is displaced to within *Scene 30.*

Scene 30

[19] *Still.*

[20] At this point we move to POLLY's bedroom, and PEACHUM's discovery of her absence takes place on-screen. POLLY then arrives immediately, the robbery of the safe by MACKIE's gang being omitted. The argument with her parents in *Scene 32* takes place in POLLY's bedroom (*Still*), and her song in *Scene 33* is omitted.

Scene 34

[21] The film at this point includes a scene in TIGER BROWN's office, in which PEACHUM threatens trouble at the forthcoming Coronation if BROWN does not arrest MACKIE and have him hanged. The dialogue is adapted from that used in *Scene 61* of the script.

Scene 35

The STREET-SINGER's song, in the film, runs as follows:

Man lives through his head,
A head fit for a mouse.
Just test it out, your little head,
It wouldn't feed a louse.

For our life in this world,
Man is very much too dim.
Never does he notice
Everyone deceiving him.

Yes, make yourself a plan,
Yes, be a shining light.
Then make yourself a second plan
And both your plans will fight.

For our life in this world,
Man is not corrupt enough.
Yet his aspirations
Provide a noble touch.

Yes, just you chase your luck,
But don't you run too fast,
Since all who push their luck too much
Find that they come in last.

For our life in this world
Man assumes too much.
So all his aspirations
Are self-deceptive gush.

Scene 36
MACKIE MESSER's headquarters, as seen in the film (*Still*), is described by Paul Rotha in *Celluloid* (see Appendix). The conversation between MACKIE and POLLY in this scene is greatly condensed, but follows the sense of that in the script.

Scene 38
[22] In the film, POLLY slaps MAT's face with the comment: *Nothing personal, of course.*

Scenes 39 and 40
These are omitted in the film, and *Scene 48* — JENNY's exchange with MRS PEACHUM (*Still*) — takes place before MACKIE's entry into the brothel.

Scene 47
[23] *Still.*
The conversation between MACKIE and JENNY is somewhat condensed in

the film. MACKIE then turns his attention to the other girls and JENNY walks over to the window and signals to the waiting policemen. Standing in front of the window, she then begins to sing 'The Ballad of the Ship with Fifty Cannon' (and not the 'Tango Ballad'). The song runs as follows:

Today I wash glasses and make up the beds
Servant to one and all, sir.
Give me a penny and I thank you well
For I live in rags in a dirty hotel,
But you don't know who I am, sirs.

But one night soon there'll be screaming by the harbour
And then they'll be in terror all the while.
Then I'll be smiling to my glasses
And they'll ask, Why should she smile?

And a ship with eight great sails
And with fifty fine cannon
Will tie up at the quay.

Dear sirs, it'll take the smile off your faces
When the walls come tumbling in.
The town will be flattened right to the ground,
Just this dirty hotel left safe and sound
And you'll wonder who lives within.

At this point MACKIE comes up, having left the other girls, and listens intently to JENNY's song.

But in the night there'll be shrieks round this hotel
And they'll wonder why it should be standing free,
And they'll see me step outside in the morning
And they'll be saying, Who is she?
And they'll be saying, Who is she?

And a ship with eight great sails
And with fifty fine cannon
Will run up her flag.

At mid-day hundreds will swarm ashore
Searching every street and hill,
Rounding up survivors who'll be shivering with fear,
Wrapping them in chains and bringing them all here,
And they'll ask me, Which shall we kill?
And they'll ask me, Which shall we kill?

At this very hour there'll fall a hush on the harbour
And they'll ask me, Who shall die?
And then you'll hear me order firmly, All.
When the heads fall I'll cry, Hoppla!

And a ship with eight great sails
And with fifty fine cannon
Will then sail off with me.

Instead of dancing MACKIE into the arms of the waiting police, JENNY now relents. She tells him he has been betrayed and hides him behind a curtain as the police search the brothel. JENNY diverts the police with the words: *He went through the window*, and MACKIE then walks nonchalantly out onto the roof.

From this point on, the sequence of events in the film departs substantially from that in the script, and the following notes therefore itemise each scene as it occurs.

Scenes 48 and 49
These are omitted, and instead MACKIE, having made good his escape, falls in with another tart in the street and disappears into her lodging with her as the police search for him outside. This episode is clearly suggested by *Scene 57* in the script.

MRS PEACHUM meanwhile returns to inform PEACHUM that MACKIE has escaped:
MRS PEACHUM: *He escaped. The girl helped him.*
PEACHUM: *Tiger Brown's the girl's name. Now for the Coronation . . .*

MACKIE emerges again from the tart's lodging, takes leave of her and walks straight into the arms of the waiting police.

We now see the STREET-SINGER, who addresses the camera as follows:
STREET-SINGER: *Ladies and gentlemen, you have seen Mackie's flippancy and boldness . . . Now see how a shrewd, loving wife alters events in a way you can't predict.*

The film then moves to a version of *Scene 64*, in which POLLY addresses the directors of the newly instituted bank, then we return to *Scene 50*.

Scene 50
This scene is substantially cut in the film. It opens with an exchange between SMITH and BROWN (this is SMITH's first appearance in the film):

BROWN: *Give him everything he asks for!*
SMITH: *Cigarettes too?*
BROWN: *No — here, give him a cigar.* He hands SMITH some cigars from his pocket.
We then move to the conversation about the handcuffs between SMITH and MACKIE, during which MACKIE is horrified to hear the sound of an execution taking place off-screen.

Scenes 51 and 52
The character of LUCY does not appear in the film at all, and it is JENNY who in fact comes and visits MACKIE in prison (*Stills*), and engineers his escape by seducing SMITH. Moreover, this episode is displaced to a later point and the film moves directly from *Scene 50* to *Scene 66* — the preparations for the procession of beggars.

Scene 66
In this scene it is not FILCH but PEACHUM who gets up on the desk and addresses the beggars, who are alarmed at the sound of the royal guard off-screen.
24 In the film PEACHUM's speech continues: *You can participate in this glamorous event. You'd all be dead but for my fund-raising schemes. I discovered that the rich can't face the misery they make. They've got cold hearts but weak nerves . . . No consideration for their nerves today! We'll tear their nerves with all our power. Our rags won't cover our wounds . . . Don't be afraid, gentlemen, the Queen won't tolerate bayonets against cripples.*
At this point MRS PEACHUM rushes in with the news that MACKIE has been arrested, and PEACHUM tries to stop the procession, which has now got under way. However, he is swept aside by the silently marching beggars. This sequence matches that given in *Scenes 75* and *76* of the script, but FILCH's leadership of the mob is not in evidence.

We then return to the STREET-SINGER, who gives his acid comment on the proceedings:
STREET-SINGER:

Yes, make yourself a plan,
Yes, be a shining light,
Then make yourself a second plan
And both your plans will fight.
For our life in this world
Man is not corrupt enough,
Yet his aspirations
Provide a noble touch.

The film next moves to the bail scene *(Scene 70)*, then we return to PEACHUM being swept aside by the advancing tide of beggars. The episode in which PEACHUM visits BROWN at the Old Bailey and gets locked in MACKIE's cell is of course omitted from the film, which next moves to JENNY's visit to MACKIE in jail — an adaptation of *Scene 52.* SMITH is just bringing MACKIE his dinner, and JENNY persuades him to let her see MACKIE with the words: *I'll let you come and see me tonight . . .* SMITH opens the cell and goes in to give MACKIE his dinner. JENNY then folds him in an embrace at the bars and gestures to MACKIE, who sneaks out of the cell, locking the door behind him.
The film then returns to the procession of beggars as they encounter the police.

Meanwhile, BROWN is receiving the news of the demonstration in his office. This is an adaptation of *Scene 68* in the script — except that SMITH is not present (being locked in MACKIE's cell) and BROWN is of course under the impression that MACKIE is still in jail. In this scene, the BANK EMPLOYEE arrives with MACKIE's bail (*Scene 79* in the script). BROWN immediately phones the cells to order MACKIE's release, only to find that he has escaped.

Amid the crowds waiting for the Coronation procession, MACKIE, on the run, encounters one of his gang in the street. The burglar informs MACKIE that he is now the managing director of a bank: *The City Bank . . . in Piccadilly.* MACKIE is highly approving and makes off towards the bank.

We now see the horde of beggars as it converges on the Coronation procession *(Scene 84* in the script). The beggars charge into the procession, and there is a dramatic confrontation as they come face to face with the open carriage in which the QUEEN is riding. Unable to bear the beggars' gaze, the QUEEN finally hides her face behind her fan, and the carriage moves on.
Now the mounted guards charge the beggars and disperse them, while BROWN — also in guard's uniform — watches in despair from his horse. (*Stills*).

The film then moves to the bank, as *Scene 85*. First there is a reunion between MACKIE and POLLY, then one of the burglars announces the news that the Coronation has been ruined by thousands of beggars. The shutters are lowered.
Outside, BROWN rides up on his horse, dismounts and goes into the bank.

We see the procession of beggars sweeping past in silence.

BROWN then blunders into the bank, where everything is in darkness. Candles are brought, and the directors gather round *(Scene 87* in the script). After BROWN has deposited the bail money, MACKIE and BROWN drink to friendship and reminisce over their times in the Indian Army — they break into ' The Song of the Heavy Cannon ', as follows:

MACKIE: *John was there and Jim was too*
BROWN: *And George was made a sergeant.*
MACKIE: *But the Army doesn't give tuppence for you*
BROWN: *As it sets its men a-marching.*

BOTH: *Soldiers depend on the heavy cannon*
From Cape to Couch Behar.
BROWN: *If they should chance to meet,*
MACKIE: *In sunshine, snow or sleet,*
BROWN: *Another sort of race,*
MACKIE: *Dark or fair of face,*
BOTH: *They chop them up to make some beefsteak tartare.*

MACKIE: *Johnny thought whisky rather warm*
BROWN: *And Jimmy was short of blankets,*
MACKIE: *But Georgie took them by the arm*
BROWN: *Crying, The Army will always vanquish.*

BOTH: *Soldiers depend on the heavy cannon*
From Cape to Couch Behar.
BROWN: *If they should chance to meet,*
MACKIE: *In sunshine, snow or sleet,*
BROWN: *Another sort of race,*
MACKIE: *Dark or fair of face,*
BOTH: *They chop them up to make some beefsteak tartare.*

MACKIE: *Johnny and Jimmy are both long dead*
BROWN: *And Georgie is broken and missing,*
MACKIE: *But blood is blood and always red*
BROWN: *And the Army's still recruiting.*

EVERYONE IN CHORUS:
Soldiers depend on the heavy cannon,
From Cape to Couch Behar.
If they should chance to meet
In sunshine, snow or sleet

Another sort of race,
Dark or fair of face,
They chop them up to make some beefsteak tartare.

The ending of the film is radically different from the script, since PEACHUM now enters (instead of passing by the bank, a broken man, as in *Scene 88*). The following conversation takes place:

PEACHUM: *Poor Peachum and rich Mackie ought to join hands.*

MACKIE: *You're bankrupt, honest Mr Peachum. A poor devil like the rest.*

PEACHUM: *Today I've seen the power of the poor . . . Your money and my experience, a mighty business.*

He sits down and produces some contracts which he and MACKIE proceed to sign.

MACKIE: *Why do they need us, if they're so powerful?*

PEACHUM: *They don't know it, but it's we who need them!*

As they sign the contracts, the STREET-SINGER is heard over:

STREET-SINGER:

Gathered for the happy ending
All crowd under the same hat.
If good money is quite handy,
Everything ends well for that.
Hinz and Kunz fish muddy waters,
Wish each other quickly dead,
Yet in the end around the table
They both share the poor man's bread.

As he continues, we see the procession of beggars filing silently past in the street outside.

STREET-SINGER:

Therefore some live in the darkness
And the others in the light,
We see those who live in the daytime
But not those who live in night.

Der Golem (1920)

From *The Haunted Screen* by Lotte Eisner (London, Thames and Hudson, 1969)

Paul Wegener had too strong a personality to be content with merely imitating Reinhardt's style. His treatment of the magical lighting-effects found at the Deutsches Theater was to adapt them to the needs of the cinema. From his previous work in natural settings he kept a fluidity of atmosphere which he managed to bring to his studio-made *Golem* (1920). An airy lightness hangs about the shots of the flower-garlanded children playing in front of the ghetto gates.

Wegener uses every one of Reinhardt's lighting-effects: the stars glinting against a velvety sky, the fiery glow of an alchemist's furnace, the little oil-lamp lighting a corner of a darkened room when Miriam appears, the servant holding a lantern, the row of blazing torches flickering in the night, and, in the synagogue, the light trembling over the prostrate, indistinct forms wrapped in cloaks, with the sacred, haloed seven-branched candelabra emerging from the darkness.

The spell of these subtle effects is never broken by clashing contrast or exaggerated Expressionist brio. A warm Rembrandt-like light floods the interiors, modelling the old Rabbi's ravaged face and casting the young disciple into gentle relief against the dark background; the shadow of a barred window stands out across a garment. The scene of the appeal to the demon with its circles of flames is even more poignant than the corresponding scene in Murnau's *Faust*: the demon's phosphorescent head, with its sad empty eyes, is suddenly transformed into a huge Chinese mask looming up in profile at the edge of the screen with a kind of prodigious ferocity.

Paul Wegener always denied having had the intention of making an Expressionist film with his *Golem*. But this has not stopped people from calling it Expressionist, doubtless because of the much-discussed settings by Poelzig, the creator of the Grosses Schauspielhaus in Berlin.

Kurtz says something to the effect that Poelzig expresses all a building's dynamic, ecstatic, fantastic and pathetic elements in the façade without extending any renewal of forms to the layout itself.

This explains why the sets of *The Golem* are so far removed from those of *Caligari.* The original Gothic forms are still somehow latent in these houses with their steeply-pitched thatched roofs. Their angular, oblique outlines, their teetering bulk, their hollowed steps, seem the none too unreal image of a distressingly insanitary and overpopulated ghetto where people actually live. The success of these sets owes very little to abstraction. The narrow gables are somehow echoed in the pointed hats and wind-blown goatees of the Jews, the excited fluttering of their hands, their raised arms clutching at the empty restricted space. This alternately terrified and exultant crowd at times recalls the flamboyant outlines and disjointed movement of a painting by El Greco. The brio of these masses has nothing in common with the mechanical use of extras found in Lubitsch, or the geometric groupings of crowds found in Fritz Lang. The shaping effect is particularly successful when the ornamental derives from the natural, as in the high-angle shot of the thora-tabernacle bordered by the great sacred trumpets.

In the interiors, a tracery of Gothic ribs and ogives transformed into oblique semi-ellipses composes a framework for the characters. This gives stability to the fluctuating intensity of the atmosphere, which is at times curiously " Impressionistic " for this authentically " Expressionistic " structure.

We do find from time to time Expressionistic shock lighting effects: for instance the conch of the spiral staircase glaring out abruptly from the darkness of the laboratory; the sudden glow of the seven-branched candelabra; or the livid, anguished faces of the faithful in the synagogue.

Nosferatu (1922)

From *The Haunted Screen* by Lotte Eisner (London, Thames and Hudson, 1969)

The complete title of Murnau's film is *Nosferatu, eine Symphonie des Grauens* (*Nosferatu, a Symphony of Horror*). And in fact, seeing this film again today, one cannot fail to be chilled by what Béla

Balázs called " the glacial draughts of air from the beyond ". The terror emanating from *Caligari* seems somehow almost artificial by comparison.

In Friedrich Wilhelm Murnau, the greatest film-director the Germans have ever known, cinematic composition was never a mere attempt at decorative stylization. He created the most overwhelming and poignant images in the whole German cinema.

Murnau was trained as an art-historian. Whereas Lang attempts to give a faithful reproduction of the famous paintings he sometimes uses, Murnau elaborates the memory he has kept of them and transforms them into personal visions. The foreshortened view of a prostrate man stricken with plague in *Faust* (the shooting angle makes the soles of his feet become enormous) is the transposed reflection of Mantegna's Christ. And when Gretchen nurses her infant in the snow among the ruins of a cottage, with her head wrapped in her cloak, this image is no more than the vague reminiscence of a Flemish Madonna.

Murnau had homosexual tendencies. In his attempt to escape from himself, he did not express himself with the artistic continuity which makes it so easy to analyse the style of, say, Lang. But all his films bear the impress of his inner complexity, of the struggle he waged within himself against a world in which he remained despairingly alien. Only in his last film, *Tabu,* did he seem to have found peace and a little happiness in surroundings which abolish the guilt-feelings inherent in European morality. Gide, once his *Immoraliste* had delivered him from Protestant austerity and its concomitant scruples, could then indulge in natural inclinations. But Murnau, born in 1888, lived under the ominous shadow which the inhuman Paragraph 175 of the pre-1918 German Penal Code, lending itself to all the horrors of blackmail, cast over him and those like him.

Murnau, a conscientious artist, German in the good meaning of the word, never resorted to the little shifts and subterfuges which can facilitate the creator's task. This is why his films seem rather heavy in places — the underlying meaning of their rhythm only becomes apparent little by little. At other times, when the big businessmen of Ufa put pressure on him for a happy ending, as in *Der Letzte Mann* (*The Last Laugh,* 1924), he scamps it with disgust, pulling the coarsest threads of comedy, and becomes as crass as the audiences that slapped their sides at Lubitsch's *Kohlhiesels Töchter,* one of his least refined farces.

In any case one is forced to admit that Murnau's genius — I think we can talk about genius in his case — has surprising weaknesses. Normally so sensitive, he sometimes commits extraordinary errors of taste and lapses into mawkishness. In *Faust*, for example, insipid images follow powerful visions bursting with creative vigour. His shy nature, burdened with a weighty heritage of typically German sentimentality and morbid timidity, led him to admire in others the muscular strength and vitality he himself lacked. This is why he allowed Jannings to show off outrageously in the role of Mephisto and failed to moderate the exuberance of Dieterle.

Murnau came from Westphalia, a region of vast pastures where enormous peasants breed heavy-boned plough-horses. The landscape had a great influence on him. Even when he was prevailed upon to film in the studio he kept his nostalgia for the countryside; and this homesickness gives *Der Brennende Acker* (*The Burning Earth*, 1922) a wild flavour which is still perceptible in *Sunrise*, made in the USA.

The landscapes and views of the little town and the castle in *Nosferatu* were filmed on location. This was far from being the usual practice in German films at that time. Directors such as Lang or Lubitsch built vast forests and entire towns so as to be able to film in the studio or, at a pinch, a few yards away on a strip of waste ground; and the reason was not merely that the frontiers were closed to them through a lack of foreign currency and sympathy. They could easily have found Gothic towns on the Baltic coast or Baroque towns in Southern Germany; but Expressionist precepts turned them away from reality.

Murnau, however, making *Nosferatu* with a minimum of resources, saw all that nature had to offer in the way of fine images. He films the fragile form of a white cloud scudding over the dunes, while the wind from the Baltic plays among the scarce blades of grass. His camera lingers over a filigree of branches standing out against a spring sky at twilight. He makes us feel the freshness of a meadow in which horses gallop around with a marvellous lightness.

Nature participates in the action: sensitive editing makes the bounding waves foretell the approach of the vampire, the imminence of the doom about to overtake the town. Over all these landscapes — dark hills, thick forests, skies of jagged storm-clouds — there hovers what Balázs calls the great shadow of the supernatural.

In a film by Murnau every shot has its precise function and is entirely conceived with an eye to its participation in the action. The momentary close-up of a detail of billowing sails is as necessary to the action as the image preceding it — the high-angle shot of the current sweeping away the raft and its sinister cargo.

The grisaille of the arid hills around the vampire's castle recalls, with its extreme and almost documentary restraint, certain passages in the films of Dovzhenko. A few years later, when Ufa obliged him to use pasteboard, Murnau filmed the famous air journey in *Faust* in the studio, with the aid of models. This prodigious chain of artificial mountains is complete with valleys and torrents; the only thing that makes them tolerable — and sometimes even admirable — is the talent of Murnau. He masks his materials with those combinations of mist and light to which the Germans are so sensitive and which they interpret with the same skill they bring to portraying the gentle glow of a hanging lamp in a stuffy room. *Faust* is the largescale deployment of all the artifice of the cinema by a man who knows every detail of his craft; but how one regrets the greyish expanses of *Nosferatu.*

In the full maturity of his talent Murnau could achieve in the studio such visions as the vast snow-covered plains against which a storm-rent tree stands out; a post in all its sad nudity rises above a demolished fence — a precarious refuge for Gretchen nursing her child.

Similarly, in the studios in America, he was to create for *Sunrise* such realistically desolate marshes that it takes the eye a long time to discern their artificiality. Murnau was one of the few German film-directors to have the innate love for landscape more typical of the Swedes (Arthur von Gerlach, the creator of *Die Chronik von Grieshuus,* was another), and he was always reluctant to resort to artifice. When he made *City Girl* (1930), according to Theodore Huff, he was moved to exaltation when he felt his camera running over the wheatfields of Oregon and sliding through the ocean of ripe grain at the height of the harvest. The coming of the sound film and the commercial ruthlessness of Hollywood destroyed this dream. To escape, Murnau fled to the South Seas, and *Tabu.*

The architecture in *Nosferatu,* typically Nordic — brick façades with stubby gables — is perfectly adapted to the film's strange plot. Murnau did not have to distort the little Baltic townscapes with contrasting lighting effects: there was no need for him to increase the mystery of the alleyways and squares with an artificial chiaroscuro. Under Murnau's direction the camera of Fritz Arno Wagner required no extraneous factors to evoke the bizarre. When *Nosferatu* is preparing a departure in the courtyard, the use of unexpected angles gives the vampire's castle a sinister appearance. What could be more expressive than a long narrow street, hemmed in between monotonous brick façades, seen from a high window, the bar of which crosses the image?

The undertaker's mutes dressed in top hats and skimpy frock-coats move slowly over the crudely hewn cobbles, black and stiff, bearing, two by two, the slim coffin of a victim of the plague. Never again was so perfect an Expressionism to be attained, and its stylization was achieved without the aid of the least artifice. Murnau was to return to this theme in *Faust*, but there the men in cowls have a quality of artificial picturesqueness rather than the starkness of the earlier composition.

But it was in the portrayal of horror that the camera of Murnau and Fritz Arno Wagner excelled. In *Caligari* the forms of the satanic doctor and Cesare often slant up in a shot left deliberately out of focus, which Kurtz defined as " the ideal and pure shot of the transposed expression of objects ". But Murnau created an atmosphere of horror by a forward movement of the actors towards the camera. The hideous form of the vampire approaches with exasperating slowness moving from the extreme depth of one shot towards another in which he suddenly becomes enormous. Murnau had a complete grasp of the visual power that can be won from editing, and the virtuosity with which he directs this succession of shots has real genius. Instead of presenting the whole approach as a gradual process, he cuts for a few seconds to the reactions of the terrified youth, returns to the approach, then cuts it off abruptly by having a door slammed in the face of the terrible apparition; and the sight of this door makes us catch our breath at the peril lurking behind it.

It is true that the opening shots of *Caligari* show the evil doctor walking straight at the camera and drawing up his replete figure in a menacing attitude; for a second his face swells up diabolically. But a diamond-shaped lens mask immediately tones down the effect. The images of Cesare advancing in the booth and crossing Lil Dagover's bedroom, or the robot coming towards us from the back of the screen in *Metropolis*, are less violent than that of the vampire slowly emerging from the darkness. (But Lang was to learn how to use this effect to advantage; in the first *Mabuse* the doctor's head appears, at first small and remote on a black background, only to be suddenly projected forward, as if by some supernatural agency, filling the whole screen.)

Murnau could also enhance the effect of a transversal movement by spreading it over the whole screen: for instance, the dark phantom vessel speeding with all sail set over a surging sea, and ominously entering the harbour; or again, the low-angle shot of the enormous silhouette of the vampire crossing the vessel to reach his prey. Here the camera angle confers on him, in addition to his gigantic proportions, a kind of obliqueness which projects him out of the screen and makes him into a sort of tangible, three-dimensional menace.

People have often wondered why Wiene never used for *Caligari*, in addition to lens masks of various shapes, the trick techniques that Méliès had already developed, which would have increased the impression of mystery and terror. In *Destiny* Lang took full advantage of superimpositions and fade-outs. The superimposed march of the dead towards the great wall, and the various transformations and apparitions, show that he had understood the resources of a technique capable of freeing itself from the limits imposed by this apparently two-dimensional art-form.

In *Nosferatu* the jerky movements of the phantom coach which bears the young traveller off to the land of the undead, or those of the coffins being piled up with an atrocious rapidity, were rendered by the " one stop one " (stop-motion) technique. The spectres of bare white trees, rearing up against a black background like carcasses of prehistoric beasts, during the rapid journey to the monster's castle, were rendered by an insertion of a few feet of negative.

Murnau used the obsession with inanimate objects much better than many fanatics of Expressionism. In the haunted hold of the sailing vessel in which all the sailors have been struck down by death, the empty hammock of the dead sailor goes on gently swinging. Or again, stripping down the details to the very minimum, Murnau shows nothing but the reflection of the sustained, monotonous, swinging of a suspended lamp in the deserted captain's cabin. Murnau was to use the same effect when his rejuvenated Faust takes the proud Duchess of Parma: a chandelier swinging above the sumptuous bed.

M (1931)

From *The Cinema of Fritz Lang* by Paul M. Jensen (New York, A. S. Barnes & Co.; London, A. Zwemmer Limited; 1969).

In 1930, Fritz Lang put a notice in the newspapers announcing that his next picture would be titled *Mörder unter Uns* (*The Murderer is among Us*). Suddenly, anonymous threatening letters began arriving and he was refused use of the studio at Staaken; it was as though he had stumbled into one of his own plots, with hindrances appearing from no known source and for no known reason. Was some secret organisation, led by an evil master-mind, plotting against him? This fanciful idea was revealed to be quite close to the truth when Lang confronted the studio head. Asked why there was opposition to a film about Peter Kürten, the child-murderer known as " The Vampire of Düsseldorf ", the executive replied, " Oh! I see ", laughed, and held out the keys to the studio. Lang, noticing the party insignia on the man's lapel, realised that the Nazis had thought the film to be about them. It was here that Lang came of age politically.[1]

The picture was shot in six weeks in a makeshift studio at the Staaken Zeppelinhalle, outside Berlin. Peter Lorre, who played the killer, performed for Lang by day while appearing on the stage in *Squaring the Circle* (a farce by Valentin Katayev) in the evenings. The original title was shortened to the single letter *M*, though the film has also been referred to as *Eine Stadt sucht einen Mörder* (*A City Searches for a Murderer*) and *Dein Mörder sieht dich An* (*Your Killer Looks at You*). Made for Nero Films, instead of UFA or Lang's own company, it opened at the UFA-Palast am Zoo, Berlin, in June 1931. Its running time was then 114 minutes, but *Variety's* review of the première noted that this was " a little too long. Without spoiling the effect — even bettering it — cutting could be done. There are a few repetitions and a few slow scenes ".[2] This advice was followed two years later when Foremco Pictures released *M* in the

[1] Siegfried Kracauer, *From Caligari to Hitler* (New York, The Noonday Press, 1959).
[2] Magnus, " *M* ", *Variety* (June 2, 1931).

USA; this version was only ninety-two minutes long. The first print shown in New York City was in German, with English subtitles, but after two weeks it was replaced with a dubbed version. Supposedly, Lang had planned for this situation by avoiding close-ups of people talking and by covering lip movements with a prop, such as Lohman's cigar, or a turn of the head. The dubbing was done in England, by Eric Hakim, and except for Lorre most of the actors involved were not the original performers. New York's Museum of Modern Art now circulates a slightly longer, ninety-seven minute copy to which is added the Museum's own prologue of printed information. (The Museum states on the film and in its catalogue that the original print was thirty minutes longer, but this is simply an exaggeration.)

Seymour Nebenzal, head of Nero Films, produced several quite original films in the early 'thirties, including *M* and Lang's *Das Testament des Dr Mabuse.* In 1950, he and Harold Nebenzal also produced an American version of *M* for Columbia Pictures. " People ask why I do not re-make *M* in English," said Lang some years earlier. " I have no reason to do that. I said all I had to say about that subject in the picture. Now I have other things to say ".[3] Instead, Joseph Losey directed the re-make, which the production code authorities agreed to pass only if it bore clear similarities to an accepted classic. " I'd seen *M* in the early 'thirties ", says Losey. " I saw it again, once in a very bad copy, just before I made it. I never referred to it. I only consciously repeated one shot. There may have been unconscious repetitions, in terms of the atmosphere of certain sequences ".[4]

As field research for *M*, Lang spent eight days in a mental institution; he had also known and studied several murderers, supposedly including Peter Kürten, who alone had killed about ten people in the period around 1925. Real criminals were used in certain scenes, resulting in a high turnover rate among the extras; a total of twenty-four cast members were arrested during the filming.

This was Lang's first use of sound, which may have hastened the transition into a realistic mode hinted at in *Die Frau im Mond.* At

---

[3] Eileen Creelman, " Picture Plays and Players ", *New York Sun* (October 6, 1944).

[4] James Leahy, *The Cinema of Joseph Losey* (London, New York, 1967), page 47.

any rate, though a concern for mob psychology still exists, the crowd is no longer the anonymous mass of *Metropolis*. Instead, all of its members are sharply delineated. Some of Lang's coldness is replaced with pity and a concern for individuals, but though he examines his subjects and characters more closely than before, his observation is still highly objective. There are really no main characters, though Lorre's is the central and most famous role, and no one with whom the viewer is allowed to identify. This gives the film a cool, documentary quality.

Lang's style now emphasises realism, but he still uses people and objects expressively, and his highly calculated structure ties many scenes together with aural and visual transitions. Though his themes remain, they have been translated into a realistic context. Duality has become homicidal schizophrenia, with an innocent, unassuming façade hiding a murderer, the line between justice and revenge is again blurred, and mob violence is associated with both; the master villain still exists, but in the slightly more down-to-earth figure of Schrenke, the criminal organiser.

This is Lang's favourite of all his own films because of the social criticism it contains. In *M*, the individual who is trapped and menaced is not an idealised Nordic hero (*Die Nibelungen*) or an innocent, hardworking young man (*Fury*); he is a fat psychopath who murders involuntarily. This important difference allows the film to make a statement, denied to Lang's other pictures, by serving a " preaching function ". It only lectures overtly at the very end, but throughout it pleads the cause of the mentally ill by showing the " hero " treated as a criminal and a disease, not as a sick man who cannot help himself. This adds a new dimension to the story.

The director himself once stated that he made *M* " to warn mothers about neglecting their children ".[5] He said this, however, in 1937, after *Fury* and *You Only Live Once* had given him a reputation for the courageous handling of social themes. Actually, the questions of mental illness and child watching are only small portions of the film's substantial content. Through the opposition of the criminals and the police (with an individual caught between), *M* really embodies the more general contrasts of disorganisation (the police in one sense, the mob in another) and order (the criminals

[5] Marguerite Tazelar, " Fritz Lang Like Hollywood, America and Social Themes ", *New York Herald-Tribune* (February 7, 1937).

and beggars), justice and revenge, Democracy and Fascism, and perhaps even the Weimar Republic and the Nazi Third Reich. All of this, however, is subordinate to the film's quality as a semi-documentary crime melodrama.

M is concerned with two types of murder and murderers. The first is that committed by Franz Becker (Peter Lorre), a disturbed child killer. The pivotal character, he is cut off from the law by his deeds and from the underworld because he is independent and compulsive. The separate worlds of the criminals and the police had previously operated in a kind of balance, but Becker, a psychotic outsider, disrupts this by causing the police to bear down heavily on all aspects of crime. When this happens, the criminals themselves organise and try to locate the killer. Becker's capture is now inevitable, since both factions are against him. The only uncertainty is about which group will discover him first, and when that will happen. This leads to the second kind of murder: that which is almost committed by the citizens and criminals who hunt him down and give him a " trial ". This action begins as simple self-concern; then, convinced it is enacting justice but in reality seeking revenge for the children's deaths, the group attempts to murder the murderer before the agents of true justice take charge. As this occurs, its methods change from the precise planning of an organisation to the emotional impulsiveness of a mob.

An equally important contrast is between the methods used by the police and those of the criminals. A police conference is inter-cut with a similar meeting in the underworld, and Superintendent Lohman's character here, and throughout the film, parallels and opposes that of Schrenke. Lohman's inefficiency typifies the organisation he serves, just as Schrenke represents the more efficient criminals. The Superintendent states at the meeting that the public won't co-operate; it refuses to see anything and doesn't care, anyhow. While he talks, however, a substantial portion of the public is gathering for the same purpose as the police. Later, at the " trial ", the criminals have been joined by other citizens, including mothers of the dead girls, and so the group even more fully represents the Public. It now cares about Becker's crimes, having forgotten its original selfish motive of removing police pressure. This unity throughout the entire underworld appears to have had precedent in the Germany of 1931, but today it appears to be an unlikely and impractical bit of romanticism supported by a slight attempt to present the criminals as magicians, or at least sleight-of-hand experts. One man does card tricks, while another produces an impressive number of watches from his pockets; such talents are echoed by the efficiency with which they take the office building apart in their search for Becker. This " magic " corresponds to the similar powers of Mabuse's men, and Schrenke, the accepted and respected head of this group, is a new version of the old master criminal. With his bowler hat, cane, gloves, and leather coat, he has a distinctive air of authority. Like Joh Fredersen, he inhabits an ivory tower: he makes the decisions, and leaves others to answer the phone and do the talking (except at the concluding trial). His past is vague, and he maintains this anonymity in the present by avoiding contact with others, symbolised by the gloves he constantly wears. But while for the moment he is completely in power (an idea represented by a shot of his hand placed on a map of the city), this is only for the duration of the search, and the temporary, emergency nature of his position helps to keep the character from slipping off into the fantasy world of a Mabuse.

The methods of the police depend mainly on chance, but this is due less to ineptitude than to a lack of information, manpower, and opportunity. Because an empty candy bag is found near one murder site, all candy stores within the radius of a mile are checked; when this proves fruitless, the circle is gradually enlarged. Such clues lead nowhere, so the police resort to indiscriminate raiding in the hope of discovering the killer or an informant. Through this hit-or-miss method brings about the arrest of several other criminals, it also causes Lohman to waste time sitting at a table, checking identity papers. It is decided to obtain from prisons, sanatoriums, and mental institutions the names of those recently released as harmless, yet capable of murder (a seemingly contradictory phrase). The result is a giant list of the mentally ill who have been freed, during the past five years, from private and state institutions. Obviously, the murderer might have been released more than five years before or he might never have been committed at all.

Paralleling the police conference is another meeting, at which all branches of criminal activity are represented. Together, these men divide the city into sections and assign one to each member of the Organisation of Beggars, who can secretly observe any children abroad on the streets without arousing suspicion. If and when the murderer reveals himself, he would be readily identified and apprehended. The planning is detailed, with each beggar's name, assignment, and membership card number recorded in a ledger, and everything is so well arranged that chance is theoretically (and practically) eliminated; the entire town is under observation and Becker has no hope at all. This is where the tension created by Lang differs from the suspense built up by a director like Alfred Hitchcock. The latter uses cutting and close-ups to create uncertainty about what will happen, while Lang forces the viewer to remain in one spot and watch the hero squirm in the net that has trapped him.

With the police doggedly checking each name on the long list of possible suspects, it is little wonder that the criminals spot and capture Becker first. Lohman's men do succeed in identifying the murderer, since his name happened to be on the list, but they haven't seen him yet and don't know where he is. While they wait for him to return to his rented room, he is already being followed by the criminals; it is only the lucky arrest of a man who had helped break into the building where Becker was hiding that allows the police to re-locate him. In fact, Lohman is so dumbfounded when told of the underworld's search, that his cigar drops from his mouth and he has to douse his head with cold water. This same man also tells Lohman where Becker was taken for " trial ", so the prevention of his murder-execution occurs through chance rather than ingenuity.

The idea that organised justice, while better, is the longer, less efficient method recurrs often in Lang's works. The police, slow but in the long run fair, are here contrasted with the violent and vengeful mob; the police are consistent, but the criminals are not. At the start of the film they are a mob, hooting and whistling at Lohman and talking back to the police. Later, when organised and regimented by Schrenke for a goal that is to their advantage, they lose this cvil quality of violence and impulsiveness. When Becker is captured they revert once more to a mob, and the " trial " is a mere formality, a prelude to the enactment of their vengeance. " There is only one just thing for you — kill you ", says the mother of one of the murdered children. They have come full circle from a mob, to an efficient organisation, and once more to a mob. Parallel to this, they have gone from being ruled by emotion, to logic and order, and back again to emotion and irrationality. By the time Becker is given an official trial, the people have been freed from the grip of such violence. They have returned to " normal ", and one of the victims' mothers now declares that sentencing the killer would not bring back her little girl.

When Becker is put on trial by the criminals, he pleads that he cannot keep himself from killing. It is as though there is a second Franz Becker who takes over his body; " I am always forced to move along the streets, and always someone is behind me. It is I. I sometimes feel I am myself behind me, and yet I cannot escape ". Afterwards, standing before a poster, he reads what he has done and remembers nothing about the incident. Though he is haunted and tortured by his deeds, they seem to have been committed by someone else within him. To Becker, the world is a frightening place, with everyone working against him, from the police to the underworld, and even including a blind, helpless beggar selling balloons. But the greatest threat to him comes from the underworld of his own mind, and the other part of his personality that lurks there waiting to destroy the everyday Franz Becker. This part consists of the emotional desires generally held in check by logic and reason. Occasionally, at times of great stress or temptation, they are freed while the individual is briefly off guard; mental illness and schizophrenia allow this other self more regular control, but in all cases a lowering of his guard can destroy the person. He himself is his own worst enemy.

In *M*, this idea is given a psychological context which it had previously lacked, with the defence attorney arguing that the uncontrollable compulsion to kill relieves Becker of responsibility, since he is ill and should be turned over to a doctor. Even the state, he says, does not have the right to kill this sick man; no one has such a right. This is the film's only didactic moment, and the " trial " setting provides a natural motive for the speech-making. The specific reference is to the misunderstood mentally ill, just as *Fury* deals with the social problem of lynching, but both pictures are just different embodiments of the general themes common to so many of Lang's films. the individual trapped, and menaced from all sides; the danger of allowing the emotions to gain control; the ambiguity of responsibility.

M marks a transition in Lang's directorial style, and contains elements of the pictorial combined with a generally naturalistic presentation. Expressionism — the use and manipulation of objective reality to reflect the inner emotions and responses of the artist — appears in certain stylised visual arrangements which sometimes, but not always, have symbolic reference beyond their factual content and artistic form. The film's opening, an overhead shot of children grouped in a circle with one standing in the centre, presents a geometric pattern which is pleasing in itself and also creates a feeling of inescapabillity like that eventually developed for Becker. He is trapped between the two outside forces and within the maze of his own mental illness, and his capture is inevitable. Other arrangements, such as the overhead view of a policeman checking Becker's round table for clues, do not contribute to this idea of being caught (though this case repeats the circle motif), but the majority of *M*'s expressionistic shots do. Most of these are taken from above to bring out geometric qualities that would otherwise go unnoticed. One such is the " X " of an intersection across which Becker is pursued, with its squares and angles reducing the human figures to pawns on a large chess or checker board. A display of knives, reflected in a store window, seems to circle Becker's head; he is trapped again, this time by his own implement of death. Some views of high stairways, looking directly down from several flights above, resemble rectangular mazes from which there is no escape; others, taken from the side, allow Lang to compose within his frame an intricate pattern of diagonals. A remnant of the anonymous masses of *Metropolis,* and the force they represent, can be seen during the raid on an underworld hangout. As the rows of policemen march in unison down the steps, the camera is placed so that their heads and shoulders are out of the frame.

This expressionistic art contains an unexpected humanism, a concern for man and his welfare. Lang's earlier films were often peopled with cardboard figures existing merely to advance the plot. They lacked depth and dimension. This is much less true in *M,* though a feeling of calculated characterisation still exists and a natural spontaneity is something quite foreign to Lang. Still, his killer, though a villain of sorts, is sympathetic in his illness. Becker and several other characters have a new sense of indiviuality, but Lang remains typically objective in his observation, and approaches realism not through feeling and emotion, but through the objectivity of a documentary. Many scenes are content to describe the workings of the police department, without any thematic " comment " by the director-author. Shots of fingerprints are accompanied by a lecture-like voice explaining their charateristics. Policemen are shown questioning the owners of candy stores, while a narrator reports their negative results. When a guard at the building where Becker is trapped pulls a warning switch, the camera follows the results, as machines click on and off and the source of the impulse is identified at headquarters. The voice of a handwriting analyst speaks of the killer's " histrionic tendencies ", as we see Becker making faces before the mirror in his room. These are not exactly examples of narration, since the voice used each time is never the same, belongs to a character (albeit an anonymous one), and speaks to others in the film instead of directly to the audience. Still, the principle is the same, and it allows for concise exposition by juxtaposing voice and image from different places and different times.

The film's structure is often admirable. Intercutting is used to contrast two concurrent incidents; one such juxtaposition compares an electric drill, used by the criminals to enter the buildings, with the broken pocket-knife that Becker uses in trying to escape. His comparative helplessness and the inevitability of his capture are again effectively set forth. Some scenes are linked together by sound bridges, as when Lohman asks the prisoner where Becker has been taken. " To the old distillery ", he answers, and his voice on the soundtrack describes the place as the screen shows the building's interior. When the talking stops, the image remains; Becker and his captors enter, and the sounds heard are now of their arrival. The scene has been imaginatively, gradually changed. Another transition made smooth by the use of sound involves the music of a street organ. A shot of an instrument being played indoors is followed by one of a man listening. This is succeeded, with no break in the song, by a shot of an instrument being played, at a later time, on a street corner.

M has been carefully thought out to make good use of sound, as in the narration and transitions already mentioned. Becker is seen whistling " In the Hall of the Mountain King " early in the film, and once he is solidly associated with this tune it is used by itself to establish Becker's presence, while the camera remains fixed on a girl gazing into a store window. Such subtlety through suggestion is also applied to Becker's crimes, with a balloon caught among telephone wires and a rolling rubber ball establishing a murder.

Towards the end, we see Becker crouching in the cluttered darkness of the building, a ray of light reflected in his sweating face. In the background, we hear the gradual approach of his pursuers. As the sound grows louder, the reaction of fear in the hunted man's face increases until a shout of "There's the swine!" ends the sequence. If *M* had been a silent film, Lang would have been required to cut away from Becker to show the searchers, but now he can establish their approach on the soundtrack and keep his camera unswervingly focused on the quarry's expression. This example epitomises Lang's approach to the thriller form: he creates tension in the viewer by forcing him, almost sadistically, to observe the writhings of a helplessly trapped victim. The development of sound made it possible for the director to avoid an emphasis on editing, which interfered with his individual style, and to make active use of silence (the utter quiet before a police raid is broken by a whistle, and then a low noise swells to the thunder of a crowd rushing to escape). Lang's style is based on fearful anticipation, hence the long takes and lack of action scenes.

M is constructed like a machine, with tightly interlocking parts, and once it is set in motion it proceeds with an inevitable logic. It is a very versatile invention: it entertains, it preaches, it creates tension, it even evokes sympathy to a degree, but nonetheless it does not live. *M* is important to any consideration of Fritz Lang's career and themes. It is also one of those significant pictures from the early 'thirties which make use of sound rather than allow it to control them. Some of its techniques, especially that of the narrator, have since become more familiar, but the ingenuity which Lang brings to his subject is something still rare among film-makers.

The Threepenny Opera (1931)

From *Celluloid* by Paul Rotha (London, Longmans Green & Co., 1933).

The scenario for *Die Dreigroschenoper* is loosely adapted from a musical extravaganza of the same name by Brecht and Weill, which in turn is distantly based on Gay's "*The Beggar's Opera*". Not a great deal of Gay's eighteenth-century spirit remains, however, in this new version. . . . Instead of an eighteenth-century London, we have substituted a most delightful, fantastic underworld set in a district approximating to Soho in the 'nineties, which is close to a romantically conceived dockland, with gay-life cafés and the most naughty yet highly diverting houses of ill-repute.

Any reader familiar with Pabst's work will at once appreciate what admirable scope such an environment gives for his love of darkly-lit, macabre settings, and for curious twists of vice and virtue. It can well be imagined how he delights in showing the romantic philanderings of Mackie Messer, the new Macheath, who is the captain of the so-called gang of London Apaches, and how Pabst portrays for our joyous entertainment the scandalous exploits of this charming hero.

At the opening of the film, Mackie falls in love at first sight with Polly Peachum, the beautiful and spirited daughter of the King of the Beggars, and marries her out of hand at a sumptuous wedding feast staged by his gang out of stolen goods in Mackie's sinister underground headquarters. When the wedding night is over, Polly steals home and breaks the news to irate parents, who promptly declare that she must divorce her newly-wed husband. Polly, of course, refuses to permit this, and Peachum goes to his friend, the Prefect of the Police, who also happens to be a good friend of Mackie, and tries to arrange at once for the latter's arrest. Warned by Polly of his danger, Mackie prepares to escape, but falls in with some old flames from the neighbouring brothel. He escapes the arm of the law, however, through the aid of his late love, Jenny the Whore, only to be caught as he leaves the abode of yet another attractive *cocotte*. The business-like Polly, meanwhile, has taken charge of the gang and has decided to fly on a higher plane by running a bank. But her father, incensed because he has not been able to obtain justice, plans to upset the Coronation procession by organizing a parade of his beggar-legions to spite the Prefect of the Police. He learns too late of Polly's success as a business woman, and fails to stop the trooping army of beggars from breaking up the procession. Whilst this is taking place, the faithful Jenny contrives Mackie Messer's escape from prison, just as Polly is arranging to pay the ransom for his release. Learning of her success, Mackie returns to Polly's extended arms, and the film comes to a happy conclusion with the launching of a new firm with Mackie and

Peachum as the directors. Borrowing from Gay's original, the picture is interrupted at regular intervals by a street singer, who gives a brief résumé of the action and explains for the benefit of the dense-minded why and wherefore the characters are behaving as they do. In all, an amusing piece of lighthearted nonsense strung together with a brilliant parade of wit and a multitude of intriguing situations.

Passing over for the moment the polish of the character-playing and the subtle handling of the incidents, I would comment principally on the architectural environment which Pabst and Andrei Andreiev have jointly contrived for this comedy of manners. Not solely on account of their individual merit as design do I draw attention to these sets, but because they are the envelope, as it were, of the film. Without the self-contained world that they create, a world of dark alleys, hanging rigging and twisting stairways, without their decorative yet realistic values, without the air of finality and completeness which they give, this film-operetta would not have been credible. It is partly by reason of the queer, fantastic atmosphere created in this dockside underworld that this film is lifted on to a plane by itself. This is due not only to the settings in themselves, but the very close relationship maintained between the players and their surroundings, which has come about because the director and the architect have to all intents and purposes worked with one mind. Each corner and each doorway is conceived in direct relationship to the action played within its limits. This factor, together with the co-operation of the camerawork, builds the film into a solid, well-informed unity.

Actual instances of such dovetailed workmanship are too numerous to be detailed in full, but I praise especially the set representing Mackie Messer's headquarters, a piece of creative set design which deserves to be put on record. Presumably situated beside the wharves, it is built on three levels, the roof reaching to a considerable height. From a door at the top, an incredibly steep and very long flight of narrow wooden steps descends to the middle level, from which the inimitable Mackie Messer dictates his questionable correspondence to his secretary, who is seated at least twenty feet below him on the lower level. What a delightful touch of humour is this! On all sides of the set rise up great barrels, ridiculous barrels of absurd height and girth, yet how admirably original. Mackie's dressing-room consists of smaller barrels placed slightly apart, behind each of which he vanishes in turn to complete his toilet. Outside there is a salubrious erection of piles and arches and small bridges, a perfect ideological world for the Apaches of London, hung about with slanting masts and drooping rigging. The most delightful part of it all is that when the gang emerge from their huge cellar by the door in the ceiling, they arrive on the normal level of the streets outside.

Quite different but equally amusing is the late-Victorian brothel, with its paper-patterned windows and antimacassars, its multitude of useless ornaments and its giant negress statues standing about the room. Every detail in these sets is placed there with a definite purpose — to create the mood for the scene. In the twisted streets, in the prison, in the angular office of Peachum, in the underground café, this same striving for atmosphere is apparent and is tremendously successful. No other films in the world can create such an architectural environment so well as those of Germany.

This intimacy between the director and the architect is not all. The camerawork and lighting also are closely related to the settings and the action. The remarkable photographic genius of Fritz Arno Wagner must be added to the creators of the environment. His lighting, camera set-ups and camera movements are worked out in careful relationship to the sets and the action. When the camera is in motion, the smoothly sliding pan glides from one figure to another across the set with a perfect respect for its material. Low-level or high-level, its set-up and path of direction is governed by the mood of the scene, which is also the mood created by the set. . . .

Moreover, especial reference should be made to the prevalence of moving camerawork in *Die Dreigroschenoper*. Since the introduction of the spoken word into film-making, there has been a growing tendency to decrease the number of direct cuts in a picture, partly because of the desire to minimise the amount of different camera set-ups and partly on account of the difficulties attendant on cutting and joining the sound strip. . . .

As far as *Die Dreigroschenoper* is concerned, the moving camera is noteworthy in that it is used not so much for economic reasons as for its assistance in establishing the relationship of the characters with their environment. Pabst is far too skilled in cinematic sense to allow mere convenience of camera mobility to interfere with his fine expression of mood. This film abounds with instances of his uncanny instinct for selection of camera angles, particularly when several characters are grouped together. In addition to which, he employs his favourite method of making every cut from one shot to another on a movement, so that the eye of the spectator is carried smoothly from image to image, aided by the sound. This style of cutting will be remembered in *Jeanne Ney* and in *Crisis*, both significant pictures in Pabst's career.

In each of his earlier films, it will be recalled that Pabst has displayed an interest in the mental and physical make-up of his feminine players, with the result that he has often brought to the screen women who have been unusually attractive in a bizarre, neurotic manner, very different from the brilliantly turned out, sophisticated but stereotyped women of American pictures, or the dreary young ladies favoured by British directors. Pabst is one of the few directors in the whole film business who has any understanding of women. Whatever part they are required to play, or whatever clothes they wear, the women in Pabst's films never fail to be interesting, and those in *The Threepenny Opera* prove no exception to the rule.

To instance a small detail of the picture, the chance meeting of Mackie Messer and the stray street-girl after the former has escaped from the brothel is one of the most amazingly well-handled incidents that I have ever seen on the screen. How it is contrived I do not pretend to know, but Pabst extracts the very last ounce of meaning out of the scene. The enticement of the woman and her physical magnetism are brought out in all their human strength despite the fact that she herself is far from being attractive in the ordinary sense of the word. Similarly, Messer's indifference gradually turning to fascination is remarkable. An effect of cynicism is not gained wholly by acting, but by Pabst's rendering of the scene, by his choice of angles and by his deep psychological understanding of the elements of the situation. The scene in itself is an admirable example of his close penetration into the depths of human behaviour, and the way in which he recreates an ordinary human experience on the screen. Further evidence of this extraordinary quality abounds in the film, as in the diverting women of the brothel, the scenes in the café, the wonderful reunion between Jenny the Whore and Mackie Messer, and the treatment of Polly throughout. To any close observer of Pabst's outlook, these are in direction tradition with certain scenes in *Pandora's Box*, *Jeanne Ney*, *Westfront 1918*, *Crisis* and *The Diary of a Lost Girl. . . .*

Under Pabst's direction all the cast of *Die Dreigroschenoper* play with an exquisite charm and purposeful deliberation of gesture to correspond with the fantasy of the plot. Rudolf Forster makes an engaging Mackie Messer in grey bowler-hat and canary-yellow gloves; Carola Neher is immensely attractive as Polly; Fritz Rasp and Valeska Gert, familiar to all followers of the German cinema, bring experience and humour to Mr and Mrs Peachum; whilst those who remember the genial Communist attaché in *Jeanne Ney* will delight once more in Vladimir Sokolov as Schmidt the Gaoler.

Good as the poised acting may be, it is the direction of this film that causes its cynical drollery and sinister melodrama to be so effective. It is the controlling, creative mentality of Pabst that combines the thrills of a crook drama with the light melodious atmosphere of an eighteenth-century operetta. Whilst the plot is essentially one of wit and humour, nevertheless we feel through it all a sense of drama. It is a supreme genius of cinematic art that can bring out the subtleties of the situations, envelop the whole delightful extravaganza in charm, and still preserve a touch of dramatic feeling. The direction of Pabst grows on one and becomes curiously fascinating. Like *City Lights, The Threepenny Opera* is at its best when seen for a second time.

Extracts from an interview by Gideon Bachmann with Jean Oser, who worked with Pabst as editor on many of his films

From *Cinemages 3: Six Talks on G. W. Pabst* (New York, the Group for Film Study Inc, 1955).

GB: You started working with Pabst on *Westfront?*

JO: Yes, I was working for " Tobis ", the company who owned the patents on sound reproduction. That in itself is quite a story. Tobis had a monopoly on all sound film production in Germany because they had bought up all the Swiss, Danish and German patents. They were the only ones who could actually make sound films. You had to rent the sound crew and equipment from them. I was working for Tobis, and so when Pabst wanted to make a sound film he got the equipment from them and I became editor for him. . . .

. . . After *Westfront 18,* he went into *Dreigroschenoper,* which he did for Warner Brothers, but again Nebenzahl (owner of Nerofilm) was involved; it was a deal between Nebenzahl and Warner Brothers. *Dreigroschenoper* was a very hot property at the time: it had come out as a big theatrical hit; in fact it was almost phenomenal how much it influenced a complete generation.

GB: You mean the play. . . .

JO: Yes. When *Dreigroschenoper* came out, it formed the entire pre-Hitler generation until 1933; for about five years. It was not just a big success like, for example, " South Pacific " — not every young American girl today would like to act and look and talk like Nellie. When *Dreigroschenoper* came out, every girl in the country wanted to be like Mackie. Apparently, the ideal man was the pimp. Warner Brothers thought that this was a big hit and they bought the rights for *Dreigroschenoper* from Kurt Weill, who had written the music, and Bert Brecht, who had written the play.

GB: Did the actors from the play work in the film too, like Kurt Gerren and Lotte Lenya?

JO: Only Lenya, the rest were different. They had Rudolph Forster as Mackie Messer: Reinhold Schunzel, as Tiger Brown; and they had a very fine actress, Klabund's wife, Carola Neher, as Polly; Valeska Gert, as Mrs Peachum, and Fritz Rasp as Peachum. This film again was made in two versions, with different actors, for release at the same time in French-speaking and German-speaking countries. In the French version they had Albert Préjean as Mackie, and a young musical actress, quite well-known in France at the time: Florelle, as Polly. After the success of *Dreigroschenoper*, she became Number One star in France. Gaston Modot was in the French version as Peachum. The film was released in France as *L'Opéra de Quait' Sous*, and was a tremendous success. In Germany it was not such a success and it was attacked quite often by the critics.

GB: Tell me something about the production of *Dreigroschenoper*.

JO: When Pabst started this film it was immediately budgeted as a very big film, and he soon had trouble with Weill and Brecht.

GB: Why?

JO: Because Brecht had a different approach, and I must say in this case I agree with Brecht, because you don't make a million-dollar movie out of a story which should practically be shot in a backyard. The charm and the power of the theatrical production was in the fact that it was an opera performed by beggars, so that nothing cost anything. And now suddenly you see a thing which is photographed on the biggest set that had ever been made for a German movie up to that time. They built the complete harbor of London. Somehow it just didn't fit the story; it was too lavishly produced. I happened to see it again in France a few years after it was made, and by that time the print had become old and scratchy and somehow it had more reality for me then, than when it was new and shiny. I must say, though, that what Pabst himself told me about his difficulties with the authors, sounded quite different. I was the editor and was not in on the script conferences, so I don't know what actually happened, but he told me that Brecht and Weill wanted to make it even a bigger production than he wanted to. He said they wanted to have 5,000 people in the wedding scene and wanted to shoot it in the big Sports Palace in Berlin, which is something like Madison Square Garden, so I don't really know who was right. Anyway, there was fighting from beginning to end, and when the picture was ready, Kurt Weill went into the act too, and they sued Warner Brothers and Nerofilm for not having hollowed the music exactly. I remember that there was one trumpet fanfare when the beggars start their march which was not officially composed by Weill, and on the basis of that, Warner Brothers and Nerofilm lost the suit. In those days, there was an interesting state of affairs: whenever an artist sued a producer, the artist generally won. But in this case I don't really think it was justified. Brecht and Weill won the suit and got — I think — 50,000 marks, which at the time corresponded to $50,000, and also — which is very interesting — the right to re-do the film if they wanted to.